THE CRISIS OF CONFIDENCE
IN AMERICAN EDUCATION

ABOUT THE AUTHOR

Robert E. Hagerty is associate professor and coordinator of the Educational Leadership Program at Grand Valley State University in Grand Rapids, Michigan. He received his B.A. degree (1955) from Western Michigan University and his M.A. (1961) and Ed.D (1970) degrees from Wayne State University. Dr. Hagerty was a regular and special education teacher, building administrator and Director of Special Education for the Hazel Park Community Schools for twenty-five years. He served as superintendent of schools for ten years, the last eight in Ionia, Michigan, where he received national recognition as the developer of the Ionia Educational Center. Dr. Hagerty lectures and consults throughout the state and nation. He received the National School Public Relation Association's Superintendent's Award of Excellence in 1987. Dr. Hagerty is president of the Michigan Association of Professors of Educational Administration.

THE CRISIS OF CONFIDENCE IN AMERICAN EDUCATION

A Blueprint for Fixing What Is Wrong and Restoring America's Confidence in the Public Schools

By

ROBERT HAGERTY, ED.D.

Associate Professor, Educational Leadership
Grand Valley State University
Grand Rapids, Michigan

With a Foreword by

Donald Burns

President, Montcalm Community College

CHARLES C THOMAS • PUBLISHER

Springfield • Illinois • U.S.A.

Published and Distributed Throughout the World by
CHARLES C THOMAS • PUBLISHER
2600 South First Street
Springfield, Illinois 62794-9265

© *1995 by* CHARLES C THOMAS • PUBLISHER
ISBN 0-398-05965-9   (cloth)
ISBN 0-398-05966-7   (paper)
Library of Congress Catalog Card Number: 94-39005

With THOMAS BOOKS *careful attention is given to all details of manufacturing
and design. It is the Publisher's desire to present books that are satisfactory as to their
physical qualities and artistic possibilities and appropriate for their particular use.*
THOMAS BOOKS *will be true to those laws of quality that assure a good name
and good will.*

Printed in the United States of America
SC-R-3

Library of Congress Cataloging-in-Publication Data

Hagerty, Robert.
    The crisis of confidence in American education : a blueprint for
fixing what is wrong and restoring America's confidence in the
public schools / by Robert Hagerty : with a foreword by Donald
Burns.
        p.   cm.
    Includes bibliographical references and index.
    ISBN 0-398-05965-9 (cloth). — ISBN 0-398-05966-7 (paper)
    1. Public schools—United States.   2. Education—United States—
Aims and objectives.   3. Educational change—United States.
I. Title.
LA217.2.H34   1995
371'.01'0973—dc20   94-39005
                                                            CIP

FOREWORD

As H.L. Mencken once said, "There is always a well-known solution to every human problem—neat, plausible and wrong."

Most of us have heard others describe, and perhaps have even had thoughts on our own, of simple ways to solve the woes of the American educational system. Prior to embracing any such thoughts, one should attempt to get some kind of overall perspective on the issue. The following text provides the reader with such an opportunity. The major issues within and forces affecting education are described in this text.

In a comprehensive and direct fashion, Bob Hagerty describes the situation—an educational system in the 1990s. He reminds us that schools are not apart from, but rather a part of, American life.

Convinced that there are solutions and that we have the spirit to pursue them, Dr. Hagerty encourages those within and those who support education. The author presents convincing solutions to the most pressing public criticism of American education. However, these solutions are not panaceas. Dr. Hagerty calls on educators and citizens to join hands, to have the resolve to abandon defensive posturing, and the courage to use collaborative planning to implement the research driven exemplary practices put forward in this book.

You will come away motivated, informed and prepared to make your community and the school the best that they can be.

DONALD BURNS

INTRODUCTION

Organizational Scheme

After examining the nature of the crisis of confidence in the public schools and the antecedents of the crisis, in Chapter I, the history of American public schools is traced with particular reference to the current crisis, in Chapter II. Chapter III, on preventing school failure, provides valuable insight into improving student success and restoring the public's confidence in the schools. Chapter IV, on urban schools, also is important because it provides credible evidence to show that urban schools can, in spite of violence and poverty, make a positive difference in the lives of children of the underclass.

The subject of character education in Chapter V has the potential of creating a national division. While character education has been ignored by most educational scholars, an ever-increasing body of evidence supports character education, in building stronger classroom learning cultures. Chapter VI, on school size, provides evidence to support some of the more profound changes which can be made to turn schools into more secure and caring learning communities. Chapter VII, on the "fossilization" of the high school curriculum, demonstrates the urgency of transforming the culture of American high schools from "holding tanks" to school-to-work laboratories.

Chapter VIII, which examines Japanese schools, dispels many of the popular myths about Japanese education. This chapter objectively looks at the Japanese system of education and makes recommendations which will make American schools more effective.

The final chapter makes a clear case for confronting and embracing change, for promoting and encouraging staff and community collaboration and planning as the only way to bring about positive and enduring school improvement. I have witnessed numerous attempts at planned educational change over the last 35 years. The benefits have rarely equalled the costs, and all too often the situation has seemed to worsen. I have attempted in this book to distill from these experiences the most powerful lessons about bringing about positive school improvement— things that make a real difference in the lives of students.

I know of no better way to restore public confidence in public schools than by promoting the ways that exemplary practice and theory can transform local schools. I offer neither prescriptions nor panaceas; but taken as a whole and given the required time for collaborative planning at the local school level, the programs and strategies contained in this book will provide positive direction and improve the educational quality of any school or school system seriously committed to improving public confidence.

ACKNOWLEDGMENTS

Because this book covers such a broad range of knowledge and experience, I accumulated an enormous debt in the course of writing it.

This book would not exist without the example set by my longtime mentor, Wilfred D. Webb, retired superintendent of schools, Hazel Park, Michigan, and the Michigan House of Representatives. As a visionary leader, many of the ideals promoted in this book were "seeds" planted by Dr. Webb over thirty years ago.

I am most grateful to the generous support and helpful suggestions of David Donovan, who died shortly after critiquing the first draft of the book. Dr. Donovan served as a valued mentor when I was superintendent of the Ionia Public Schools. As associate superintendent of schools for the state of Michigan, Dr. Donovan encouraged and became an influential advocate for many of the strategies described in the book as they were implemented by the Ionia Public Schools.

I am unusually fortunate in my professional associations to have obtained support and mentoring from some of the most eminent contemporary educational leaders. I am thankful particularly to have learned from Philip Runkel, former superintendent of public instruction for the state of Michigan, Elmer Vruggink, Dean, Davenport College, Don Shebuskey, Superintendent of the Ingham Intermediate School District, Don Burns, President of Montcalm Community College, and John Marrs, Educational Consultant and Pollster. These experts have taught me what I have learned about restoring confidence in the public schools.

Several of the strategies discussed in the book were pioneered at the Ionia Education Center, a comprehensive high school, a community college, and an area technical high school under a common roof. This would not have been possible without the loyal and consistent support of Board of Education presidents David Pinnow and Harry Larkin; treasurer, Spiro Mann; secretary, Lynn Sterner; and trustees, Don Lehman and Lyle Clover.

The enduring dedication of Ionia Public School administrators, Charles Seguna, Scott Hubble, Donald Wilcox, and Daniel Evans, associate superintendent, assistant superintendent, director of finance, and middle school principal, respectively, made possible the implementation of several strategies described in this book. I also wish to acknowledge the indomitable spirit and hard work of former assistant superintendent Michael Freeland, who is now superintendent of the Bullock Creek Schools.

The manuscript has been critiqued by public school teachers, school administrators, and both graduate and undergraduate faculty. I am most grateful to Mary Doyle, Thomas Jackson, Robert Cross, Janet Springer-Gabelli, Linda McCrae, Marie Ortez, James Trent, Richard Carlson, Michael Bozym, Morris Appleton, and Weston Wocholtz for both suggestions and affirmations.

I am also grateful for the confidence of Alan Ten Eyck, Dean, School of Education, Grand Valley State University, Brenda Lazerus, Assistant Dean, and Professor Dorothy Armstrong who has been a wise and valued mentor.

I could not have undertaken this project without the willing support of my family, including my wife Barbara, sons Mark and Scott, daughter-in-law Amy, and granddaughter Barbara. They loyally supported my research and left me alone for extended periods of time to work on the manuscript.

My profound appreciation goes to my typist, Ginny Dozeman, who displayed unbelievable patience and forbearance during the process of typing, editing, and re-editing the manuscript.

Lastly, I am thankful to the editors and staff at Charles C Thomas Publisher for their care in preparing the manuscript for publication.

CONTENTS

THE CRISIS OF CONFIDENCE
IN AMERICAN EDUCATION

Chapter I

EVIDENCE OF A CRISIS

The problem I address in this book, simply stated, is how American educators can restore public confidence in our schools. Support for the public schools in America is at a low ebb. State support has grown slightly in recent years but has not made up for earlier losses incurred by a declining economy, taxpayer revolts, and cutbacks in federal programs. Federal government officials have pressured both Congress and some of the more vulnerable state legislatures to create incentives in the form of tuition tax credits or voucher plans, both of which threaten to erode attendance in, and support for, public schools.

A flood of reports since 1983 have criticized schools and more recently colleges for all manner of shortcomings. These critical reports have eroded confidence in many schools. Charles Achilles and Nan Lintz found that 45 percent of the administrators in schools with reputations for excellence and 70 percent of samples of teachers and administrators from Nebraska and Texas did not feel that public confidence had been improved by the reform reports (Wayson et al., 1988). Educators in many communities have objected because the weaknesses noted in the reform reports do not apply to their school districts; yet the public assumes they do. Extensive media coverage of the reform reports, whether intentional or not, has tended to undermine confidence in public education.

Demographic and economic trends show that the public confidence crisis likely will intensify. Schools will have a larger proportion of poor, minority, and latchkey children and more children from single-parent families than ever before. These are the children that the schools have been least able to educate in the past (Hodgkinson, 1988; Lewis, 1986). At the same time, the American economy, which in the past was able to absorb dropouts or undereducated high school graduates and immigrants, now is in need of a better educated work force with advanced technical skills. Even the more constructive reform reports, such as *A Nation Prepared: Teachers for the 21st Century* (Carnegie Forum on Education and the Economy, 1986), express doubts as to whether schools can meet the challenge, and they leave open the option for other institutions to fill the need:

> There is a growing awareness that further progress is unlikely without fundamental changes in structure. In fact, we suspect that dramatic change may be easier to achieve than incremental change, given the growing frustration with political gridlock and the increasing awareness that the biggest impediment to progress is the nature of the system itself. (p.16)

Governors and other leaders leave no doubt that the present structure of our public school system will have to change dramatically if it is to meet future needs (National Governors' Association, 1986).

These are old refrains; yet they may not be sufficient to arouse a lethargic system to respond. Some of the criticism from the reform reports is exaggerated and the recommendations simplistic or unrealistic. But the cry for reform is strong, and the pressure for change is persistent and supported in high places. At the same time, educators are more vulnerable than ever, because they are divided internally and are themselves suffering a crisis of confidence.

The system also has lost some of its allies. The historic coalition that united labor, middle-class parents, church groups, and government agencies in support of public education has fallen into disarray. The strongest supporters of education traditionally have been those with children in school, but no more than 25% of taxpayers now have children in school (NSPRA, 1986). Without this once solid front of support, America's public schools may be at risk of becoming pauper schools serving only the working class and welfare families.

Other signs of declining confidence are the failure to pass school levies in many communities and middle-class flight from urban areas to suburban or private schools. To compound the problem, as education has become more "professionalized," it has become more isolated from the community. The need to re-establish links between school and community is an obvious step toward developing public confidence. Many schools need help in designing programs and practices that foster good community relationships.

WHAT OPINION POLLS TELL US
ABOUT LOSS OF PUBLIC CONFIDENCE

Public confidence in the schools was at an apex in the 1950s despite accusations that Johnny could not read and that administrators were building school palaces. Public confidence began to decline about the time the Soviet Union launched Sputnik in 1957 and continued to decline into the 1970s.

One measure of public confidence can be found in the Gallup Poll of Public Attitudes Toward Education. A recurring question in the Gallup polls since 1974 asks respondents to give their schools a "grade" of A, B, C, D, or F. In 1986 schools were given high marks (A or B) by 41%, compared to 48% who gave those grades in 1974. Those assigning D's and F's increased from 11% in 1974 to 17% in 1992 (Elam et al., 1994). Despite some ups and downs over the years, these figures do indicate a gradual decline in public confidence. Although respondents with children in schools tend to grade their schools higher than those without children in school, the proportion of such respondents has declined to less than one-fourth of the voting public.

OTHER GROUNDS FOR LOSS OF PUBLIC CONFIDENCE

Some educators may view discussions of public confidence as so much academic quibbling. They are not having any trouble in their schools at the moment, so why worry about it? Such sentiments ignore the fact that *confidence affects action.* Confidence, or lack of it, leads to actions that have consequences for every person in the school system and every citizen in the community. Consequences are evident in the choices people make about schools.

Public schools are facing greater competition for resources and enrollments than ever before. In the last two decades public schools experienced aggressive competition in the form of private schools, both non-sectarian and church related, home schooling, magnet schools, and other alternative types of schools. Some experiments with voucher systems in the late 1960s were short-lived, but the idea persists with strong support from proponents of market-driven schools, a trend which will be investigated in Chapter IX.

A major study on alternative education choices by Bridge and Blackman (1978) concluded that the following factors are influential in parents' decisions about choosing a school:

1. Parents' child-rearing values may affect their choices. Their own education and work experience has taught them that certain things

are necessary for "success." They look for those things in rearing their children and in choosing a school.

2. Geographic proximity is an important factor in choosing a school, particularly among poorer parents. However, as these parents' children become teenagers and as the parents learn more about the choices available, proximity becomes less important. When alternatives are available within a school district, these parents make educationally relevant choices.

3. Better-educated parents use more sources of information in making choices about schools. They make more use of school publications and direct talks with teachers than do other parents.

4. About one-third of parents choose a school because of what is taught and how it is taught. However, curriculum factors are not of major importance in selecting a school.

5. About one-fifth of parents choose a school because of the school staff. After the choice is made, a good relationship with staff is the most important factor contributing to continuing satisfaction.

6. When lower-class parents choose an alternative school, they tend to select those with highly structured programs that stress basic skills and strict discipline. More affluent and better-educated parents tend to choose more flexible programs that stress social relationships, independent learning, and creativity.

Although parents who have no options take their public schools for granted, some parents use the quality of the schools as a primary criterion when buying or renting a house. Included in this group are affluent parents and also poorer parents who are willing to make great sacrifices to get their children in a preferred school.

Criteria used in making choices about school include the general pedagogical approach, unique course offerings, quality of teaching staff, nature of the student body, and general atmosphere of the school (Kyle & Allen, 1982). Other studies show that parents choose private schools because they are dissatisfied with, or cannot find what they want in, public schools (Williams, Hancher, & Hutner, 1983). Oakley (1985) studied choices made in an affluent suburb, where parents had several private schools as well as one alternative program within the public system from which to choose. His findings confirm earlier studies, which show that direct contact with school personnel and testimony from students, neighbors, and acquaintances influence the choices parents make.

Boyer and Savageau (1985, p. 3), in their rating of cities for quality of life, concluded: "If there is one area of public service in which shoddy performance pushes families to change their address, it is the kind of education their children are getting in public schools."

The identified criteria help to determine the level of confidence the public will have in a school. Confidence influences decisions and impels action. Sociological and political factors influencing education in the 1990s require that educators become more knowledgeable about how to address the crisis of confidence in American public schools.

By many accounts, the American education system is not working well. Children appear to be learning less in school today than they did a generation ago. Some 25 percent of the nation's high school students drop out before graduating, and in large cities, whose poor and minority children desperately need quality education, the figure can climb to 50 percent (Lewis, 1986).

More troubling still, these problems have stubbornly resisted determined efforts to solve them. During the last quarter century, successive waves of education reform have swept the country, most recently in the wake of the publication of *A Nation at Risk*. For most of that time, the middle and upper classes in American society strongly supported the public schools. Its leaders were prestigious public officials. The small number of parents who opted for independent schools never really threatened public education, and its authority was widely respected. Public education's favorable political and educational environment has been eroding, gradually but unmistakably. The outcome will not be limited to increased support for private education. It will also include a major reorientation of entry into the labor force. At the present time, media treatment of education is dominated by college preparation and college admissions; relatively little attention is devoted to school failure to prepare young people for the world of work. The costs of this failure cannot be sustained indefinitely. Inevitably, business may gradually replace secondary education as the primary education and training agency for many students currently forced to invest their time in public schools.

DEFINING PUBLIC CONFIDENCE

Public confidence is not something that is easy to see or measure, but we know it is there. And we know that it disposes people toward actions that directly affect both communities and schools. *The Handbook for Developing Confidence in Schools* concluded in 1988 (p. 221) that public confidence in education was a concept worthy of study and after considerable deliberation adopted the following working definition: *Confidence is belief in, faith in, pride in, loyalty to, understanding of, and willingness to support and defend a school or school system.*

Another problem in defining "public confidence" is that there is not one public, but many whose expectations sometimes conflict with one another. Yet many studies show that persons with widely different views nevertheless share basic values about the outcomes of schooling (Achilles, 1984; Hodgekinson, 1990; Oakley, 1985).

RATIONAL AND EMOTIONAL FACTORS INFLUENCING PUBLIC CONFIDENCE

Public confidence is based on both rational and emotional factors. Consideration must be given to both. The rational approach to building confidence in the schools is to give the public the facts that show why a school is good. But emotional factors may cause a person to believe that a school is the best (or worst) in the world despite facts showing that it is not. When emotional factors cause the public to lose faith and trust in the schools, restoring confidence is difficult no matter what the facts are. Negative attitudes tend to persist; and even when facts are available, they may be used selectively to maintain negative attitudes.

The present crisis of confidence is far more, however, than a public relations problem. There is no quick fix. While the public schools have done a remarkably good job of educating children in a time of increased crime, dysfunctional families, poverty, and influx of immigrants, the public's perception is, particularly in urban centers, that the schools are woefully inadequate, broken.

Undeniably, the current debate about schools has included plenty of nonconstructive turmoil and rancor. Still, those who work in schools must welcome the scrutiny. After all, it is a rare and overdue moment when education leaps to the top of the national agenda—and it is during unstable periods like this one that true change often begins. So no matter what misgivings we might have about the current era of school reform, one thing is certain: millions of Americans are currently thinking hard and talking urgently about their schools.

Our schools are assuredly not as dismal as the most strident critics complain, nor as good as they should be or can be. In order to discern why the public's confidence level in its schools has become diminished, the history of American education must be understood against the background of the political, social and economic forces which have impacted American public education over the past 200 years.

Chapter II

ANTECEDENTS OF THE CRISIS

Knowledge of both schools and communities is a prerequisite for understanding the crisis of confidence in American public education. What are these two social entities, the school and the community, between which good relationships ought to exist? Furthermore, why should we care about such a relationship? The answers are found in the historical roots of the American school and society.

Most of those studying the crisis of confidence in the public schools have a rather substantial personal experience within the public schools. What else is necessary? Broad as it may be, one's idiosyncratic experience is, in the last analysis, unique and limited, even though it may extend over decades and have occurred in various geographic locations. A comprehensive view of America's public schools is necessary for a reasonable examination of the present crisis.

Educational professionals like myself with three or more decades of experience in public education are sometimes amused and often frustrated to see the periodic reoccurrence of familiar problems, as well as suggested solutions, without recognizing previous success or failure by others. For example, asked to review the literature about "school size in relationship to effectiveness," a student recently reported on an article published in the early 1960s and concluded, "If this research had been implemented we would have avoided many of the problems we face today." We seem to keep falling into the same trap again and again because we have limited memories. History does repeat itself, perhaps because people were not taught history or, if they were, failed to learn their lessons. Educators are certainly not immune.

Cuban (1990, p. 1) noted the phenomenon in education of "reforming again, again, and again." The education reforms noted by Cuban have often been disguised in a slightly different fashion, with slightly changed labels (for very similar behaviors) and under slightly different conditions. He suggests that by studying the history of education's attempts to solve its problems, one could define preexisting patterns and avoid old mistakes and the repetition of the same attempted reforms. Callahan says that "education is always influenced by the time and place in which it occurs. Education never exists in a vacuum or in the abstract; it always goes in a particular society at a particular time" (1960, p. 107). Such comments could not be better stated; they serve as an appropriate introduction to understanding the present crisis of confidence in American public education.

THE ENGLISH COLONIAL ORIGINS
OF AMERICAN SCHOOLING

Not every citizen of the United States had ancestors who came over on the Mayflower or fought in the American Revolution. Not every Caucasian-American had ancestors who owned slaves. Not every African-American had ancestors who were slaves. Not every citizen is a Christian, nor is every citizen an entrepreneur running a business for profit. Yet the events suggested in the above ancestral scenarios profoundly influenced the configuration of today's public schools in the United States.

Many cultures and historic events shaped the history of the United States, enriched its culture, and influenced today's schools. We are unique in the wide range of native cultures, including Native Americans, Aleuts, Eskimos, and Hawaiians, that augment the immigrant cultures. The Spanish were in the Southwest before the English were at Plymouth, Russians settled Alaska before anyone else, and the French populated the Mississippi Valley from St. Paul to New Orleans. To this is added later immigrations of many peoples that newly comprise our "heritage" and influence our school curriculum.

Yet, when speaking of the nation and its public schools in particular, the English tradition is entrenched. In de Tocqueville's classic observations of American democracy (1945), the Frenchman notes again and again that it was the English traditions, the English language, the English colonists and their religions that dominated the building of the American democracy. When describing the democracy he observed in the early 1800s, he particularly noted the important role of the public schools. Historian after historian of American education also makes that point. The views of these notable scholars are accepted on merit and meaning for fair comparison with today's public schools.

RELIGION IN AMERICAN EDUCATION

In what remains a classic work after thirty years, Callahan (1960) indicates the important role of the schools in the English colonies, as well as their continuing influence on today's schooling. He says, "Similarities are apparent in a comparison of education in colonial and modern America, especially if one looks beneath the surface, for both were in the stream of Western civilization" (p. 107). Additionally, he states, in concert with others, that always in colonial days the notion of schooling was tied closely to the pursuit of religion and piety.

While the early establishment of public education in the development of American democracy was important, education was not the primary concern among colonists. Thus, Callahan notes, "It is not surprising that schools and the means of supporting education were neglected" (p. 121). A logical conclusion is that, except during occasional periods in our history, excellence in public education and the means to provide it were and still are often neglected.

Cremin, in his monumental *American Education: The Colonial Experience* (1970), establishes the fact that the majority of colonies made provision for the schooling of their young during the last half of the seventeenth century and that religion and Bible reading were always of major importance, if not prime motivators of the colonists' interest in schooling. Furthermore, closely related to the considerable importance to the present structure of the curriculum and organization of the public school in the United States, the home was *always* a central element in schooling (pp. 127–131). Nash, in his *History and Education* (1970), sees religion as central in the establishment of schooling in colonial America. In this edited collection of the works of ten others, three chapters are devoted solely to the role of religion in education, and many other chapters mention religion in some way. Cremin (1970) titled the first chapter of his work "The Practice of Piety" and the second "The Nature of Civility" before launching into "The Advancement of Learning" as a background for understanding American education. He has a chapter on the church before presenting his chapter on the school. While noting the pluralist nature of America even in colonial days, Cremin calls attention to the central influence of the English tradition.

> Seventeenth century America was as much a label of religion as it was of social class and ethnicity: in addition to English . . . there were French and Spanish Catholics, Swedish Lutherans, Dutch Calvinists, French Huguenots,

and Spanish Jews, to say nothing of Indian and African. . . . Yet, in this realm as in others, English forms and customs came to predominate, providing the context within which other traditions developed, waned, or changed. (p. 148)

Both Cremin (1970) and Callahan (1960) point to Massachusetts as the keystone of American public education. Callahan emphasizes a quote from the 1642 Massachusetts law establishing public schooling, expressing the primary educational concern of the colonists as "especially of their ability to read and understand the principles of religion and the capital laws of this country" (p. 109). He continued by quoting the "Old Deluder Satan Act" of 1647: "It being the chief project of the old deluder, Satan, to keep men from the knowledge of the Scriptures. . . . It is therefore ordered that every township . . . should then forthwith appoint one within their towne to teach all such children . . . " (p. 115). Cremin concludes that "the schools were established and supported by public taxation for the welfare of the community and that set a precedent" for what was to follow (pp. 114–115).

Like others, Spring (1986) begins his discussion in *The American School* with the chapter "Religion and Authority in Colonial Education." Here again are the two themes in public education in the United States: (1) its English colonial origins and (2) its religious connections. Another theme suggested in Spring's work is the close tie of public education in America to a third influence, the family and parental control. Spring acknowledges this consistent tie between family and public schooling in colonial America but makes an important point:

What distinguishes education in pre-Revolutionary and post-Revolutionary America is the concept of service to the broader needs of government and society. After the Revolution, many Americans began to believe that a public system of education was needed to build nationalism. (p. 28)

The individual and the family began to become submerged within the larger society. This constitutes a shift in emphasis but not a break with the family as an influence in public education in the United States.

In his more politically oriented work, Spring (1989) returns to the theme of religion in American education and the right of the family to make decisions regarding the education of its children. Two important points emerged, each shaping and reordering important threads in American education. Both emanate from constitutional amendments. It is pertinent, however, that for all the discussion of the rights of citizens in the preamble to the Constitution of the United States, the constitution itself guarantees almost no rights for citizens. Attention and concern for citizens' rights came with the first ten amendments and have played major roles in shaping today's public schools. The First Amendment directs that "Congress shall make no law respecting the establishment of religion" (U.S. Constitution).

This last concept was later interpreted to mean that there is a "wall of separation" between all levels of government in the United States and any church or religion. The issue, for the present, was settled by the *Engle v. Vitale* (1962) U.S. Supreme Court ruling that prayers may not be offered. More recent Supreme Court rulings protect the rights of students to pray and conduct religious studies in public schools as long as these activities are student initiated and student led.

Despite the *Engle v. Vitale* ruling, knowledgeable school people will recognize violations of this ruling in some areas of the nation today. However, if based on tenents of colonial education, it would appear that such religious activities in publicly supported schools are not a traditional violation of American schooling but rather a continuation of traditional values.

Those who fear federal legislative and administrative interference in public education should note: it is clearly unconstitutional for the federal government to establish a single public education system for the nation. That is left to the mores and traditions of the American people and the legislatures of their states. However, the federal judicial branch can and has reestablished and restructured public education with rulings based on the First and Fourteenth Amendments. Perhaps the two major shifts in American public education from colonial days to the present are (1) the separation of public education from religion, based on the Fourteenth Amendment and affirmed in the "wall of separation" decision in *Illinois ex. re. McCollum v. Board of Education* (1948), and (2) the establishment of the principle that separate but equal schools are neither equal nor constitutional under the First Amendment as affirmed one hundred years later in the decision *Brown v. Board of Education in Topeka* (1954). It must be noted that both rulings broke with long established traditions in American education and restructured the public schools of America without providing any money to accomplish those purposes. The costs of compliance were left to the states and their people. Also, note that it took a century after those rights were established by constitutional amendment for those same rights to be affirmed and operationalized for all citizens. Traditional and cultural change occurs slowly and with considerable pain in any society and in its schools.

In spite of such changes, the U.S. Supreme Court has, with some consistency, upheld the tradition in American public education that parents have the fundamental right to decide how their children will be educated. Spring (1989) cites numerous cases, the vast majority of which must be interpreted to mean that parents have the right to be prime deciders about what and how their children learn. They may also establish their own "private" schools to provide education. This upholds the colonial tradition that the school shall supplement the education given by the parents at home.

There is also the matter of the predominant upper-class influence in public schools also having its roots in colonial America. Many have noted the predominantly white, male, upper and middle class, Anglo-Saxon composition of local and state school boards (Spring, 1989) and of school administration, although this condition is changing. In addition, a related, and perhaps more insidious influence has been noted by some: the inordinate influence of American business in public education. Spring (1986) calls attention to the influence of American business and capitalism in determining the nature and curriculum of American public schools. He points to the hornbook and McGuffey readers and refers to the scholarly controversy regarding whether public education most serves public need or corporate greed. Perhaps it is Callahan (1960) who best posits that question in his statement about the influence of business in American education:

> What was unexpected [at the outset of research] was the extent, not only of the power of the business-industrial groups, but the strength of the business ideology in the American culture on the one hand and the extreme weakness and vulnerability of schoolmen, especially school administrators, on the other. (pp. ii–iii)

GAINING STABILITY AND
BECOMING A NATION, 1800–1865

Recognizing that "we should honor our colonial forefathers for their efforts to provide schools," Good (1960, p. 421) suggests that the colonists did not envision the bureaucratic institutions that American public schools were to become. Noting that growth in the number of chief state school officers (superintendents) from the 1830s until 1861, when "of 36 states and organized territories, 30 had provided state school officers," he concludes that "the development of the state school office may be regarded as an index to the growing will of the American people to develop public education" (p. 421). The establishment and growth of the state superintendency does measure an intent and a determination to see to it that the nation would provide free public education for its youth.

During the period between 1800 and 1860, not only did the state superintendency grow so that every state in the union had a chief school officer by 1861, but the number of schools and the curriculum also grew. By 1860, the basis for a public school system extending from kindergarten through twelfth grade had been laid, although it had not been completely realized. This was to be supplemented by virtually free state-supported higher education in many states during the 1930s and the 1940s, and aided by the federally legislated education benefits in the G.I. Bill of Rights following World War II.

Two other problems surfaced and were virtually solved during this period. The first was the question of whether some citizens should be taxed for the education of the children of others. The second was the question of whether the public schools should be nonsectarian, teaching values but leaving religion completely to the church. Both issues were reaffirmed under the leadership of Horace Mann, the premier state school superintendent in the history of public education. He led the fight for universal taxation for nonsectarian schools. The years between 1860 and 1865 were truly a test of whether the nation would last. "Equality," "opportunity," "freedom," "destiny" were the things the nation was founded on and floundering toward in 1860. However, the reality for many during this period was slavery, disenfranchisement, poverty, lack of educational opportunity, and actual prohibition from being educated. Surviving the Civil War, our nation moved during the next 130 years, haltingly and slowly, toward those high goals, with the public schools always in the midst, if not on the front lines, of the battle.

WESTWARD EXPANSION AND THE
INDUSTRIAL PERIOD, 1865–1900

With the Civil War over but its value conflicts not resolved, the nation turned its full attention to accomplishing what it saw as its Manifest Destiny. Good (1960) asserts:

The political evils of the congressional plan of reconstruction increased the sectional hatred aroused by war and the fear of Negro control, the burning issue of mixed schools, the outright opposition to Negro education even in separate schools tended to paralyze the agencies which might have developed public education. (p. 435)

In similar fashion, Butts and Cremin (1953, p. 293) note that "the years between 1865 and 1918 mark the transition from the old to a modern America." They see the Civil War as essentially "a struggle between two alternative ways of life, the decentralized agricultural way of the South and the centralized industrial way of the North." The victory, they say, was a "triumph of individual capitalism" (pp. 299–300). The "mopping-up" operation from that victory is still being felt by rural America, reflected in the education reforms of the 1980s and 1990s.

The period between 1880 and 1910 saw corporate America become a dominant force with a series of corporate mergers and the growth of industry, unparalleled since until the time of the Reagan administration nearly a century later. As industry grew, so did the urban areas and the urban schools. This was fueled by immigrants swarming to America to fill jobs largely unwanted by citizens who were the product of earlier immigrations. Consequently, the nature of the population changed as well. Not unlike today, large groups of newcomers with different faces, languages, and religions created fear and suspicion among long-settled citizens. By the end of World War I, immigration to the United States would virtually dry to a trickle for half a century (Butts & Cremin, 1953).

The period between 1880 and 1910 was a period of national growth and expansion for industry; the corporate giants were in control and were aided by a government that believed that the "business of the United States is business." This fact was not lost on public education. Spring (1986) notes that while some historians, such as Cremlin, label all

educational changes of the late nineteenth and the twentieth centuries . . . progressive, . . . many scholars have opposed [that] . . . view [and assert] . . . that the political and administrative structure of education changed to assure elite and corporate control of the educational system and to produce cooperative and docile workers. (pp. 152–153)

Both of these positions, as Spring suggests, are probably overdrawn. Certainly everything done by corporate America is not altruistic. Neither does big business care to control, or try to control, everything in government and surely not everything in public education. As Dahl

(1961) so clearly points out, power in the United States is unequally distributed. That is, the United States is not ruled by any single oligarchy of corporations. Issues at all levels of government are decided by shifting polyarchies of power, coalescing because of shared interest in some particular issue.

Industrial corporations in the United States are interested in having a pool of capable workers who can be motivated by "reasonable" wages and who will produce a "reasonable" profit. They are also interested in assuring that the public schools, whose job it is to provide that pool, do not become so expensive, and taxes so high, that the profit margin is not reasonable or that the market price is driven too high. To this end, private business and corporate America have always exercised a considerable influence in our public schools. Although perhaps not a Machiavellian plot to produce docile workers, corporate influence may not always have been seen as in the "best interest" of public education. Iannaccone (1990), reviewing Callahan's work, sees the decade of 1890–1900 as a "turning point" in American education politics. Agreeing with Burnham (1970) and Schattschneider (1960), Iannaccone sees this period as establishing the basis for three decades of conservative policy in education. This political watershed was created partly by a conservative fear of the massive immigrations of the late 1800s and the fear, particularly in the South, of the African-American population, recently freed and struggling for equality.

While agreeing that American business is influential in public education, as it is in all American politics, Iannaccone (1990) thinks that "ideologically the two systems are profoundly different" (p. 162). The one, business, is operationally exclusive and secret, concentrates power and fosters inequality; the other, American democracy, is broadly egalitarian and public and rests in "disbursed inequalities. . . . Thus the business system with its values and the governmental system with its dissimilar ones are the Gemini twins of American society and its governance as a whole" (p. 163).

Westward expansion went forth until the last of the western territories became part of the continental United States during the early 1900s. The influence of business continued at least through the administrations of Harding, Coolidge, and Hoover in the 1920s and early 1930s. The growth of the immigrant population continued until World War I. These major influences, (1) westward expansion and Manifest Destiny, (2) the heavy influence of business in government and public education, and (3) the growth and change of the population of the United States centering largely in the cities, were all established by 1890 but continued well into the first third of the twentieth century and were marked by conservative ideas and the growth of urban schools.

NATIONAL CONSERVATISM AND GROWTH IN URBAN SCHOOLS, 1900–1950

The United States was an emerging world power during the early 1900s. Its industrial wealth and world influence were growing. Butts and Cremin (1953) make this clear: "The years before 1918 also witnessed growing American influence in the political and economic life of Europe and Asia, a fact which was ultimately destined to change the power structure of the world" (p. 309). Unlike Europe, the United States emerged from World War I stronger than it went in. While Europe was economically and socially decimated, the United States, having fought a "war to end all wars," drew back and became more conservative. Its urban schools grew and thrived, although in many places African Americans were still segregated and undereducated. They and other minority groups were not encouraged to enter the professions or even to stay in school beyond attaining the minimal skills in reading, writing, and figuring needed to succeed in the marketplace. Nonetheless, even individuals with few skills could find employment during the first half of the twentieth century, when laboring jobs were abundant.

It was during this period that Frederick Taylor (1947) laid out his principles of "scientific management," addressed management groups, and published his "theory" throughout the world. The efficiency movement swept public education, its administration, organizations and the newly developing university programs in educational administration. There were three major influences during this period: (1) the work of Counts and Dewey, (2) the adoption of scientific management as a model for education, and (3) a great world depression straddled by two major world wars. The first, not so overt or immediately felt, resulted from the ideas of two educators: John Dewey and George Counts.

Two Great Education Thinkers

"Dewey's philosophy of education took the form of a restatement of the aims of education in the light of the rapid changes that had taken place in American society in the nineteenth century," according to Butts and Cremin (1953, p. 480). Dewey, in his "progressive school" at the University of Chicago, stressed both the social and psychological aspects of the "whole" child, always emphasizing "experimentation" and "experience" as essential elements of the learning process. In such a manner Dewey broke with the usual separation espoused in traditional education, that of mind and body and of the rote learning style and punishment. In many ways Dewey's ideas ran counter to the conservative nature of American politics and business during the first half of the twentieth century. Dewey's commitment to experience as an important aspect of education fitted nicely with the business need and demand for vocational education, and those programs expanded during this period.

George Counts, a social reconstructionist, was prominent from the 1930s to the 1950s. He proclaimed public education as the means of social reform, a means out of poverty and ignorance for the sweltering masses in the American urban slums and into a magnificent world society of free people. For him this was the great possibility of public education in the United States.

Counts conceived of an education system that would move the American nation out of the past and into the future. He suggested that "the present age calls for a great education, for an education liberally and nobly conceived . . . for an education that expresses boldly and imaginatively the full promise . . . and the strength of America" (1952, p. 21). In words clearly suggestive of the preamble to the first National Defense Education Act, Counts stated, "If the democracies are to triumph in this *struggle for the minds and hearts of men,* they will be compelled to derive from the civilizations conceptions of equal power" (p. 37). Therefore, he says,

> the time has arrived to relate our thought about education to the whole sweep and substance of our American civilization — its history, its finest traditions, its present condition, and its promise. We must fashion a conception of civilization that will respect the rights of all nations and champion the cause of liberty at home and before the world. Such an education would prepare the American people to discharge with honor and strength the heavy responsibilities which history has placed on their shoulders. (pp. 37–40)

In other words, Counts saw public education in the United States as the center of a changed society which gives public education its purpose.

The ideas of these two giants in American educational thought remain unrealized but still visible in educational thought today. Probably, with the possible exception of Thomas Jefferson, no two Americans contributed more to the conception of what public education in the United States should be.

Scientific Management

The second major influence in public education during this period was the finalization of a movement that started in the last period. As previously mentioned, Frederick Taylor (1947) had developed his method of scientific management and it was becoming widely accepted as a method of management in the private business sector. Callahan (1962) documented scientific management's movement into public education administration in the 1940s and 1950s and noted its use as the basic framework in newly emerging university programs to train educational administrators. Educational administrators therefore became "school executives" rather than scholars of education who make administrative decisions. It is the period between 1900 and 1950 that clearly established the management orientation in educational administration that continues to dominate the field into the 1990s. This is, therefore, one of the significant events of this period.

The Great Depression

We speak today of recession and unemployment in terms of single-digit numbers. In 1930, 30 percent or more of the work force was unemployed and that work force consisted mostly of persons from single-wage families. A depression of that magnitude could not help but affect the public schools. Even the noblest of school boards had to reduce teacher salaries, and some were required to issue "script" instead of paychecks.

Actually this period and the years following it, climaxing in the 1940s and 1950s, could be referred to as the "Golden Years" for urban public schools in America. Still, many citizens were left out. Dropping out of school after grade six or eight was an accepted practice for male children of poor families in the 1930s. Earning only a very small wage was sufficient for many. Females were generally not encouraged to go beyond high school, or if so only to normal schools or teacher colleges. Entrance into engineering, law, medicine, or politics was nearly unheard of for women. African Americans largely attended segregated schools, which were clearly below the standard of white schools. Even in nonsegregated schools, African Americans were usually not encouraged to aspire to high achievement, such as going to college or entering the professions. In fact, they were often deliberately discouraged from doing so, accomplishing such goals, when they did, largely because of support from parents and family or some close friend.

The economy and the conservative nature of waging a war in the 1940s, followed by enjoying the benefits of victory in the 1950s, left the schools larger but little changed.

Vocational Education, High School, and Higher Education

Two additional influences of importance emerged during this half century. One was the vast expansion of the numbers of students continuing on to high school, particularly after 1935, and the inclusion of greatly expanded vocational education programs in those high schools.

Following the end of World War II and the enactment of the G.I. Bill of Rights, tens of thousands of veterans entered college with the education benefits provided for them in that bill. The result was threefold: (1) colleges and universities grew extensively and their curricula became more practical and more student oriented, and faculties grew proportionately between 1950 and 1965; (2) the university was democratized and no longer seen as a place for only the wealthy; and (3) high schools were forced to be concerned about the possibility that any and all students, regardless of wealth, race, or sex, might be applying to colleges and universities and thus could not be ignored by college preparatory programs.

A HALF CENTURY OF EDUCATIONAL REFORM, 1950–1990

The history of education through the 1940s tends to represent a stream of progress toward better, more expensive, more comprehensive and inclusive public education. Many of these advances, shifts, and changes in public education prior to 1950 were labeled "school reform." Certainly the press to make schools "efficient" through scientific management from 1900 to 1930 was also labeled "reform." Plank (1986) has argued that education reform is often more rhetoric than reality. That is, reform seems to push public education farther and deeper in the direction it has been going. Yet historic events labeled "reform" have been major catalysts for "recharging" and "revitalizing" public education. There were several events during the latter half of the twentieth century that, though not called reform, had a major influence on public education and could be thought of as reform.

The National Defense Education Act

Passed by Congress in response to the USSR launching the first space satellite, *Sputnik,* and enacted by the single Republican president between the Hoover and Nixon administrations, Dwight D. Eisenhower, this reform was designed to help the nation regain superiority in space technology and weaponry. The act was couched, both in its title and its preamble, in defense, military terms and values. It was hardly a broad education support bill, but was aimed at improving education for the college bound in math, science, and foreign languages. However, it did infuse large amounts of money into public education in an effort to specifically increase student achievement in these areas.

The Great Society

Lyndon Johnson, like Franklin Roosevelt, had a distrust of professional educators. Johnson's Great Society, like Roosevelt's New Deal, was not centered in the philosophy of George Counts. Johnson placed his confidence in areas of the private and public sector largely outside organized public education. Although the first Elementary and Secondary Education Act was passed during the Johnson administration, supplying federal money for the first time to public schools across the board, most of the effort and money of the Great Society to help the condition of the poor went to other agencies, often for literacy education and job training outside of the public education bureaucracy. The Great Society was a continuation and extension of the New Deal of Franklin Roosevelt and the Fair Deal of Harry Truman.

The period from the mid 1960s to the mid 1970s was tumultous. There was unrest and rioting in the cities. There was a major civil rights revolution. There was a war in Vietnam, the only war the United States ever lost. Whether because the war absorbed too much money or because it was ill conceived, or perhaps both, the Great Society reform, largely not a public education reform, failed.

The Vietnam War stimulated vigorous protests on college campuses. The issue came to a head in 1974 at Kent State University when several students were shot to death by government forces. These campus incidents helped influence public opinion and undoubtedly helped bring the war to an end.

The loss of the war, the resignation of Richard Nixon as president, and the hostage situation of the Carter administration left the American public decimated psychologically. There was probably no period during which national morale was lower.

Education for the Handicapped

New rights for handicapped students were ushered in with the passage of PL 94-142, the Education for All Handicapped Act. In 1975, President Gerald R. Ford signed this federal law guaranteeing a free and appropriate education to all handicapped children, ages 3–21 (Hagerty & Howard, 1978). This law guaranteeing every handicapped student's right to a quality education placed the United States at the forefront of all civilized countries in providing educational opportunities for its least able citizens.

Failed Expectations

The post-*Sputnik* crisis in the 1960s spawned the development of large-scale curriculum innovations and the advocacy of inquiry-oriented revisions in chemistry and physics, open education, individualized instruction, and so forth. This decade has become known as the *adoption* era, because people were preoccupied with how many innovations of the day were being "taken on," or adopted. Innovations, the more the better, became the mark of progress.

The public schools started naively in the 1960s pouring scads of money into large-scale national curriculum efforts, open plan schools, individualized instruction, and the like. It was assumed, but not planned for, that something was bound to come of it. Educators have never really recovered from the profound disappointment experienced when expectations turned out to be so far removed from the realities of implementation. Indeed, the term implementation was not even used in the 1960s, not even contemplated as a problem.

That world of innocent expectations came crashing down around 1970 when the first implementation studies surfaced. People, especially those toiling in the schools, no doubt already knew something was terribly wrong, but the problem crystallized almost overnight in Goodlad et al.

(1970), Gross et al. (1971), and Sarason's (1971) major studies of failed implementation.

Up to this point, then, one could say that the 1960s' educators had been busy developing and introducing innovations, while in the first half or so of the 1970s they were busy failing at putting them into practice. The negative lessons of these first two periods were not lost, and a number of more positive though hitherto unrelated themes began to converge in the late 1970s. It would be stretching the point to characterize this period (1978–1982) as universal implementation success, but compared with what preceded it, more pockets of success were in evidence. Confidence in their validity was buoyed by the fact that the evidence was coming from a variety of research and practice traditions that were compatible but were arrived at seemingly independently. Implementation research and practice, school improvement, effective schools, staff development (e.g., coaching), and leadership (e.g., the role of the principal) all more or less independently documented success stories and provided lists of key factors and processes associated with these accomplishments.

The futility of attempting to implement one innovation at a time, even serious ones, was attacked with force by the National Commission on Excellence in Education in the watershed document, *A Nation at Risk* (1983). Its subtitle contained the new call to arms, "The imperative for educational reform." The report was an attention getter and both galvanized and reinforced a number of major developments. The Carnegie Forum's (1986) *A Nation Prepared: Teachers for the 21st Century* and the National Governors' Association's (1986) *A Time for Results* were two among several high-powered, nationwide mandates for the action that followed, not to mention the even more prolific omnibus reform efforts at the state level across the United States.

The *Nation at Risk* Reforms

President Reagan used the "bully pulpit" to criticize public education, on the premise that schools were not doing their job. The report of President Reagan's education commission (*A Nation at Risk*) implied that the federal government's responsibility was to point out the failure of public education and then let states and local government devise methods and provide monies to improve it. Thus the education reforms of the 1980s were launched. All were to be *state* reforms. Most consolidated centralized power in state education agencies, requiring new tax money at state and local levels, and were oriented toward producing a pool of more skilled workers so corporate America could compete in world markets. The reforms of the 1980s increased standardization of curriculum, centralization of state authority, and a drive for accountability similar to the "cult of efficiency." The reforms struggled between a quest of meritocracy (raising achievement standards) and egalitarianism (a concern for reducing dropouts). In many of the states in the U.S., intensively so in some states, curricula were specified and mandated, competencies for students and teachers were detailed and tested, salaries of teachers were raised, and leadership competencies were listed. Overlapping these top-down regulatory efforts was another movement which began after 1985. In the U.S. it went under the name of restructuring (Elmore, 1990; Murphy, 1991). Here the emphasis was on school-based management, enhanced roles for principals and teachers, and other decentralized components.

Events of the 1980s had a tremendous impact on our large urban centers. Their infrastructure had been neglected for several decades and was crumbling. Roads, sewage, water, transportation, bridges—all the things people had become accustomed to in large urban centers—could no longer be taken for granted. As poverty, homelessness, drugs, and crime increased in urban centers, more money was needed and given to combat crime. As the cost of crime fighting and prison construction increased, crime accelerated and politicians pontificated.

Additionally, legal immigration to the United States increased during the 1970s and skyrocketed in the 1980s. Unlike previous waves of immigration, most of the new immigrants were from Asia or from Central and South America. "In 1988 alone, the U.S. admitted 643,025 immigrants, a 52-year high. Two hundred thousand people or more also entered illegally that year, pushing the total close to the record highs set during the so-called 'Great Wave of Immigration' " (Sawhill, 1987, p. 16). What all of this suggests is that American schooling, particularly urban education, will change again, whether by plan or fiat.

At this point there is much debate but little evidence that the *Nation at Risk* reforms are succeeding. There is much discourse about "restructuring" schools, but the reforms seem to reemphasize rather than restructure. Assessing the impact of the reforms of the 1980s, it is important to note that local school boards were largely neglected as an instrument for implementing the reforms. The reforms quite clearly were intended to

increase the power of state agencies and decrease the power of local
boards.

THE INFLUENCE OF CORPORATE AMERICA

Some scholars claim that the influence of American business in public
education has been in its own self-interest and pervasive, even to the
detriment of the people, and has contributed in no small part to the
present crisis of confidence in American public education. Others suggest that while the influence of business in public education has been
pervasive, it has benefitted education and the changes resulting from
business influence have been progressive. None, however, argue that
American business does not influence public education. No one or no
group is likely to spend time, energy, and money influencing politics
against their own interest. The United States is not ruled by an oligarchy
but by different polyarchies. The American political system is a system
of inequalities, but in that system of inequalities some are *more* unequal
than others. Corporate America is clearly *not* among the least equal, and
this inequality is often to their advantage.

Business and politics have different systems of valuing and operating.
Corporate America concentrates power and decision making among a
few and decisions are usually made away from the public eye. On the
other hand, American politics is generally egalitarian and public and
requires support in one form or another, usually in the form of votes.
Thus, we have a system of "dispersed inequalities." Corporate America
has considerable power and money; those working for a salary or those
unemployed have little money individually, but they represent a very
large number of votes. Still the resources of corporate America can be,
and have been, used to influence the course of public education and the
votes of middle class and poor in America.

Generalizations do not fit every corporation or every corporate leader.
Many American business people have altruistically served American
education, whether on local boards or through supporting higher taxation in order to improve education. Generalizations need not hold true
in every case in order to be useful. Corporate America has consistently
influenced public education in ways of interest to corporate America.
Educators, it can be argued, ought to be more sensitive and to pay closer
attention to the needs and interests of corporate America. American
democracy, particularly public education, so long as it remains governed

largely by locally elected school boards, results in the American people getting about what they want by going to the polls and voting. Therefore, it can be contended that in the United States, insofar as public education is concerned, the people get more or less what they deserve.

CONCLUSION

The public school system in the United States is unique. The two-party system in its role in political realignment, along with the local school board, represents structures peculiar to American politics. The local governance of public education has its roots in the basic idea of American democracy. It is uniquely American. The local governance of American public education is as much a product of history as is the freedom to participate or not to participate in the governance process. Both are essential to liberty. Local governance notwithstanding, powerful interest groups who have access to the media can influence positively or negatively the public's confidence in public education.

This chapter is not a substitute for the study of history of education, nor for reading any of the many fine works written by scholars of the history of education. Rather, this chapter is intended to provide a brief overview of the history of American education as a basis for the study of the current crisis of confidence in the public schools. Those who study the confidence crisis in public education should understand the foundations of both the American school and the American community.

The following eight chapters are hopeful. They provide a blueprint for fixing what is wrong and restoring America's confidence in its public schools. Built on a foundation of research and exemplary practice, these pages, hopefully, will help to transform American public education.

Chapter III

PREVENTING SCHOOL FAILURE
IN THE TOUGHEST SCHOOLS

The inability to solve the persistent problem of preventing early school failure has contributed to the erosion of confidence in the American public schools. The shameful waste of human resources, particularly in large urban districts, can no longer be ignored and must be immediately addressed.

The evidence presented in this chapter unequivocally undermines the proposition that school failure is inevitable for any but the most retarded children. Further, the programs and practices that, either alone or in combination, have the strongest evidence of effectiveness for preventing school failure for virtually all students are currently available and replicable. None of them is exotic or radical. At the policy level, one can choose to eradicate school failure or one can choose to allow it to continue. It is irresponsible to pretend that there are no choices.

The many changes now occurring in early childhood education are taking place against a backdrop of the public's crisis of confidence in the public school and a growing concern about the effectiveness of our nation's schools, particularly for the children of the poor. This concern is certainly warranted. The National Assessment of Educational Progress (NAEP) (Mullis & Jenkins, 1990) has found steadily increasing reading scores for African-American and Hispanic students, but these students still fall far behind non-minority students.

In schools serving large numbers of disadvantaged students, the situation is, of course, much worse. In research on the Success for All program (Slavin, Madden et al., 1992), the lowest performing quarter of students could hardly read at all at the end of first grade. They averaged a grade equivalent of 1.2 (first grade, second month) on individually administered measures.

One outcome of widespread reading failure is a high rate of retentions in urban districts. In many, 20 percent or more of the children repeat

29

first grade, and more than half of all students have repeated at least one grade by the time they leave elementary school (Lloyd, 1978). In the early grades, performing below grade-level expectations in reading is the primary reason for retention.

The consequences of failing to learn to read in the early grades are severe. Longitudinal studies find that disadvantaged third graders who have failed one or more grades and are reading below grade level are extremely unlikely to complete high school (Lloyd, 1978; Kelly, Veldman, & McGuire, 1964). Remedial programs, such as Chapter 1, have few, if any, effects on students beyond the third grade (Kennedy & Berman, 1986).

Almost all children, regardless of social class or other factors, enter first grade full of enthusiasm, motivation and self-confidence, fully expecting to succeed in school (Entwistle & Hayduk, 1981). Toward the end of first grade, many of these students have already discovered that their initial high expectations are not being verified, and they have begun to see school as negative and demeaning. Trying to remediate reading failure later on is very difficult because by then students who have not experienced success are likely to be unmotivated, to have developed poor self-concepts as learners, to be fearful about reading, and to despise it. Reform is needed at all levels of education, but no goal of reform is as important as ensuring that all children start their school careers with success, built upon a firm foundation in basic skills. Success in the early grades does not guarantee success throughout the school years and beyond, but failure in the early grades does virtually guarantee failure in later schooling. This is one problem that must be solved.

PREVENTING SCHOOL FAILURE: THE OPPORTUNITY

The knowledge that school failure is preventable should fundamentally and profoundly make a difference in the education of students at risk of school failure. Many politicians, business leaders, and even educators believe that adding significant resources to schools, particularly inner-city schools, would simply be misspent or mismanaged. Many others have serious doubts about whether the problems of urban schools are solvable under any circumstances until "underclass" parents begin to behave like middle-class parents. A clear understanding that at least one key problem, early school failure, is essentially solvable would go a long way toward dispelling the belief that money doesn't matter.

Presently, a unique opportunity exists as a result of the emergence of two trends: a growing recognition that early school failure can be prevented, and a political willingness to spend money on programs that are known to work. With continued research, continued development, continued dissemination of effective strategies, and a political will to do what it takes to eradicate it, early failure for nonretarded children could become rare.

CAN PRESCHOOL ALONE PREVENT EARLY LEARNING FAILURE?

There is a strong belief among educators and the general public that early childhood education is a good investment, especially for promoting later school success for disadvantaged students. Support for public investment of preschool programs continues to be high and includes endorsements from such organizations as the Committee for Economic Development, the National Governors' Association, the Council of Chief State School Officers, and the National Association of School Boards.

Many factors have helped create and maintain support for public preschool programs. Demands for public preschool have been fueled by the growing number of children under the age of five who are living in poverty, the increasing number of children from diverse cultures and language backgrounds, and a dramatic increase of parents in need for child-care arrangements.

Perhaps the best known study of the effects of preschool, the Perry Preschool Project, has now followed its initial sample of preschoolers for over two decades after their enrollment in preschool as three- and four-year-olds. This study documented that quality preschool programs benefit those attending them in several important ways, including short-term cognitive gains as well as longer-term positive effects on such outcomes as higher rates of school completion, lower unemployment rates, and lower teenage pregnancy rates (Lazar & Darlington, 1982).

Other critics suggest that it is overly optimistic to expect that a one- or two-year school program at age three or four could have sufficient impact to permanently affect the education and occupational achievements of a child brought up in poverty. For example, Fuerst and Fuerst (1991) argue that preschool by itself is not enough to alter the life chances of children born and reared in poverty. They document that sustained intervention over a period of years, not just a brief shot in the arm, is needed to make a difference for disadvantaged children. The Fuersts base their claim on a long-term study of children enrolled in Chicago's Parent Child Center and in subsequent follow-through programs. In the case of the children studied in Chicago, Fuerst and Fuerst found that it took four to six years of sustained intervention for the girls and seven to nine years for the boys for a detectable achievement difference to be sustained. They argue that a one- or even two-year preschool program may be of value, but that it is not the kind of intervention that makes a significant contribution to the school success of those born into poverty. There is no simple short-term solution for long-term complex problems, they argue.

The implications the Fuersts draw from their research is that "what funds are available for early childhood education should be used for a smaller number of students, but for more years, rather than spending the money on a maximum number of children, for only one year" (Fuerst, 1992, p. 19).

BIRTH TO THREE YEARS: INTERVENTIONS

It is clear that both child-centered and family-centered interventions with at-risk children can make a substantial and, in many cases, lasting difference in their IQ scores. The child-based interventions are ones in which infants and toddlers are placed in stimulating, developmentally appropriate settings for some portion of the day. Family-centered interventions provide parents with training and materials to help them stimulate their children's cognitive development, to help them with discipline and health problems, and to help them with their own vocational and home management skills.

The IQ effects of the programs for children from birth to age 3 were mostly seen immediately after the interventions were implemented, but in a few cases longer-lasting effects were found. The extremely intensive Milwaukee Project (Garber, 1988), which provided 35 hours per week of infant stimulation, including one-to-one interaction with trained caregivers followed by high-quality preschool, parent training, and vocational skills training found the largest long-lasting effects. At age 10, the children (of mildly retarded mothers) had IQ's like those of low-risk children, and they were substantially higher than those of a randomly selected control group of at-risk children (ES = 1.77).

The studies of interventions for children from birth to age three have rarely studied effects on indicators of actual school success, such as reading performance, retentions, or special education placements, but they have demonstrated that IQ is not a fixed attribute of children; it can be modified by changing the child's environment at home and/or in special center-based programs (Ramey & Campbell, 1984). Intensive intervention maintained over a period of several years produces *lasting* effects on measures of cognitive functioning, but even the least intensive models, which often produced strong immediate effects, may be valuable starting points for an integrated combination of age-appropriate preventive approaches over the child's early years.

PRESCHOOL: INTERVENTIONS

In comparison to similar children who do not attend preschool, those who do attend preschool have been found to be higher in IQ and language proficiency scores immediately following the preschool experience, although follow-up assessments typically find that these gains do not last beyond the early elementary years. In addition, there is little evidence to indicate that preschool experience has any effect on elementary reading performance. The most important lasting benefits of preschool are on other variables. Several studies have found lasting effects of preschool experience on retentions and placements in special education. Long-term impacts of preschool on dropouts, delinquency, and other behaviors have also been found (Berrueta-Clement et al., 1984). The effects of preschool on outcomes for teenagers are due, perhaps, to the shorter-term effects on retentions and special education placement in the elementary grades. Retention and special education placements in elementary school have been found to be strongly related to high school dropout rates (Lloyd, 1978).

Attendance at a high-quality preschool program can have long-term benefits for children, but it is equally clear that in itself preschool experience is not enough to prevent early school failure, particularly because preschool effects have not been evident on students' reading performance. Preschool experiences for four-year-olds should be part of a comprehensive approach to prevention and early intervention, but a one-year program, whatever its quality, cannot be expected to solve all the problems of at-risk children. Prekindergarten programs implemented as part of comprehensive programs for children from birth to age five or in connection with changes in the early elementary grades are much more likely than one-year programs to have lasting achievement effects.

KINDERGARTEN

Since the great majority of children now attend kindergarten or other structured programs for five-year-olds, the main questions about kindergarten in recent years have focused on full-day versus half-day programs and on effects of particular instructional models for kindergarten. Research comparing full- and half-day programs has generally found positive effects of full-day programs on end-of-year measures of reading readiness, language, and other objectives. However, the few studies that have examined full-day kindergarten effects have failed to find evidence of maintenance even at the end of first grade.

Several specific kindergarten models have been found to be effective on end-of-kindergarten assessments. Among these were Alphaphonics, Astra's Magic Math, MECCA, TALK, and MARC (Slavin, 1991; Karweit, 1989). These are all structured, sequenced approaches to building prereading and language skills felt to be important predictors of success in first grade. However, of these, only Alphaphonics presented evidence of long-term effects of student reading performance. IBM's Writing to Read computer program had small positive effects on end-of-kindergarten measures, but longitudinal studies have failed to show any carryover to first or second grade reading (Karweit, 1989).

ORGANIZATION IN BEGINNING READING

The major conclusions of research regarding school and classroom reorganization to promote greater success in reading in the early grades are as follows:

Class size. The effects of substantial reductions in class size on reading in the early grades are clearly positive but small, and they tend to fade beyond the first grade even if students remain in small classes (Bain et al., 1988).

Aides. Provision of instructional aides to assist classroom teachers has rarely been found to have any effect on achievement, although it may improve the quality of life for teachers. On the other hand, aides using structured one-to-one tutoring programs can make a substantial difference in student reading achievement (Word et al., 1990; Hicks, 1976).

Ability Grouping. Assignment of students to classes on the basis of ability or achievement level has few effects on student achievement. Regrouping for reading and use of within-class ability grouping (reading groups) have not been adequately studied at the early grade levels to permit any conclusions to be drawn. However, there is evidence of strong positive effects of the Joplin Plan (in comparison to use of multiple reading groups within the classroom). The Joplin Plan involves grouping students across grade lines according to reading levels, so that whole-class instruction (or at least a smaller number of reading groups) can be used (Slavin, 1987; Bremer, 1958).

Nongraded primary. The term *nongraded primary* or *elementary school* refers to a range of practices intended to allow students to move through the grades at their own pace, progressing through a series of levels in major content areas rather than following a lockstep grade-to-grade progression. Some nongraded programs have used individualized instruction, learning stations, team teaching, multi-age grouping, and other strategies, whereas others have simply used nongraded grouping as a means of flexibly grouping students across grade lines for instruction (Goodlad & Anderson, 1963).

Research from the first wave of implementation of the nongraded primary support the use of simple forms of this strategy but not complex ones. Simple forms are ones in which students are regrouped across grade lines for instruction (especially in reading and mathematics) and are taught in groups. In their very simplest versions, this strategy is essentially identical to the Joplin Plan, cross-grade grouping for reading only (Slavin, 1987). These simple nongraded programs primarily have the effect of allowing teachers to accommodate instruction to individual needs without requiring students to do a great deal of seatwork (as is customary in many traditional reading groups). In contrast, complex forms of the nongraded primary that made extensive use of individualized instruction, learning stations, and open space were not generally effective in increasing student achievement (Gutierrez & Slavin, 1992).

Clearly, changing school and classroom organization practices is not in itself an adequate strategy for preventing early reading failure. However, in combination with other interventions, such practices as reducing class size in first grade and using grouping methods that allow for whole class instruction in reading while providing instruction appropriate to students' needs can contribute to the chances that students will be successful in reading the first time they are taught, and as such they can be important elements of a comprehensive prevention strategy.

RETENTION, DEVELOPMENTAL KINDERGARTEN AND TRANSITION FIRST GRADES

Many schools attempt in one form or another to identify young children who are at risk for school failure and give them an additional year before second grade to catch up with grade level expectations. Students who perform poorly in kindergarten or first grade may simply be retained and recycled through the same grade. Alternatively, students who appear to be developmentally immature may be assigned to a two-year developmental kindergarten or junior kindergarten sequence before entering first grade. Some schools have a transitional first grade or "pre-first" program designed to provide a year between kindergarten and first grade for children who appear to be at risk.

Interpreting studies of retention and early extra-year programs is difficult. Among other problems, it is unclear whether the appropriate comparison group should be similar children of the *same age* who were promoted or similar children in the *same grade* as the one in which students were retained. That is, should a student who attended first grade twice be compared to second-graders (his or her original classmates) or first-graders (his or her new classmates)?

Studies that have compared students who experience an extra year before second grade have generally found that these students appear to gain on achievement tests in comparison to their same-grade classmates but not in comparison to their age-mates. Further, any positive effects of extra-year programs seen in the year following the retention or program participation consistently wash out in later years (Banerji, 1990). Clearly, the experience of spending another year in school before second grade has no long-term benefits. In contrast, studies of students who have been retained before third grade find that, controlling for their achievement, such students are far more likely than similar nonretained students to drop out of school (Lloyd, 1978).

CLASS SIZE AND INSTRUCTIONAL AIDES

A popular policy in recent years has been to reduce class size markedly in the early elementary grades. Because it is so politically popular (albeit expensive) to implement, class size reduction should in a sense be the standard against which all similarly expensive innovations should be judged.

Decades of research on class size have established that small reductions in class size (e.g., from 25 to 20) have few, if any, effects on student achievement. However, research has held out the possibility that larger reductions (e.g., from 25 to 15) may have educationally meaningful impacts (Cahen et al., 1983).

The largest and best controlled study ever done on this question was a statewide evaluation in Tennessee (Word et al., 1990) in which students were randomly assigned to classes of 15 with no aide, 25 with an aide, or 25 with no aide in kindergarten and then maintained in the same configurations through the third grade. This study found moderate effects (ES = +.25) in favor of the small classes as of the third grade. A year after the study, this difference had fallen to a mean of +.13 (Nye et al., 1991). Other statewide studies of class size reduction in the first grade in South Carolina (Johnson & Garcia-Quintana, 1978) and Indiana (Farr et al., 1987) found even smaller effects of substantial reductions in class size.

The Tennessee class size study also evaluated the effects of providing instructional aides to classes of 25 in grades K through 3. The effects of the aides were near zero in all years. This is consistent with the conclusions of an earlier review by Schuetz (1980). However, evidence did find that aides could be effective in providing one-to-one tutoring to at-risk first-graders.

Reducing class size may be a part of an overall strategy for getting students off to a good start in school, but it is clearly not an adequate intervention in itself.

ONE-TO-ONE TUTORING

Of all the strategies reviewed, the most effective by far for preventing early reading failure are approaches incorporating one-to-one tutoring of at-risk first-graders. Evidence of positive effects of tutoring has been found with Success for All (Slavin et al., 1992), Reading Recovery (Pinnell, 1989), and Prevention of Learning Disabilities (Silver & Hagin, 1990) which use certified teachers as tutors; the Wallach Tutorial Program (Wallach & Wallach, 1976) and Programmed Tutorial Reading (Ellson et al., 1965) use paraprofessionals and are correspondingly much more prescribed and scripted.

The immediate reading outcomes for all forms of tutoring are very positive, but the largest and longest-lasting effects have been found for the three programs that use teachers rather than aides as tutors. Reading Recovery is a highly structured model requiring a year of training and feedback. It emphasizes direct teaching of metacognitive strategies, "learning to read by reading," teaching of phonics in the context of students' reading, and integration of reading and writing, and is limited to the first grade. Two follow-up studies of this program have found that strong positive effects seen at the end of first grade do maintain into second and third grades.

Prevention of Learning Disabilities focuses on remediating specific perceptual deficits as well as improving reading skill and usually operates for two school years. Reading effects of this program were substantial in three studies at the end of the program and in follow-up studies remained very large as of the end of third grade. The tutoring component of Success for All resembles that of Reading Recovery, in that it emphasizes "learning to read by reading" and teaching of metacognitive strategies, but it is different from both Reading Recovery and Prevention of Learning Disabilities, in that it is closely coordinated with the regular classroom instruction in reading.

Success for All tutoring is provided for at-risk students until they are performing adequately, and may therefore continue into second grade in some cases. However, most students who receive any tutoring remain in tutoring for one semester in first grade. The Success for All program includes many components in addition to tutoring, such as improvements in curriculum and instruction from preschool to grade five and a family support program, so the unique effects of tutoring cannot be separated out. However, reading effects for the lowest achievement quarter of students have been substantial in several evaluations and have maintained through the third grade (Slavin et al., 1992; Haxby & Madden, 1991). In addition, substantial reductions in retentions and special education placements have been found.

The Tutoring Model

An effective teacher teaches within a child's zone of proximal development (Day, Cordon, & Kerwin, 1989; Vygotsky, 1978). In other words, the teacher neither teaches children at their actual level, because they would not be challenged, nor does the teacher teach beyond what the children are currently capable of doing. Instead, the effective teacher instructs the students in their zone of proximal development with material that is well within their grasp but that also challenges their potential.

With a group of 25 to 30 students who all have varying cognitive abilities, it is difficult to teach within *each* student's zone of proximal development. However, the one-to-one tutoring partnership creates the perfect situation for working within a student's zone of proximal development. The tutor can determine what the child knows about reading, what reading strategies he or she uses, and how he or she processes information. The tutor can tailor the instruction for each student's needs.

Affordability of One-To-One Tutoring

It does not come as a surprise that one-to-one tutoring of primary grade students is effective. A more important question is whether it is effective enough to justify its considerable costs. One way to address this question is to compare tutoring to expensive interventions. For example, experiments in Tennessee, New York City, Toronto, and Indiana have reduced class size by almost half. This is the same as hiring an additional teacher for each class, who could instead be used to provide one-to-one tutoring for 20 minutes per day to about 15 students. The best and most successful of these class size experiments, a Tennessee statewide study, found a cumulative effect of substantially reducing class size from kindergarten to third grade of about +.25 (Word et al., 1990), less than that found in any of the tutoring models. Other studies of halving class size have found even smaller effects. The effects of having aides work in the classroom have been found to be minimal in many studies (Schuetz, 1980); the same aides could be used as tutors using models designed for that purpose, or replaced by teachers for a greater impact.

On the other hand, it is not yet established that a heavy investment in first grade will pay off in permanent gains for at-risk students. Tutorial programs such as Reading Recovery and Prevention of Learning Disabilities results hold out significant hope for lasting gains, and the cumulative effects of Success for All also show promise for maintaining initial gains. Reductions in retentions and special education referrals, seen in the tutoring models, have both immediate and long-term impacts on the costs of education for low achievers. Substantial savings due to reduced retentions and special education placements have been shown for Reading Recovery (Dyer, 1992) and for Success for All (Slavin et al., 1992).

However, if first grade tutoring models prove to have long-term effects, either without additional intervention (as in Reading Recovery and Success for All), cost effectiveness will not be the only criterion for deciding to use these models. If it is known that large numbers of students can be successful in reading the first time they are taught, and that the success not only lasts but also builds a basis for later success, then educators and legislators would feel compelled to do whatever it takes to see that all students do in fact receive that which is necessary for them to succeed.

Although much more information is needed about how tutoring works and how to maximize its effectiveness and minimize its cost, *it is clear from the research that one-to-one tutoring is an effective means of preventing student reading failure.* As such, preventive tutoring deserves to be a primary consideration in the reform of compensatory, remedial, and special education. Because current research shows educators how to ensure that students will learn to read in the early grades, there is an ethical and perhaps legal responsibility to see that they do. Preventive tutoring is the best available possibility for providing a reliable means of abolishing illiteracy among young children who are at risk for school failure.

The most important component of early reading success is that the school must continue with every child until that child is succeeding. If prevention is insufficient, the child may need tutoring. If tutoring is not enough, the child may need help with behavior or attendance or eyeglasses. If this is not enough, the child may need a different reading program. In a Success for All school, "good enough" is never good enough (Slavin et al., 1992). The school does not merely provide services to children, it constantly assesses the results of the services it provides and keeps varying or adding services until every child is experiencing success.

INTEGRATING SERVICES ACROSS THE YEARS

There is a consistent pattern seen across most of the programs and practices reviewed. Whatever their nature, preventive programs tend to have their greatest impacts on variables closely aligned with the intervention and in the years immediately following the intervention period. The positive effects seen on these variables were strongest immediately after the program and then faded over time.

Some might conclude from the observation that effects of early interventions often fade in later years as an indication that early intervention is ultimately futile. Yet such a conclusion could be too broad. What research on early intervention suggests is that there is no "magic bullet"—no program that, administered for one or two years, will ensure the success of at-risk children throughout their school careers and beyond. However, it is equally clear that there are key developmental milestones that children must successfully achieve in their first decade of life and that it is known how to ensure that virtually all of them do so.

The first hurdle, for children from birth to age 5, is development of the cognitive, linguistic, social, and psychological basis on which later success depends. Second, by the end of first grade, students should be well on the way to reading. Each year afterward, students need to make adequate progress in basic and advanced skills, at least enough to avoid any need for remedial or special education and to be promoted each year.

Research on programs for children from birth to age three, on preschool, and on kindergarten shows that educators know how to successfully teach first grade children with good language skills, cognitive skills, and self-concepts, no matter what their family backgrounds or personal characteristics may be. Research on tutoring, instruction, curriculum, and organization of early grades education shows that educators know how to successfully teach third grade students who can read, regardless of their family and personal backgrounds. While early interventions have been the focus of this chapter, it is important to note that there are many programs and practices with strong evidence of effectiveness for at-risk students throughout the grades (Slavin, Karweit, & Madden, 1989). Rather than expecting short-term interventions to have long-term effects, at-risk children must be provided with the services they need at a particular age or developmental stage.

Intensive, "preventive" services must be provided for a very small proportion of those now served in special education for several years. But for the great majority of students, including nearly all of those currently served in compensatory education programs and many of those now called "learning disabled," Slavin and associates believe that *intensive* intervention will only be needed for a brief period, primarily one-to-one tutoring in first grade. After these students are well launched in reading, they still need high-quality instruction and other services in the later elementary grades to continue to build on their strong base.

Improving instruction by means of implementing research-based curriculum and exemplary instructional practices, quality professional development, and improved school organization is relatively inexpensive. Intensive early intervention for at-risk children without following up with improved instruction is unlikely to produce lasting gains, and mild interventions over extended periods may also fail to bring low achievers into the educational mainstream. Yet intensive early intervention followed by long-term improvements in instruction, curriculum, and other services can produce substantial and lasting gains.

HOW MANY STUDENTS CAN SUCCEED AND AT WHAT COST?

Evidence from the Success for All, Reading Recovery, and other tutorial programs suggests that it is possible to ensure the school success of the majority of disadvantaged, at-risk students using the Chapter 1 funds already allocated to these schools in different ways, i.e., to improve curriculum, instruction, and classroom management in the regular classroom. However, ensuring the success of all at-risk students takes a greater investment. There is a large category of students who would fail to learn to read without intervention, but succeed with good preschool and kindergarten experiences, improved reading curriculum and instruction, perhaps short-term tutoring at critical junctures, family support, or other relatively inexpensive assistance. A much smaller group of students might require extended tutoring, more intensive family services, and so on. A smaller group still would need intensive intervention before preschool as well as improved early childhood education, tutoring, and other services to succeed in school.

The costs of ensuring the success of at-risk children increase exponentially as the degree of risk increases. By making wise use of limited funds, the success of most at-risk students could be ensured. Ensuring success for each additional child beyond this costs an increasing amount per child.

Nothing in this chapter should be interpreted as suggesting that dollars can magically be turned into success. This chapter has noted many types of investments that have failed to make any marked impact on achievement. Money does not ensure success, but the programs that do ensure success cost money.

PREVENTING EARLY READING FAILURE

The most important objective of compensatory education ought to be to ensure that children are successful in reading the first time they are taught and never become remedial readers. The importance of reading success in the early grades is apparent to anyone who works with at-risk students. The consequences of failing to learn to read in the early grades are severe. For example, disadvantaged students who have failed a grade and are reading below grade level are extremely unlikely to graduate from high school. Chapter 1 itself has few effects beyond the third grade (Kennedy, Birman, & Demaline, 1986), which suggests the difficulties inherent in intervening too late. Retentions and special education referrals are usually based on early reading deficits.

The evidence presented in this chapter indicates that reading failure in the early grades is preventable. Well-structured programs incorporating one-to-one tutoring can greatly reduce reading failures. A coordinated combination of preschool, kindergarten, early reading and family support approaches can virtually eliminate reading failure even among the most disadvantaged and at-risk students. This and other evidence suggest that reading failure is preventable for nearly all children, even a substantial portion of those who are typically categorized as learning disabled.

Reading failure *can* and *should* be prevented! Chapter 1 is the logical program to take the lead in giving schools serving disadvantaged students the resources and programs necessary to see that all children learn to read.

ENHANCING PREVENTION AND REGULAR CLASSROOM INSTRUCTION

One of the most fundamental principles of Chapter 1/Title I has been that compensatory funds must be focused on the lowest-achieving students in qualifying schools. In principle, this makes sense, in that it avoids spreading Chapter 1 resources too thinly to do low achievers any good. But in practice, this requirement has led to many problems, including a lack of consistency or coordination between regular and Chapter 1 instruction, disruption of children's regular classroom instruction, labeling of students who receive services, and unclear responsibility for children's progress.

However, without an investment in staff development, Chapter 1 services will always be rowing against the tide, trying to patch up individual children's deficits without being able to change the environment in which Chapter 1 students spend the great majority of their day, the regular classroom. Under current regulations, schools can use a portion of their Chapter 1 dollars for staff development, but this rarely goes into the kind of training, follow up, and assessment needed to effectively implement validated programs which concentrate services at first and second grade levels to provide effective prevention and intervention.

Chapter 1 is extremely important to the most vulnerable children. For more than 25 years it has focused attention and resources on low-achieving students in disadvantaged schools. Yet Chapter 1 can become proactive in preventing learning problems rather than primarily reactive in remediating problems that are already serious. It can ensure literacy for every child; it should become a major force in bringing effective programs into schools serving disadvantaged students.

SUCCESS ONE YEAR AT A TIME

Instructional programs must help students maintain success at each critical stage of development, assuring that all students leave first grade well on their way to success in reading and other critical skills. This requires effective kindergarten and first grade instruction and curriculum, family support programs to ensure parental support of the school's goals, and one-to-one tutoring or other intensive interventions for students who are having difficulties in reading. As students move into second and third grades and beyond, this means continuing to improve regular classroom instruction, monitoring student progress, and intervening intensively as frequently as necessary to maintain at-risk students at a performance level at which they can fully benefit from the same instruction given to students not at risk.

The school mission ought to be to organize school and nonschool resources and programs to relentlessly and systematically prevent students from becoming academically handicapped from their first day of school to their last. Rather than just trying to adapt instruction to student heterogeneity, the original problem must be attacked at its source, attempting to remove the low end of the performance distribution by preventing whatever deficits can be prevented, intensively intervening to identify and remediate any remaining deficits, and maintaining interventions to keep at-risk students from sliding back as they proceed through the grades.

PREVENTION OF SPECIAL EDUCATION PLACEMENT

It is too early to say precisely what proportion of the students now identified as having academic handicaps can be prevented from ever having learning deficits serious enough to warrant special education. It may be that as educators' knowledge and experience grow, it will become possible to avoid separate special education for many students currently categorized as learning disabled (about 4.8 percent of all students ages 3 to 21 [Hagerty & Howard, 1978, p. 80]), plus some proportion of those identified as mildly mentally retarded and behaviorally handicapped. For example, more than 80 percent of at-risk students in Reading Recovery are successfully discontinued and then continue reading adequately through the upper elementary grades (Pinnell, 1989).

CONCLUSION

Early school failure can be prevented for nearly every child. The knowledge that this is a practical and attainable reality must have consequences for this country's policies toward at-risk students. If educators know how to prevent school failure and do not take advantage of this knowledge, then the blame lies with educational and political leaders, certainly not the children who fail or their parents or their communities. If we, as a society, decide to make school failure a thing of the past, we can do so.

Do today's political and budgetary imperatives make a major new commitment to preventing school failure, particularly for America's most disadvantaged children, seem illusory? Do the costs of first-class programs, in dollars and professional resources, preclude elected officials from allocating substantial funds to meet the needs of such a powerless constituency?

The writer hopes that enlightened realism will prevail. All Americans will benefit from the prevention of school failure. All Americans are burdened by the high cost of not making the required investment. Reaching out to the hard to teach and helping the disadvantaged learners do not represent idle sentiment but a practical response to an urgent American problem.

The chilling effects of budgetary deficits ought not be allowed to deter action. Doctor Isabel V. Sawhill, senior economist at Washington's Urban Institute, explains it this way: "Large deficits make it difficult to argue for new spending [because they lower the rate of economic growth and threaten future standards of living]. Unfortunately, a failure to invest in the next generation has precisely the same effects" (Sawhill, 1988, p. 11).

Knowing now that effective prevention strategies and interventions can significantly reduce the number of children who experience failure in the early elementary grades, we must make sure that these newly available tools are put to work. We know how to provide the relentless one-to-one tutorial and small group tutorial services required by the needy children. We know how to intervene so that virtually all children can arrive at the third grade *functioning at grade level* and to help break the cycle of educational retardation that reaches succeeding generations. Unshackled from the myth that nothing works, we can assure that children without hope today will have a real chance to be contributing citizens tomorrow.

Chapter IV

THE AGONY OF UNDERCLASS SCHOOLS

S ince the early 1980s the media have proclaimed the failure of American public schools. However, the drumbeat of bad news about the schools which contributes to the "crisis of confidence" does contain some faulty data. For example, the top 20% of American students outscore the top 20% of Japanese students, and American students in the upper 50% of American classes score as well as or better than Japanese students in the upper 50% of Japanese classes. Furthermore, the recent scores from the Iowa Test of Basic Skills show that test scores are at an all-time high in every grade except eighth and twelfth. "Virtually all the widely used standardized scores are up and rising" (Bracey, 1993).

The data of significance is in the scores of American students in the lower 50% of their classes. These students are far behind both the upper half of American classes and the upper half of Japanese classes. Concern for the academic performance on the lower half students has contributed to the decline in confidence in the public schools. In a very real sense, America has two school systems: perhaps three-quarters of American students attend decent public and private schools, while the other fourth attend those big-city schools that are often weighed down with grievous problems. Only by averaging these two separate and different systems can one derive the picture, the false and misleading picture, that America's main educational problem is mediocrity.

The American bottom half, largely the urban and the rural poor, are in serious difficulty and will remain in difficulty unless a moral and financial commitment is made to put in place the most exemplary educational practices and programs in the inner cities and rural areas where the schools are in terrible shape.

In order to make a difference in schools with large numbers of disadvantaged children, the nature of the problem from a cultural and sociological perspective must be understood. Educators also must "get over" the idea that the most exemplary research-based practices won't work in urban schools. Both of these issues will be addressed in the chapter.

INSUFFICIENT FAMILY-SOCIAL CAPITAL

As the primary influence on the life of the child, the family should be the basic institution upon which other socializing institutions within society build. It is estimated that over one-half of all young people will live in a single-parent home at some time (Kirst, McLaughlin & Massell, 1990). Given the nontraditional nature of the vast majority of families in urban areas, it makes sense that any given family is best understood within its own context, what Ogbu (1981) termed a "cultural-ecological perspective," rather than by comparison with other groups (Wagstaff & Gallagher, 1990).

Trends in key indicators about the family suggest that many families, especially those in urban areas, are troubled. In female-headed families, 10% are Asian Americans, 12% white Americans, 24% Hispanic Americans, and 52% African Americans (Kirst, McLaughlin, & Massell, 1990). In 1985, "20% of all children, 54% of children in female-headed families and 78% of black children in female-headed families lived in poverty" (Wagstaff & Gallagher, 1990, p. 103). As Hoffer and Coleman (1990, p. 123) noted, there is a "pattern of growing inequality of family background which one would expect to find reflected in measures of educational outcomes." If this hypothesis is correct, then school achievement is likely to be adversely affected, as family structures continue to change for urban populations. Both common sense and research tell us that as family stress, *regardless of its source,* increases, the capacity for nurturing decreases and the likelihood of abuse and neglect increases. Whether the stress stems from insufficient income, a difficult child, an impaired adult, family violence and discord, inadequate housing, chronic hunger and poor health, or surroundings of brutality, hopelessness, and despair—these are circumstances in which affection withers into hostility, discipline turns into abuse, stability dissolves into chaos, and love becomes neglect (Hoffer & Coleman, 1990, p. 151). Such stress on the family can become most dysfunctional in those neighborhoods that have the lowest levels of supportive mechanisms, namely, the poorest of the inner-city neighborhoods.

Thus, the total social capital available within the neighborhood in which poverty is extreme and concentrated and social isolation is characteristic is insufficient to support families in need. Other neighborhoods with a greater reservoir of social capital might be able to bolster a family in stress. But inner-city neighborhoods in extreme poverty cannot, so child rearing under stress is much more difficult. Where informal supports are not forthcoming, there is a greater dependence on formal supports of social service institutions. When those formal supports are not present or are insufficient in quality or scope, the family under stress is forced to depend on its own resources, which often are simply not enough to insure adequate child rearing.

One stress that inner-city families must face is the absence of fathers and the high incidence of unmarried mothers. W. J. Wilson (1989) argued that such an occurrence was based on the effects of joblessness and economic exclusion for inner-city residents. Citing the work of Testa et al. (1989), Wilson noted that employed fathers are two-and-a-half times more likely to marry the mother of their firstborn child than are unemployed fathers. Therefore, joblessness is central to the fact that many children in the ghetto do not have married parents. This effect of joblessness pertains not only for African Americans but also for Puerto Ricans, Mexican Americans, and white Americans. This is but another indication that dysfunctional elements in the inner city have a systemic basis related to broader forces of the economy and the urban context. The responsibility which urban high schools have for joblessness will be discussed in detail in Chapter VII.

RESTRUCTURING

Currently, urban school districts are the locales of numerous experiments in the restructuring of schools. In Chicago, parents and community members have been given substantial power on locally elected school councils, including the authority to hire and fire principals (Wilkerson, 1989). The school district of Chelsea, Massachusetts has been taken over by Boston University, which manages the district under a special management contract (Watkins, 1990).

Neither centralization nor local control has served as a panacea for solving the problems of urban school systems. Each has its advantages and disadvantages, which cause a pendulum movement over the years from one form to the other. When school officials have known what they wanted to do and how to do it, then faith in centralization was strong, as in the early nineteenth century and in the 1890s. But when both the means and the ends of schooling seem confused and uncertain, and when the political legitimacy of the educational authorities appeared doubtful, there has been a trend to decentralize control of the schools.

URBAN SCHOOL LEADERSHIP

The principal needs to identify local urban resources with which the school can link to better serve its community. These resources include cultural institutions, universities, businesses, financial institutions, private foundations, churches, and the like, as well as various social service agencies. A catalog of these is an indispensable resource. A principal needs to develop a network of contacts with such organizations and agencies in order to develop broad community support for the school and its goals. The principal must recognize that the urban school is entangled with the broader urban community (Hill, Wise, & Shapiro, 1989). Consequently, the principal must constantly look for ways to build bridges between school and community.

The successful urban principal should have a healthy distrust of the status quo. The principal needs to be able to disrupt routines and ask basic questions, including "What is going on here?" (Florio-Ruanne, 1989). Simply because something has traditionally been done a certain way is not a justification for its continuance. The good leader constantly examines what others take for granted and looks for ways in which the organization can continuously improve itself. This is a necessary characteristic of a reformer.

The literature on successful programs time and time again emphasizes that active leadership is a crucial ingredient of success. The principal must have a moral purpose, the attitude that he or she can make a difference. As some researchers have observed, "it is well known that administrative leadership, particularly on the part of the building principal, frequently is the crucial characteristic associated with successful inner-city schools" (Levine, Levine, & Eubanks, 1987, p. 84).

REDUCING STUDENT ALIENATION

As James Comer (1989) has noted, the possibility of school success for urban children will be greatly enhanced if schools can reduce the alienation of children, families, and other groups within the school community. The framework for analyzing and reducing student alienation is based primarily on the work of Newman (1989). When discussing alienation, Newman draws on a long history of psychological and sociological literature referring to the fragmentation, estrangement, and separation felt by individuals, as well as objective structural conditions that are political, economic, and social. Newman (1990) argues that the possibility of reducing alienation creates a moral obligation to do so.

> The fact that schools vary considerably in the extent of student and staff commitment and engagement indicates that the ills of modernization do not fall uniformly on all schools. The evidence that some schools are operated in ways that minimize the alienating features of modern life offers reason enough to continue the quest. (p. 257)

A strategy for reducing alienation involves reorganizing the schools so that the units of student identification are in fact small. Schools within schools, a house system, and homerooms are all strategies that have potential for contributing to student identification. The more time children spend in these units and the greater substantive role they play, the more they are likely to reproduce the desirable effects of small schools. Because student alienation has been identified as problem of increasing magnitude, Chapter V will deal specifically with the issue of student alienation.

ORGANIZATION OF THE SCHOOL DAY

"The schedule should be the servant of instruction, not the boss. It is a significant purpose of leadership to make it that" (Maehr et al., 1992, p. 423). Flexible scheduling is an extremely important facilitating feature of achievement-oriented schools. In itself, it does not guarantee a task focus, but it is more suited to a task focus than traditional scheduling, which accommodates lecturing. Flexible schedules can promote heterogenous grouping, student choices, independent student work, variety in instructional styles, instructional innovation, learning task variety, field trips, project work, variety in evaluation technique, and other possibilities related to a task focus and improved motivation. The traditional schedules of many urban schools are unnecessarily restrictive for students and teachers. The organization of the school day can be a powerful tool to create variety and excitement, while carefully giving students more responsibility and control over their learning.

INVOLUNTARY MINORITIES AND IMMIGRANTS

A major focus of the urban educators' efforts to improve motivation to learn in school should be the larger cultural environment. Because of the particular challenge represented by the significant presence of minority populations in urban communities, long the victims of restricted opportunity, prejudice, and racism, this discussion is based on the cogent and important analyses of John Ogbu (1981) and Signithia Fordham (1988). If school can give hope to the urban underclass and engage their children sufficiently to succeed in school, the likelihood is that all children, including those who come from advantaged families, will benefit.

Ogbu identifies two distinct types of minorities: immigrants and involuntary minorities. Immigrants voluntarily come to the host country with hope of improving their lives. They also compare their present situation favorably with the situation in their native country and very significantly, they retain an identity with a primary culture, usually with its own language. For these reasons, immigrant children tend to do well in the school of their newly adopted country (Ogbu, 1981). Their voluntary status results in a culture that enhances attitudes and behaviors that are associated with success in school (Ogbu, 1981).

Involuntary minorities tend to respond to their exploitation by developing oppositional identities and oppositional cultural frames of reference (Ogbu, 1988, p. 176). The oppositional identity forms in response to perceived patterns of discrimination and exclusion. For blacks, it is a social identity system "which they perceive and experience not merely as different but more particularly as in opposition to the social identity system of their dominators" (p. 176). Behaviors and attitudes associated with the dominant culture are deemed inappropriate for the dominated culture. An oppositional cultural frame of reference emerges "which includes devices for protecting their identity and for maintaining boundaries between them [blacks] and white Americans" (Fordham, 1986, p. 181).

For involuntary minorities, there exist two conflicting cultural frames of reference, one for the dominant culture, and one for theirs. Theirs is an oppositional culture, defining attitudes and behavior appropriate for the minority and inappropriate for the dominant culture. "The oppositional cultural frame of reference becomes particularly important in the school context because black Americans (like similar minorities) generally equate school learning with the learning of the culture of the dominant group, or white culture" (Ogbu, 1988a, p. 177). Thus, for members of involuntary minorities to succeed in school, they must turn their backs on their own cultural frame of reference, their own identities, and act white (p. 177).

Especially within the peer group, acting white can be viewed as cultural betrayal. However, defining behaviors and attitudes as white (such as working hard for grades, punctuality, speaking standard English, and the like) creates serious problems for minorities, since many of these are behaviors and attitudes necessary for success in school (Ogbu, 1988b, pp. 177–178). Minority students who want to succeed in school must adopt some strategy to cope with the conflict between their oppositional culture and the dominant culture of which the school is a part. Ogbu identifies eight coping strategies based on ethnographic research on the black experience (1989, pp. 198–199).

1. Assimilators are those who adopt a white cultural frame of reference. They have come to believe that they cannot be successful in both cultural frames and they have chosen to be successful in school. They are generally successful but often suffer isolation and criticism.
2. Emissaries play down black identity and cultural frame of reference to succeed, but they do not reject them. They follow the rules and remain marginal members of the black peer group. Their motto is "Do your Black Thing but know the Whiteman's Thing."
3. Alternators adopt the immigrant approach, accommodation without assimilation. They do not reject their black identity or cultural frame of reference, but they also play by the rules. They tend to adopt secondary coping strategies such as being involved in "black activities" or playing the clown.
4. The Reaffiliated are students who may have rejected the black cultural frame of reference until they encountered powerful examples of racism. They may become more involved with their black peers, but they may also continue to do well in school.
5. The Ivy Leaguers are black youths who exhibit middle-class behaviors. They belong to middle-class social organizations, are well-liked, and appear to be good students.
6. The Regulars are members of the street culture but do not go along with it entirely. They are good students, have close family ties, follow the rules and know how to stay out of trouble.
7. The Ambivalents need to be with their black peer group and they also need to succeed in school. They do not resolve this conflict and so their school performance tends to be erratic.
8. The Encapsulated equate success in school with "acting white," which they refuse to do. They do not try to learn or follow the rules. Generally they do not succeed in school.

The learning and performance difficulties resulting from the burden of acting white should be made the focus of educational policies and remediation effort.

> The black community has an important part to play in changing the situation. The community should develop programs to teach black children that academic pursuit is not synonymous with one-way acculturation into a white cultural frame of reference or acting white. To do this effectively, however, the black community must reexamine its own perceptions and interpretations of school learning. Apparently, black children's general perception that academic pursuit is "acting white" is learned in the black community. The ideology of the community in regard to the cultural meaning of schooling is, therefore, implicated and needs to be reexamined. (Ogbu, 1989, p. 203)

The relationship between motivation to learn and culture conflict, based on the research and theoretical perspectives of John Ogbu (1981) and Signithia Fordham (1986), is informative. The formation of an oppositional cultural frame of reference, in response to repeated patterns of exclusion and discrimination by those termed involuntary minorities such as American-born blacks and Native Americans, represents a reality that urban educators need to face objectively. In the last 30 years, the oppositional culture has defined success in school as "acting white," producing conflict and stress for involuntary minority students who seemingly must choose between their own cultural identity and success in the schools of the dominant culture. Although minority children have developed some coping mechanisms to mediate the conflict, a more satisfactory solution would involve the modification of the oppositional cultural frame of reference in such a way that success in school is not identified as abandoning one's culture or acting white. Principals, and teachers, especially those who are members of minority groups, can help precipitate discussions and actions that make it acceptable for children to succeed in school, regardless of their identity and culture.

PARENTAL AND COMMUNITY INVOLVEMENT

Research has found that the parents of minority students are excluded from school involvement and do not know exactly how to help their children academically even though they want their children to succeed in school and would like to become more involved in helping them to succeed (Cummins, 1986).

While parental involvement appears to be especially important for student success in low-income communities (Wilson, 1988), it is often not high in the inner cities. Is this the fault of the family or the school? Research evidence indicates that the "school's practices to inform and to involve parents are more important than parent education, family size, marital status, and even grade level in determining whether inner-city parents get involved" (Center for Research on Elementary and Middle Schools, 1989, p. 10; also, Epstein & Dauber, 1989). This means the onus for establishing appropriate levels of parental involvement in inner cities rests with the school.

The level of community that includes families', businesses', churches', and social service agencies' involvement in schools is integral to meeting the needs of diverse student groups. Existing research suggests that school-community partnerships are more likely to be successful when they are designed with high expectations for community involvement, when they recognize that communities are changing, when they provide a variety of ways for community members to be involved, and when they accommodate the needs of the communities to be involved. Schools that encourage frequent and meaningful interaction and networking of families and neighborhood organizations and agencies find that school effectiveness, student attendance, and student achievement are improved (Coleman & Hoffer, 1987; Comer, 1986; Eastman, 1988; Epstein, 1988).

In urban schools, involving communities suggests coming to terms with the discrepancy between the attitudes of communities and of educators (Nettles, 1991). Parents especially are interested in being involved in schools at all levels, from tutoring to decision making. Educators frequently, however, continue to consider traditional limited roles of community involvement.

The design and implementation of family, community, and school partnership programs should include a wide range of options designed to meet diverse interests, expertise, and service needs of families and communities. Urban school administrators have to improve access to information about school programs and services, instruction and training in how to work with children at home, encourage assistance with classroom activities, and participation in school-based management committees. Increased participation means that authority does not reside with the principal and teachers alone. The greatest possible distribution of authority at the school is required. School-based management requires that the school community should have the authority to make and implement decisions that enable it to adapt to the needs of the school's students, to have the flexibility to change when needed, to establish a wide leadership base, and to initiate and implement school improvement efforts that can have significant results.

SCHOOL-BASED TEAMS

An approach initiated to develop school-based teams in which school staff, parents, organizations, and community agencies work collaboratively to deliver school, social services, and community support has been particularly effective in urban settings. In this approach, the school serves to facilitate the communication of information both in and out of the school (Manning, 1987). A Comprehensive Social Service Support model uses a school-based team to join the school, parents, and community resources in order to address attendance, counseling, special education, parent involvement, public services resources, and staff development needs. The school is considered to be the most stable institution in the community and it creates an important social network that children and families can benefit from.

Core Teams

Other kinds of urban workers across the country have discovered the power of *core teams,* for example, to assist primary providers of service in meeting the needs of those to be served. Core school support teams consisting of administrators, teachers, community members, and representatives from outside social agencies can be assembled on a voluntary basis by the principal to redesign an urban school's internal parent support groups and a wide variety of drug-free activities by assisting the development of an effective human infrastructure for these activities (Madden, 1991). Urban principals may be surprised to find so many voluntary advisors and intermediaries who care.

The widespread concern about the failure of many urban schools and the inability of educators in many urban environments to be successful teaching urban students has prompted various urban reform movements. In a backhanded and ironic way, mainstream school reform has actually endorsed old modes of schooling. Many experts have never really questioned the basic day-to-day process and content of American education; instead they blindly assume that if the same activities are conducted within an enhanced framework, with more time, more money, more teachers, more tests, then student achievement and outcomes will improve. In this version of reform, you simply do the same things harder and longer.

Urban schools also have suffered enough one-shot efforts, quick fixes, here-today-gone-tomorrow fads, and erratic and unpredictable budgetary support. Priority outcomes and exemplary practices must be clearly identified and resources conserved and dedicated to their sustained achievement. Conserving one's resources for the most important priorities is advisable, rather than squandering them on demands to be and do all things for everyone.

EXEMPLARY INSTRUCTIONAL PRACTICES FOR UNDERCLASS SCHOOLS

It is important to emphasize that the evidence is clear: the unrelenting application of exemplary instructional practices will be effective in all kinds of schools, particularly in urban schools. If this book fails to encourage urban educators to apply exemplary instructional practices, its mission will have failed.

On a very optimistic note, the last nine or ten years of tumultuous national debate, though it certainly hasn't concentrated upon instruction and curriculum, has nevertheless indirectly prodded further research in these areas. All the people in this uncoordinated reform movement, the teachers, instructional researchers, and educational leaders have been rethinking the substance, the content, the processes, the methods, and the dynamics of schooling. As a result, we now have recent summary reports, meta-analyses of instructional research, reports from pilot classrooms, pilot schools, and landmark sets of professional recommendations. Today, there is a consensus about the adoption of exemplary instructional practices in American public schools, including those instructional practices which will be effective in schools which serve the poor and disadvantaged.

One might expect that when experts and practitioners from such disparate fields as science, mathematics, reading, writing, and social science sit down to define their own field's exemplary practices, the results would be some very different visions of the ideal urban classroom, contradictory ways of organizing subject matter, and divergent models of what good teachers do. But, in fact, such polarities are not representative of these reports. Whether the recommendations come from the National

Council of Teachers of Mathematics, the Center for the Study of Reading, the National Writing Project, the National Council for the Social Studies, the American Associates for the Advancement of Science, the National Council of Teachers of English, the National Association for the Education of Young Children, or the International Reading Association, the fundamental insights into teaching and learning are remarkably similar. Indeed, on most key issues, the recommendations from these diverse organizations are unanimous. Below is a list of these common conclusions, features that begin to define a coherent pattern of learning and teaching across the whole curriculum which will improve the quality of teaching and learning in underclass schools (and in fact all schools).

Common Recommendations of National Curriculum Reports

- LESS whole-class, teacher-directed instruction, e.g., lecturing
- LESS student passivity: sitting, listening, receiving, and absorbing information
- LESS prizing and rewarding of silence in the classroom
- LESS classroom time devoted to fill-in-the-blank work sheets, dittos, workbooks, and other "seatwork"
- LESS student time spent reading textbooks and basal readers
- LESS attempt by teachers to thinly "cover" large amounts of material in every subject area
- LESS rote memorization of facts and details
- LESS stress on the competition and grades in school
- LESS tracking or leveling students into "ability groups"
- LESS use of pullout special programs
- LESS use of and reliance on standardized tests
- MORE experiential, inductive, hands-on learning
- MORE active learning in the classroom, with all the attendant noise and movement of students doing, talking, and collaborating
- MORE emphasis on higher-order thinking; learning a field's key concepts and principles
- MORE deep study of a smaller number of topics, so that students internalize the field's way of inquiry
- MORE time devoted to reading whole, original, real books and nonfiction materials
- MORE responsibility transferred to students for their work: goal-setting, record-keeping, monitoring, evaluation

- MORE choice for students, e.g., picking their own books, writing topics, team partners, research projects
- MORE enacting and modeling of the principles of democracy in school
- MORE attention to affective needs and the varying cognitive styles of individual students
- MORE cooperative, collaborative activity; developing the classroom as an interdependent community
- MORE heterogeneously grouped classrooms where individual needs are met through inherently individualized activities, not segregation of bodies
- MORE delivery of special help to students in regular classrooms
- MORE varied and cooperative roles for teachers, parents, and administrators
- MORE reliance upon teachers' descriptive evaluation of student growth, including qualitative/anecdotal observations (Anderson et al., 1985; Bybee, et al., 1989, 1991; Harste, 1989; Hillocks, 1986; National Council of Teachers of Mathematics, 1989; National Science Teachers Association, 1985; American Association for the Advancement of Science, 1989; National Commission on the Social Studies, 1988, 1989)

There is an underlying educational philosophy of this emerging model. Ten principles characterize this model of education.

1. Child Centered. Schooling should be child centered, taking many of its cues from students' interests, concerns, and questions. Making school child-centered involves building on the natural curiosity children bring to school. But child-centered schooling does not mean passive teachers who respond only to students' explicit cues. Teachers also draw on their deep understanding of children's needs and enthusiasm to design experiences that lead children into areas they would not choose but that they do enjoy and that engage them. Teachers also bring their own interests and enthusiasms into the classroom to share, demonstrating how a learner gets involved with ideas. Thus, child-centered education begins by cordially inviting children's whole lives into the classroom; it solicits and listens to their questions; and it provides a balance between activities that follow the children's lead and ones which lead the children.

2. Experiential. Schools, especially underclass schools, should stress learning that is experiential. Children learn most powerfully from doing, not just hearing about, any subject. This simple psychological fact has different implications in different subjects. In writing and reading it means that students grow more by composing and reading whole, real texts, rather than just doing work sheets and exercises. With mathematics, it means manipulating objects, sorting, counting and building patterns of number and shape; and carrying out real-world projects that involve collecting data, estimating, calculating, drawing conclusions, and making decisions. In science it means conducting experiments and taking field trips to investigate real problems. For social studies, students can, for example, prepare group reports that teach the rest of the class, and role-play famous historical events, conflicts, and political debates. The key is to help students think more deeply, to discover the detailed implications of ideas through direct or stimulated immersion in them, and enhance retention.

3. Reflection. Effective learning is balanced with opportunities for reflection. Too often, school is a process of stimulus-response. But learning is strengthened when children have time to look back on what they've learned, to debrief, to recognize broader principles, to appreciate their accomplishments and understand how they overcame obstacles. Adding reflective thinking to school learning is one of the simplest of all instructional innovations. Many teachers have found that the simple addition of a student learning log for each subject, with time set aside each day for responding to well-structured teacher "prompts," builds reflection into the day and moves students into a new level of thinking.

4. Authentic. Learning activities need to be authentic. There is a natural tendency in schools to offer children in underclass schools simplified materials and activities, so that they are not overwhelmed with complexity. But too often children are underestimated and we oversimplify things, creating materials or situations that are synthetic as to not be lifelike and, ironically, of marginal educational worth.

What does authenticity mean in the curriculum? In reading, it means that the rich, artful, and complex vocabulary of classic fairy tales is far more educational than watered-down, "cleaned up" versions in basal readers. In math, it means that children might investigate ways of dividing a pizza or a cake rather than re-working the odd-numbered fractions problems at the end of the chapter. Authenticity also means that children are reading and writing and calculating and investigating for purposes that they have chosen not just because the teacher gave an assignment or because a task appears in a textbook. Teachers can and should sometimes give assignments that a whole class can work on, to share and compare the resulting ideas they've generated. If teachers in urban schools don't also take steps to turn schoolwork into something real and into something the children can truly own, then the results will be a mechanical exercise in dutifully following directions rather than in real valuing of thought and knowledge.

5. *Unified.* Learning in all subjects needs to be unified. In the traditional American curriculum, and in far too many urban classrooms, information and ideas are presented to children in small "building blocks." While the teacher may find these subparts meaningful and may know they add up to an eventual understanding of a subject, their purpose and significance aren't always apparent to the children. This part-to-whole approach undercuts motivation for learning, because children don't understand why they are doing the work. But it also deprives children of an essential condition for learning—encountering material in its full lifelike context. When the "big picture" is put off until later, later often never comes.

Children do in fact need to acquire skills and abilities that are parts of a larger whole—skills such as spelling and multiplying and evaluating good evidence for written arguments. But unified learning means that children gain these abilities most effectively by going from whole-to-part, when children read whole books, write whole stories, and carry out whole investigations of natural phenomena. Brief lessons on use of quotation marks are learned fastest and remembered longest when the class writes scripts for plays they've decided to put on. And meanwhile, the focus on a rich story text ensures that children are simultaneously making more mental connections than the teacher has time to directly teach within the one or two or three "skills" that he or she covers.

6. *Interaction.* Teachers should tap into the dynamics of classroom social interaction to promote learning. Much research has shown how social interactions in the family and community support early language learning. This occurs unconsciously and naturally in families and groups of children playing together. Such social helping is often called "scaffolding" because, just as a temporary scaffold allows bricklayers to construct a wall which finally stands on its own, these interactions support young language-builders along the way but ultimately leave the child independent. Children are far from passive in this scaffolding process. They learn not only by imitating grownup behavior but by taking an active part, constructing and testing hypotheses, and initiating behavior

themselves. Babies learn language swiftly and effectively without being directly "taught" because they are learning words that can help them get their needs met in their families. Following this model, schools can reverse counterproductive patters of isolation by encouraging responsible social interaction to promote learning.

7. *Collaboration.* Some of the most efficient social learning activities are collaborative. When we think of the social side of learning, we most readily envision group discussions, kids listening to one another's work, carrying out projects and writing letters and stories for one another. Collaborative learning goes on to promote children's learning with one another. Even in the workplace, managers recognize how much collaboration actually goes on in American life and how valuable group problem solving is, compared to competitiveness and isolation. Collaborative small-group activity has been shown to be an especially effective mode for school learning, in all kinds of classrooms, including those in underclass schools. Solid achievement gains have been documented across the curriculum by David Johnson and Roger Johnson (1985), Robert Slavin (1984), and others. Collaborative work allows learners to receive much more extensive feedback from fellow students than they can ever get from a single teacher who must spread his or her time among all students. Group work requires the training of students and carefully designing meaningful, authentic activities, lest the effort of groups be inefficient and shallow. Cooperation works very well when teachers employ student training techniques that have been refined in recent years. Cooperation pays off both in time better used in the classroom and, later on, as a valuable skill in life.

8. *Developmental.* Children's learning must be approached as developmental. This is one of the most carelessly used words in current educational parlance, enlisted in the support of all sorts of contradictory ideas. Developmentally oriented teachers know that variance in the school performance of different children often results from differences in their general growth. Such variations in the speed, but not the direction or the ultimate degree of development, should not be grounds for splitting up groups, but are diversities to be welcomed and melded into the richness of a group.

In developmental schooling, children are helped by recognizing and encouraging beginning steps when they occur, whether on schedule or not. The knowledge of research on how children actually advance in math or spelling is used to develop instructional programs. In math, for example, along with review and exploration of the week's topic, challenging, enjoyable activities that go beyond the textbook unit are included so the teacher can discover what various kids are really ready for. In many urban classrooms, children of the underclass have been robbed of developmental schooling.

9. Psycholinguistic. Influencing many of these principles is the psycholinguistic base of children's learning. It's no accident that in discussing many of the above principles the example of child language acquisition has been used. Indeed, the universal phenomenon of child language acquisition has provided educators with a most important body of knowledge about learning. Childhood language development is the most powerful, speedy, and complex learning any of us will ever do in our lives. Children learn to speak without being directly "taught" and without conscious intention to learn. It happens in the social setting of families and it becomes internalized through play and crib talk. Once learned, oral language becomes the main tool for future learning and provides the base for reading and writing. Outer speech gradually becomes storable as inner thought.

Practitioners recognize that lessons of psycholinguistics aren't restricted to preschool children at home. The concept of scaffolding representing the special kind of help provided by parents and siblings in a family can be explicitly built into the structure of work in school. The fact that language is learned tacitly, during socializing and play, suggests that classrooms be made more interactive. Perhaps above all, the fact that children learn to talk by talking implies that children should be allowed to interact more than they currently do in school. Silent classrooms should be discouraged; ironically, when teachers, especially in underclass schools, enforce the standard of silence, they are in a very real sense restricting learning.

10. Challenging. Following all these principles means that school is challenging. While some people might think of experiential or collaborative tasks as "easier" for students, teachers using state-of-the-art practices know that the opposite is true. Students are expected to take considerable responsibility, monitor their own learning, be sure they apply the abilities they've acquired, keep their own records, and elect new projects when they're finished with something, rather than just fill in an extra ditto sheet. As the students in a classroom gradually assume more responsibilities, the teacher attends to the needs of individual children, provides a safe space for experimenting with newer and more difficult tasks, and adds challenges as children are developmentally ready for them. In classes where these approaches abound, children respond to the challenge (Johnson & Johnson et al., 1984).

A Word About Phonics

The goal of teaching word analysis is meaning. The research findings on phonics have engendered fierce professional and public partisanship for nearly forty years. Both sides insist that the case is closed in their favor. The fact is that most kids will learn all the sound-symbol strategies they'll ever need from naturalistic, real reading. However, some children, which disproportionately includes at-risk children, don't acquire their sound-symbol ideas in this embedded, automatic way but can learn and use these strategies when they receive direct phonics instruction. Therefore, effective teachers have a broad-based approach to teaching word analysis that includes wide contextual reading experiences, focused word study, and student writing. They spend their instructional time judiciously; they carefully balance direct phonics instruction with more unified, integrated reading and writing activities, and are alert to the potential boredom of decontextualized drills (Harste, 1989). In any case, well-designed lessons in phonics should normally be concluded by the end of second grade.

Teacher Ownership

Teachers need to be involved in decision making and to re-create their own understandings of how learning can work for children. There are a host of reasons why this ownership is vital, and an abundance of literature, including books about change in the corporate business world, to explain them. Why is it so crucial for teachers to "buy in" in order for change to take root?

1. The teacher working with students daily knows best what the specific needs, conditions, and obstacles are.
2. No matter what changes are prescribed from the outside, their success in the classroom depends on teachers' own choices and interpretations as they move through the school day. So if choice isn't involved sooner, it will inevitably come later, with less likelihood of positive commitment.

3. The most important changes needed in education are not superficial but involve the teacher's deeply held beliefs, expectations, and relationships.

4. Many key changes involve giving responsibility and ownership to children, which will be undermined if ownership is not there for teachers.

The centrality of teachers' role in decision making is gradually being recognized by those researching and experimenting with school change. Ann Lieberman and Lynn Miller (1988, 1990) have written strong statements about collaborative leadership that redefines the relationship between teachers and principals. Henry Levin's (1988) "Accelerated Schools" concept features school-based governance with input from all parties—teachers, students, parents, administrators—and uses the strengths of the particular teachers who work in a building. John Goodlad (1988) describes the need for faculty dialogue and organizational "health" if schools are to escape from passive, uninspired classroom experience. Truly changing the urban teacher-administrator relationship means asking the teachers to set their own agenda at the beginning of a meeting or inservice session, asking for their analyses of problems in the school or in children's learning, and respecting the realities within their answers, even when we sometimes disagree with them. The importance of collaboration and cooperative planning will be expanded upon and treated in greater detail in Chapter X.

STUDENT EVALUATION—TESTING AND GRADING

Plainly, teachers and schools spend too much time formally evaluating students. Many teachers spend far more time worrying about test scores than developing ways to increase student learning, which would actually raise achievement scores. Instead, educators tinker with their measuring devices, planning and conducting more and more evaluations, tests, and exams. America seems to be a country of measurement-driven bureaucrats, politicians and educators who believe that you can raise the temperature either by improving the thermometer or checking it more often (Wheelock, 1992).

The socioeconomic function of evaluation in American education needs to be called into question. Grading and testing have historically been harnessed to the sorting and classifying of children into categories of "merit" or intelligence." These so-called categories of students are then allocated current or future rewards, such as invitations to honors classes, admission to good colleges, or entry to high-paying careers. Scholars like Michael Katz (1968), Joel Spring (1972), Stephen Jay Gould (1981), and Alan Chase (1947) have shown over the past twenty-five years that American meritocracy is suspect. School tests are part of a system that camouflages the replication of the existing social hierarchy: children from socially mainstream homes are certified by schools as "achievers," while students from poor, culturally different homes are proven by tests to be unsuccessful, to need special education, alternative education, or to be "unable to benefit" from a college preparatory program. The social consequences to closing opportunities to the lower class are frightening. The schools should take steps to de-emphasize the role of tests as "gate-keepers" and to open up more opportunities for upward mobility (Chase, 1947).

We have told students that only their academic achievement, not their character, really counts. Each turn of the academic screw snuffs out the confidence of more children and tells them that they are incapable and not going to "make it," falsely so for many students.

Overvalued and too limited measures of academic achievement tend to rob students, particularly in underclass schools, not just of their self-confidence but also of the empowering ideal of human excellence to which to aspire and work to achieve. Until the shackles of the national obsession with test scores are broken, schools will not be free to create classrooms that come to grips with the educability of today's youth. Schools will remain sterilizing and so less effective places than they could be; the educational reform movement will continue to stumble and eventually fail.

Graduates of Oxford and Cambridge represent examples of students who later became eminent British politicians and judges who had "academic records that nowadays would be viewed as catastrophic" (Hudson, 1976). Hudson found that even eminent scientists could not be identified from the level of their university honors.

A study of three hundred of this century's most eminent political, literary, artistic, and scientific figures belies contemporary parental views that not attending college condemns a youngster to eternal failure (Taylor & Ellison, 1967). Sixty percent of such eminent people had disliked or even flunked out of school; only 50 percent had gone on to college. Singular examples such as Einstein or William Gates, founder of Microsoft and one of America's wealthiest people, illustrate how school grades don't predict high creativity. However, there is sufficient evidence for us to conclude that academic grades account for between 5 and 10 percent of why individuals vary in later adult creative achievement, more so in some fields, such as the sciences, than perhaps in others, such as the arts. Clearly, high grades help but are not essential to achieving eminence later in life in many areas. If high academic achievement were essential, how shall we explain why the Japanese have received only five but Americans more than two hundred Nobel prizes for eminent achievement? Underclass schools represent warehouses of human potential, much of it unrecognized or undeveloped. The tyranny of testing and grading must be replaced by exemplary instructional practices, high expectations and standards for all urban students.

ABILITY GROUPING

Another factor which limits the numbers of students (particularly those at risk) who are able to experience school success is tracking and ability grouping. One of the conclusions of recent educational research has been the rejection of tracking and the affirmation of heterogeneous grouping. One of the most unproductive practices in American schools has been the routine division of children into different classrooms or instructional groups on the basis of "ability." Indeed, one of the earliest common experiences of most American schoolchildren is being assigned to either the low, middle, or high reading group, sometimes disguised with clever and, to the children, transparent, euphemistic names like "Bluebirds," "Sparrows," and "Cardinals." Researchers Jeannie Oakes (1985) and Anne Wheelock (1992) have provided strong evidence that ability grouping is academically damaging to kids labeled "low" and "middle." Their measured achievement is actually depressed when they are segregated by levels. The evidence of tracking's benefits for "high" kids is slight, ambiguous, and still under debate among achievement researchers. These findings do not provide support for the widespread grouping practices that exist in most schools. Interpersonally, tracking is harmful for all students and promotes elitism and social segregation (Oakes, 1985).

When teachers say they prefer tracked classes or claim that mixed ability groups are harder to teach, they are being sincere. But they are also usually envisioning traditional classes: teacher directed, presentational, and whole-class. Indeed, the durability of ability grouping in schools stems from teachers' dedication to this single model of teaching (Wheelock, 1992). In this familiar kind of classroom, the teacher is the center: he or she tells, presents, explains, and gives assignments. When they are not listening to the teacher and taking notes, students work quietly and individually at their desks, writing answers to questions about what the teacher has presented. The teacher represents the fountain of knowledge; students are vessels being filled. For students, the day is usually filled with transforming what they have heard into short written repetitions: blanks filled in, bubbles darkened, and, infrequently, sentences or paragraphs composed.

In this classroom model, a premium is placed on silence and "listening close." The spontaneity and enthusiasm of many at-risk students is systematically destroyed. Teachers often find it convenient to sort kids into groups by ability or IQ or whatever factor will make them more amenable to this style of teaching. Experience and research evidence shows that when teachers become aware of the much wider repertoire of available classroom organizational structures, ones that work to teach "content" subjects like math and science to heterogeneous groups, their feeling that tracking is "necessary" dissipates (Oakes, 1985).

CLASSROOM CLIMATE

As classroom teachers in my graduate classes tell me, they are well aware of the year-to-year variation of "good" and "bad" classes of students. Yet, the research literature on classroom climate clearly indicates that groups are mainly made, not inherited. There are well-researched, dependable methods for teachers to establish a productive classroom climate and thus open the way to many promising innovations. According to the literature on group dynamics and group development, a field of study often neglected by educators, there are specific ingredients that teachers must, and can, control to shape and create that initial climate (Schmuck & Schmuck, 1988):

- positive expectations
- mutually developed norms
- shared leadership
- diffuse friendship patterns
- open channels of communication
- mechanisms for resolving conflicts.

Wise teachers in all types of schools nurture these factors, especially during the early life of a class, to create a widely overlapping network of positive interdependence. They consciously distribute acquaintance, power, responsibility among all students, opening up every possible means of communication, verbal, nonverbal, written and artistic. Once a richly interdependent community has been created, students are able to adjust to varying complex instructional strategies and make the transition.

CONCLUSIONS

Urban schools must accept and adopt long-term strategies to improve education. Inner-city school districts are under enormous pressure to show improvements quickly. Some of the worst abuses in public education, such as changing and manipulating tests, constantly shifting personnel, and erecting impenetrable bureaucratic fortresses, are due at least in part to pressures for short-range solutions. Recommendations are as follows: (a) Do not institute programs, curriculum changes, and so on without at least a five- to ten-year commitment from decision makers and funding sources; (b) start in preschool and the early grades because expecting dramatic changes at the high school level is unreasonable; and (c) provide support and aid for long-term solutions to nonschool problems.

For new ideas to take hold in urban classrooms, beyond an enthusiastic few, a critical mass of advocates must be established. A "movement" needs enough people to encourage and support one another, to share a vision, to have a moral purpose, to exert some social pressure on the others, and to demonstrate that the new approaches work not just for the far-out risk takers but for any ordinary professional who wants to try them, not only in suburbia, but in inner-city schools as well. However, too many urban districts provide training for one or two "experts" per buildings, one or two "lighthouse" schools. These programs usually don't spread because it's easy for the "risk takers" to be kept isolated and ultimately discouraged and burned out. It is therefore incumbent on school districts, particularly those in urban centers, to make a long-term commitment to develop their own teams of in-house professional assistance and development trainers.

Chapter V

AMERICA'S FRAYING SOCIAL FABRIC

Concern over the fraying of America's social fabric is fast becoming a national obsession. "Three out of every four Americans think we are in moral decline. Two of three think the country is seriously off track" (Zuckerman, 1994, p. 88). Social dysfunction seems to haunt the land.

There are signs of the emergence of a great yearning in the country to provide our national life and institutions with a larger moral dimension. The growing hunger for a public commitment to social and moral betterment is not a simple nostalgia for the greater simplicities of yesteryear; the clock cannot be turned back. It is a profound and anxious desire to arrest decay. "But if the dysfunctional trends continue, that anxiety will turn to fear, and even panic. And when fear comes to dominate social policy, reason and tolerance are at risk," argues Mortimer Zuckerman (1994).

The crisis of confidence in American public education has escalated in no small part because of a public perception that the schools are not doing enough to help parents raise good children. For well over a decade, every Gallup poll that has asked parents whether schools should teach morals has come up with an unequivocal yes. "Typical is the finding that 57 percent of parents with school-age children in 1994 say they want the public schools to provide instruction that would deal with morals and moral behavior, up from 45 percent in 1987" (Elam, Rose, & Gallup, 1994).

Values represent the emotional rules by which a nation governs itself. Values summarize the accumulated folk wisdom by which a society organizes and disciplines itself. And values are the precious reminders that individuals obey to bring order and meaning into their personal and social lives. Moral virtue is a most essential element of a just society.

EVIDENCE OF MORAL DECLINE

Should the schools teach character? Just a few years ago, if you put that question to a group of citizens, it was sure to start an argument. If anyone said yes, schools should teach children values, somebody else would respond, "*Whose* values?" In a society where people held different values, it seemed impossible to get agreement on which ones would be taught in our public schools. Pluralism produced paralysis; schools for the most part ended up trying to stay officially neutral on the subject of values.

With remarkable rapidity, that has changed. Escalating moral decline in society—ranging from greed and dishonesty to violent crime to self-destructive behaviors such as drug abuse and suicide, are bringing about a new consensus. Now, from all across the country, from private citizens and public organizations, from liberals and conservatives alike, comes a summons to the schools: take up the role of moral teachers of our children.

Of all the moral problems that have fueled the national concern, none has been more disturbing than rising youth violence. From 1978 to 1988, according to FBI statistics, rape arrests for 13- and 14-year-old males nearly doubled. Over a 20-year period (1968 to 1988), there was a 53 percent increase in all violent crime—murder, rape, robbery and assault—for males and females seventeen or under (Lickona, 1991, p. 3). Moreover, juvenile crimes of violence have of late combined new lows in brutality with a seeming total lack of conscience or remorse.

In recent years, crimes committed by young people have reached unprecedented levels. The number of arrests per 1,000 persons aged 14–17 increased from 4 in 1950 to 117 in 1989. In 1989, about 15 percent of all offenders were under 18 and another 30 percent were aged 18–24. Over 50 percent of arrests for murder, nonnegligent manslaughter, and forcible rape were from these two age groups (Morrow, 1988, p. 3). A 1992 FBI report showed that the juvenile arrest rate for violent crime had increased by 27 percent since 1982; all races and social classes showed an increase, although not to the same extent. In fact, some authorities have identified the growing frequency of violent crime by teenagers and subteenagers as the most ominous trend in the criminal justice system. The rate of juvenile arrests for weapons violations reached an all-time high in 1990, while arrests for drug use or sale increased by 713 percent from 1982 to 1992 (*Newsweek*, 1992, p. 8).

In contemporary America, nearly one in seven American children has lost his or her virginity by the age of thirteen (National Center for Health Statistics, 1988). Millions of teenagers see little meaning in life other than to have a child, without having a serious commitment to their infants. Marriage for many has become a disposable relationship. It is all too often entered into like a rental agreement—with an escape clause that if it does not suit the parties involved, they may look for another apartment. Contemporary couples are no longer clear if and when they ought to marry or if fidelity in marriage is to be expected. And if they beget children, it is unclear what they owe them.

SCHOOL VIOLENCE

These trends have had a significant impact on public education. For instance, the fifteen largest school districts recently reported that their three major problems were weapons on campus, gangs, and drugs. According to a government estimate, 500,000 violent incidents occurred every month in public secondary schools in 1988 (Touflexis, 1989). Obviously, safety and security problems of this magnitude are bound to have adverse effects on many aspects of education.

Under such conditions a larger proportion of scarce resources must be spent on measures to improve safety and security. Despite such increases, however, a growing number of parents are concerned about the safety of their children in public schools. Private schools are becoming a more attractive option, especially since they are not as restricted as public schools in coping with crime and delinquency. Also, justified or not, many citizens regard public schools as partially responsible for crime and delinquency among young people.

While juvenile crime and delinquency have been increasing, school authority to cope with them has been eroded in various ways. Recent Supreme Court decisions have made it more difficult for public schools to expel or suspend students, search their lockers, regulate their dress, or regulate their publications, to cite some restrictions that render it more difficult for public schools to cope with undesirable student conduct.

There is today a seemingly widespread, deeply unsettling sense that children are changing—in ways that tell us much about ourselves as a society. And these changes are reflected not just in the violent extremes of teenage behavior but in the everyday speech and actions of younger children as well.

THE GROWING INSTABILITY OF THE FAMILY

There is growing evidence that schools can make a difference in the character development of the young. But what is the role of the family? The family is the primary moral educator of the child. Parents are their children's first moral teachers. They are also the most enduring influence: Children usually change teachers every year but typically have at least one of the same parents all through their growing years. The parent-child relationship is also laden with special emotional significance, causing children to feel either loved and worthwhile or unloved and unimportant. Finally, parents are in a position to teach morality as part of a larger world view that offers a vision of life's meaning and ultimate reasons for leading a moral life. All this is confirmed by numerous studies pointing to the power of parental influence (Damon, 1988). The family has undeniable clout as a moral socializer of children. But families are changing.

Most families have been touched, in one way or another, by divorce. One of two U.S. marriages now ends in divorce. America's divorce rate, which has more than doubled since 1960, is the highest in the world. About 60 percent of children whose parents break up will spend the rest of their childhood in a single-parent home (London, 1987, p. 667).

Nearly always, women are the ones who must shoulder the responsibility of raising their children without a helpmate and often must do so with the additional burden of poverty. By 1988, according to a National Commission on Children report, 55 percent of families headed by a single mother were poor (compared with 12 percent of two-parent families). For the first time in history, more than half of all children under 18 have a mother who works outside the home, often out of economic necessity. Nearly half of all mothers of one-year-olds are now in the labor force (London, 1987, p. 671). Families are also more mobile than ever before. Every year, one of five families in America moves away from the people who give parents a support network and children a sense of who they are (p. 672).

Many parents, despite adverse circumstances, make raising their children a high priority, and their children manage to thrive. All too often, however, fractured families and the stress of outside commitments carry a cost that children pay. The impact of broken homes, social science is beginning to reveal, may be greater than anyone had supposed. In the early 1970s, Doctor Judith Wallerstein, psychologist and senior lecturer at the University of California at Berkeley, embarked on what she thought would be a one-year study of middle-class families that had just been through a divorce. Her thesis was that "normal, healthy people would be able to work out their problems following divorce in about one year's time." Instead, she ended up doing a 10-year study documenting how flawed her original assumption was (Wallerstein, 1989, p. xv).

Both parents need to bond with children. It is no accident that in a wide variety of human societies (from the Zulus to the Inuits, from ancient Greece and ancient China to the present), there has never been a society that did not have two-parent families (Zelditch, 1955). Societies have varied a great deal in the roles they assigned to other members of the family (aunts, uncles, grandparents) and in the educational roles of other members of the tribe. They have also varied a great deal in the specifics of the relationship between the parents and between the parents and the child. But in the hundreds of known societies throughout recorded history, two-parent families have been the norm (Zelditch, 1955).

To be quite clear: To argue that the two-parent family is "better" than the single-parent family is in no way to denigrate single parents. Many single parents do an admirable job of child rearing.

Gang warfare in the streets, massive drug abuse, a poorly committed work force, and a strong sense of entitlement and weak sense of responsibility are, to a large extent, the product of poor parenting. True, economic and social factors also play a role. But a lack of effective parenting is a major cause, and the other factors could be handled more readily if we remained committed to the importance of the upbringing of the young. The fact is, given the same economic and social conditions, in poor neighborhoods one finds decent and hardworking youngsters right next to antisocial ones. Likewise, in affluent suburbs one finds antisocial youngsters right next to decent, hardworking ones (Patterson & Dision, 1985). The difference is often a reflection of the homes they come from.

Schools are left with the task of making up for undereducation in the family and laying the foundation for character and moral conduct. This is where the various commissions that have studied educational deficits missed a major point, because they argued only for loading students with more hours of science, foreign language, math, and other skills and bodies of knowledge. They neglected the need for character education!

THE RISE OF "PERSONALISM"

Social change had been building slowly in the first half of the twentieth century. In the 1960s it accelerated dramatically. The 1960s saw a worldwide surge of "personalism." Personalism celebrated the worth, dignity, and autonomy of the individual person, including the subjective self. It emphasized rights more than responsibility, freedom more than commitment. It led people to focus on expressing and fulfilling themselves as free individuals rather than on fulfilling their obligations as members of groups such as family, church, community, or country.

A central meaning of the American tumult of the sixties was the shift of moral authority from externalized symbols of conscience to each individual's feeling about what was best for his or her own fulfillment, which is interpreted by many to mean "If it feels good, do it."

During the watershed-rebellious sixties and seventies, relationships with traditional authorities were permanently altered. They lost their ordained power. Role and position no longer automatically commanded respect and obedience. People no longer trusted anyone to tell them what their values should be. People began to regard any kind of constraint on their personal freedom as an intolerable restriction of their individuality. The emphasis on individual freedom fostered general rebellion against authority and, in many cases, a reluctance on the part of authority figures (including teachers and parents) to exercise their legitimate authority. In the United States, the abuses of power represented by Vietnam and Watergate hastened the general erosion of respect for authority.

The death of traditional authorities spawned self-fulfillment as the *raison d'être* of being the arbiter of our choices. But in the absence of restraint and maturity, self-fulfillment deteriorates into a self-seeking pursuit of greed and pleasure. All through the turbulent 1960s and into the 1970s, individualism held high the banner of human freedom and the value of the individual person.

Peronalism spawned a new selfishness. Books with titles such as *Looking Out for Number One* became best-sellers. Slogans such as "Get all you can" influenced popular thinking about the pursuit of happiness. Polls revealed the emergence of a "new breed" of parents, who considered self-fulfillment more important than the old parental ethic of self-denial and sacrifice for one's children (Yankelovich, 1981). The sexual revolution, which elevated short-term gratification above values of restraint and long-term commitment, was another socially destabilizing manifestation of the new ethic of individualism.

The key question to ask about the modern conscience is: "Who now decides what is right, true, or good?" Whom do youth respect? Traditional authorities no longer automatically command respect and obedience for increasingly more Americans. No longer does role or position, whether of president, Supreme Court justice, labor boss, principal, teacher, or even parent, guarantee respect and acknowledged acceptance of authority.

DECLINE OF BUSINESS AND INSTITUTIONAL ETHICS

As society celebrated the individual and schools stayed neutral on values into the 1970s, clouds appeared on the moral horizon. There was accumulating evidence of a moral decline in society at large. Initially, "the establishment" represented the source of unethical, unlawful conduct. Institutional scandals broke with regularity. By the late 1970s, the media reported that more than a hundred American companies had admitted to paying large sums to buy special treatment from U.S. politicians and foreign government officials.

The 1980s brought more of the same and then some. *Yale Alumni Magazine* (p. 22), in an article titled "Ethics in the Boesky Era," noted tersely: "Perhaps more than at any time in recent American history, high-level greed and deceit are being seen as business as usual." But the moral slippage wasn't limited to high-level wheelers and dealers. For many ordinary people, personalism's emphasis on the individual had made selfishness a respectable life-style.

Simultaneously, a wave of greed and materialism has threatened to engulf society. Money increasingly has driven society and shapes the values and goals of the youth. Making money has become the justification for breaking rules. In a recent survey, two-thirds of U.S. high school seniors said they would lie to achieve a business objective (Kidder, 1990, p. 13).

As evidence that more people are joining in the rule-breaking, Doctor Jerald Jellison, a University of Southern California psychologist who specializes in moral trends, cites rising employee theft (which as of 1984 cost department stores and specialty chains $16 million a day) and increasing misrepresentation of job qualifications (e.g., submitting a phony résumé). Discouraging data on the state of personal ethics also came from a *Psychology Today* survey in 1981 (pp. 34–50). More than 24,000 readers completed the 49-item questionnaire, titled "Making Ethical Choices." Respondents ranged in age from 13 to 81, but the majority—67 percent—were young adults in their twenties and thirties. The average level of education of respondents was unusually high; 48 percent of those over 24 had attended graduate school (compared to 7 percent in the general population). Here are some of the moral behaviors that this relatively youthful, highly educated group of persons reported:

- 41 percent had driven while drunk or under the influence of drugs.
- 33 percent had deceived their best friend about something important in the past year.
- 38 percent had cheated on their tax returns.
- 45 percent of the respondents—including 49 percent of the men and 44 percent of the women—had cheated on their marriage partners (compared to 38 percent of all respondents in a 1969 *Psychology Today* survey of sexual behavior).

An abundance of examples have been cited as evidence of an ethical-moral decline. Thoughtful scholars and ordinary citizens as well as businesses and political leaders have called attention to this "crisis of character."

TWO IMPERATIVE GOALS OF EDUCATION

Developing knowledge and character represent the goals of education. John Adams wrote that our form of government was only meant for a virtuous people, and Jefferson, Madison, and Washington concurred. A government of the people would work only as long as the people were good people (Proctor, 1988).

To put it in more general terms: No society can function well unless most of its members "behave" most of the time because they voluntarily heed their moral commitments and social responsibilities (Etzioni, 1993, p. 30). There can never be enough police and FBI, IRS, and customs agents, inspectors, and accountants to monitor the billions of transactions that occur every day. And who will guard the guardians? Even if half the society were to police the other half, who would police this vast police to ensure that it obeyed the law? The only way the moral integrity of a society can be preserved is for most of the people, most of the time, to abide by their commitments voluntarily. The police powers of the government should be called upon only as a last resort to deal with the small number of sociopaths and hard-core recalcitrants, those who do not have moral commitments or sufficient impulse control to heed those commitments.

"The supreme end of education," said Samuel Johnson, "is expert discernment in all things—the power to tell good from bad, the genuine from the counterfeit, and to prefer the good and the genuine to the bad and the counterfeit" (Kirk, 1974, p. 159). Thoughtful teachers know that academic excellence and character are inseparable. Research supports their intuition. The U.S. Office of Education commissioned a study of 12,000 students from financially poor homes to identify those most likely to achieve and to pull themselves out of their dismal poverty. Those who succeeded had valued high academic achievement, enjoyed working hard in school, had parents who expected them to achieve, and were religiously committed (Strom, 1980). If you ask what is the good of education, said Plato, "the answer is easy—that education makes good men, and that good men act nobly" (Bok, 1988).

Aristotle also made an important distinction relevant to the roots of moral ordering. There are, he argued, two kinds of virtue. The first is intellectual virtue, which is the cerebral process of discovering truths through instruction and study. The second is moral virtue, which is more fundamental and is the product of habits learned early in life from family, class and community. Moral virtue teaches the values of courage, justice, responsibility, self-restraint, and compassion (Kirk, 1956).

Realizing that smart and good are not the same, wise societies since the time of Plato and Aristotle have made moral education a deliberate aim of schooling. They have educated for character as well as intellect, decency as well as literacy, virtue as well as knowledge. They have tried to form citizens who will use their intelligence to benefit others as well as themselves, who will try to build a better world.

THE CASE FOR CHARACTER EDUCATION

An illiterate and uneducated person can still be in touch with the moral inheritance of his culture. In *The Moral Life of Children*, Robert Coles (1986) shows how, even in the slums of Rio or in a sharecropper's shack in the rural South, children continue to learn the common ideals through church attendance, Bible stories, and adult precept and example. In most societies, these informal attempts at inculcating moral culture are supplemented and complemented by the formal educational system. The two reinforce each other.

But when the schools stop contributing to the fund of shared moral knowledge, the informal systems are put under enormous strain. And when they start to break down, we begin to get a picture of what a society looks like when each person makes up his own "morality." By withholding the moral culture from a whole generation of youth, we are not helping them to "think for themselves" but only forcing them to patch together crude codes of behavior from the bits and pieces they pick up on television or in the streets.

No sector of our national personality has been so affected by the social and technological whirlwinds of recent decades as have our values. We are immersed in a transitional epochal moment of change, marked by uncertainty, social disintegration, and doubt.

To be sure, even in the face of problems like these, considerable controversy still surrounds the proposition that schools should teach morality. Character education is one of the most burning topics in education today. Some groups, on both the political right and left, are deeply suspicious about any kind of values teaching in the schools. But beneath these battles is a steadily growing conviction: Schools cannot be ethical bystanders at a time when our society is in deep moral trouble. Rather, schools must do what they can to contribute to the character of the young and the moral health of the nation.

Standing on the threshold of the twenty-first century, there are several good reasons why schools should be making a wholehearted commitment to teaching moral values and developing good character:

1. There is a clear and urgent need. Young people are increasingly hurting themselves and others, and decreasingly concerned about contributing to the welfare of their fellow human beings. In this they reflect the ills of society in need of moral renewal.

2. Transmitting values is and always has been the work of civilization (Morrow, 1988, p. 4). A society needs character education both to survive and to thrive, to keep intact, and to keep itself growing toward conditions that support the full human development of all its members. Historically, three social institutions have shared the work of moral education: the home, the church, and the school. In taking up character education, schools are returning to their time-honored role.

3. The school's role as moral educator becomes even more vital at a time when millions of children get little moral teaching from their parents and where value-centered influences such as church or temple are also absent from their lives. These days, when schools don't do character education, influences hostile to good character rush in to fill the values vacuum.

4. There is common ethical ground even in our value-conflicted society. Americans have intense and often angry differences over moral issues such as abortion, homosexuality, euthanasia, and capital punishment. Despite this diversity, we can identify basic, shared values that allow us to engage in public moral education in a pluralistic society. Indeed, pluralism itself is not possible without agreement on values such as justice, honesty, responsibility, democratic process, and a respect for truth (Grant, 1985).

5. Democracies have a special need for moral education, because democracy is government by the people themselves. The people must care about the rights of others and the common good and be willing to assume the responsibilities of democratic citizenship.

6. Value-free education doesn't exist. Everything a school does teaches values, including the way teachers and other adults treat students, the way the principal treats the teachers, the way the school treats parents, and the way students are allowed to treat school staff and each other. If questions of right and wrong are never addressed in classrooms, that, too, teaches a lesson about how much morality matters. The relevant question is not "Should schools teach values?" but rather "Which values will they teach?" and "How well will they teach them?"

7. The most serious questions facing both the individual person and the human race are moral questions. For each of us as individuals, a question of the utmost existential importance is: "How should I live my life?" For all of humanity, "How can we live with each other?"

8. There is broad-based, growing support for character education in the schools. It comes from school boards which have passed resolutions calling upon school districts to teach the values necessary for good citizenship and a law-abiding society. It comes from business, which recognizes that a responsible labor force requires workers who have character traits of honesty, dependability, pride in work, and the capacity to cooperate with others.

Significantly, of 25 possible goals for education ranked by respondents, the Gallup poll reported that "To develop standards of what is right and wrong" came in second to, only barely behind the schools traditional academic mission—"To develop the ability to speak and write correctly"—and ahead of goals such as "To prepare students for a high paying job" (Gallup Poll cited in Bill Honig, p. 85).

9. A commitment to character education is essential if schools are to attract and keep good teachers. If you want to do one thing to improve the lives of teachers, says Boston University educator Kevin Ryan (1994), make moral education—including the creation of a civil, humane community in the school—the center of school life.

10. Character education is a doable job. Given the enormous moral problems facing the country, their deep social roots, and the ever-increasing responsibilities that schools already shoulder, the prospect of taking on moral education can seem overwhelming. Character education, however, can be done within the school day, is happening now in school systems across the country, and is making a positive difference in the moral attitudes and behavior of students, with the result that it's easier for teachers to teach and students to learn.

Until recently, calls for school reform have focused on academic achievement. Character development is needed as well. That awareness cuts across all spheres of society; our nation appears to be recovering a foundational understanding: Just as character is the ultimate measure of an individual, so it is also the ultimate measure of a nation. To develop the character of the nation's children in a complex and changing world is no small task. It is time to take up the challenge.

What Values Should Schools Teach?

The natural moral law defining the public school's moral agenda can be expressed in terms of two important values: respect and responsibility. These values constitute the core of a universal, public morality. They have objective, demonstrable worth, in that they promote the good of the individual and the good of the whole community. These values of respect and responsibility are necessary for:

- Healthy personal development
- Caring interpersonal relationships

- A humane and democratic society
- A just and peaceful world

Respect and responsibility are the core values that schools should teach if they are to develop ethically literate persons who can take their place as responsible citizens of society.

Finally, just as the value of respect is involved in the smallest everyday interactions, it also underlies the major organizing principles of a democracy. It is respect for persons that leads people to create constitutions that require the government to protect, not violate, the rights of the governed. The first moral mission of our schools is to teach this fundamental value of respect for self, others, and the environment.

Responsibility is an extension of respect. If we respect other people, we value them. If we value them, we feel a measure of responsibility for their welfare. (Responsibility emphasizes our positive obligations to care for each other.)

Respect, by comparison, emphasizes our negative obligations. It tells us for the most part what *not* to do. Philosopher Jon Moline points out the importance of these moral prohibitions: They tell us our duty exactly. "Thou shalt not murder" has a precision that "Love your neighbor" does not (Moline, 1982, p. 306).

Respect and responsibility are the two foundational moral values that schools should teach; others are: honesty, fairness, tolerance, prudence, self-restraint, helpfulness, compassion, cooperation, courage, and a host of democratic values. These specific values are forms of respect and/or responsibility or aids to acting respectfully and responsibly.

Developing a List of Objective Values

Even if a school begins with respect and responsibility—which are helpful starting points—and ends up with most or all of the supporting values listed above, educators and parents benefit by going through the process of working up their own list of values to teach. That process provides the opportunity to bring together teachers, administrators, other school staff, parents, students, and community representatives to get broad-scale support. Moreover, the actual list that a school or district comes up with in this way is likely to bear its own special stamp and distinctive priorities.

Good character is what the best of parents desire for all children. Good character includes self-oriented virtues (such as self-control and moderation) as well as other-oriented virtues (such as generosity and compassion), and the two kinds of virtue are connected. We need to be in control of ourselves—our appetites, our passions—to do right by others.

Character, observes contemporary philosopher Michael Novak (1986, p. 1), is "a compatible mix of all those virtues identified by religious traditions, literary stories, the sages, and persons of common sense down through history." No one, as Novak points out, has all the virtues, and everyone has some weaknesses.

Building on these classic understandings suggests a way of thinking about character that is appropriate for values education: Character consists of applied values, values in action.

HOW CHARACTER CAN BE TAUGHT

Within the classroom, a comprehensive approach for teaching character calls upon the teacher to:

1. Act as caregiver, model and mentor, treating students with dignity and respect, setting a good example, supporting prosocial behavior, and correcting hurtful actions.
2. Create a moral community in the classroom, helping students know each other, respect and care about each other, and feel valued membership in the group.
3. Practice moral discipline, using the creation and enforcement of rules as opportunities to foster moral reasoning, self-control, and a generalized respect for others.
4. Create a democratic classroom environment, involving students in decision making and shared responsibility for making the classroom a good place to be and to learn.
5. Teach character through the curriculum, using academic subjects as a vehicle for examining ethical issues. (This is simultaneously a schoolwide strategy when the curriculum addresses cross-grade concerns such as sex, drug, and alcohol education.)
6. Use cooperative learning to teach children the attitudes and skills of helping each other and working together.
7. Develop the ethic that "hard work brings success" by fostering

students' academic responsibility and their regard for the value of learning and work.

8. Encourage moral reflection through reading, writing, discussion, decision-making exercises, and debate.

9. Teach conflict resolution so that students have the capacity and commitment to solve conflicts in fair, nonviolent ways.

10. Foster caring beyond the classroom, using inspiring role models and opportunities for school and community service to help students learn to care by giving care.

11. Create a positive moral culture in the school, developing a total school environment (through the leadership of the principal, schoolwide discipline, a schoolwide sense of community, democratic student government, a moral community among adults, and time for addressing moral concerns) that supports and amplifies the values taught in classrooms.

12. Recruit parents and the community as partners in character education, supporting parents as the child's first moral teacher; encouraging parents to support the school in its efforts to foster good values; and seeking the help of the community (e.g., churches, business, and the media) in reinforcing the values the school is trying to teach (Lickona, 1991).

Character education in the classroom necessarily begins with the relationship between the teacher and child. That is the foundation for everything else. If students do not experience the teacher as a person who respects and cares about them, they are not likely to be open to anything else that teacher might wish to teach them about values.

Realizing the importance of this teacher-student relationship requires that a teacher have a moral purpose. To have a moral purpose requires seeing the moral significance of social interactions and even small events, imagining the long-range effects of children's experience at school on their values and character and the kind of society they will someday help to create, seeing teaching as it was once seen—as a special calling, a "moral craft." This is a role that large numbers of teachers are naturally attracted to. A great many already function as models and mentors, though they might not call it that. Many went into teaching in the first place not just because they liked kids but also because they wanted to make a difference in students' lives, to teach them good values as well as reading and math, affect the kind of human beings they would become.

Creating a Moral Classroom Community

A great many teachers take pains to form positive relationships with students based on respect and caring. Teachers are often at a loss, however, as to how to foster a similar level of respect and caring among their students, distressed by an increasing tendency among students of all ages to be egocentric and abusive in their treatment of schoolmates. Teachers sense correctly that much of what they are doing to try to build students' respect for self and others can be eroded by peer cruelty.

Left to its own devices, the peer group often ends up being ruled by the worst tendencies in children. Domination, rejection, and ridicule can become the prevailing social norms. Education fails, John Dewey (1934) asserted, when it neglects school as a form of community life. To succeed in teaching respect and responsibility, teachers must make the development of a classroom moral community a central educational objective.

Children learn morality by living it. They need to *be* a community—to interact, form relationships, work out problems, grow as a group, and learn directly, from their first-hand social experience, lessons about fair play, cooperation, forgiveness, and respect for the worth and dignity of every individual. Finally, for all students, there is a better atmosphere for academic learning when they're not preoccupied by worries about peer rejection and abuse.

What creates a moral community in the classroom? Three conditions are basic:

1. Students know each other.
2. Students respect, affirm, and care about each other.
3. Students feel membership in, and responsibility to, the group.

DISCIPLINE, A TOOL FOR TEACHING CHARACTER

Fewer students today come to school with an attitude of respect toward adults; many are astonishingly bold in their disrespect for teachers and other authority figures. Children's disrespectful behavior at school all too often reflects the miseducation, neglect, or outright abuse they have received at home.

It is not a kinder and gentler world for millions of children. And so it is a more difficult world for their teachers. Trouble with discipline is one of the leading sources of teacher stress and burnout. Discipline, however, is not just a problem; it is also, fortunately, a moral education opportunity. As the French sociologist Emile Durkheim (1973) observed, discipline provides the moral code that makes it possible for the small society of the classroom to function (p. 149).

A moral education approach to discipline uses discipline as a tool for teaching the values of respect and responsibility. This approach holds that the ultimate goal of discipline is self-discipline, the kind of self-control that underlies voluntary compliance with just rules and laws, that is a mark of mature character, and that a civilized society expects of its citizens. Discipline without moral education merely represents crowd control, managing behavior without teaching morality.

Moral discipline, by contrast, has the long-range goal of helping young people to behave responsibly in any situation, not just when they're under the control of a particular adult. Moral discipline seeks to develop students' reasoned respect for rules, the rights of others, and the teacher's legitimate authority; students' sense of responsibility for their own behavior; and their responsibility to the moral community of the classroom.

Teachers who practice moral discipline do four things:

1. They project a clear sense of their moral authority, their right and duty to teach students respect and responsibility and to hold them accountable to those standards of behavior.
2. They approach discipline, including rule-setting, as part of a larger ongoing effort to develop a good moral community in the classroom.
3. They establish and enforce consequences in an educational way, one that helps students appreciate a rule's purpose, make amends for wrongdoing, and take responsibility for improving their behavior.
4. They convey caring and respect for the individual student by trying to find the cause of a discipline problem and a solution that helps that student become a successful, responsible member of the classroom community.

WORK AS A MORAL IMPERATIVE

The literature on moral education typically treats moral learning and academic learning as separate spheres. But moral education includes academic work, because work has moral importance.

What gives work moral meaning? If students fail to work in school, they will also fail to learn, thus giving work a moral purpose. Adults spend most of their waking lives working. Work is one of the most basic ways adults affect the lives of others and contribute to the human community. When people do their jobs well, everyone benefits. When people do their jobs poorly, everyone pays the price. Competent people caring enough to perform their jobs competently are a major determinant of the quality of life in any society.

Work done well is a fundamental source of our dignity and sense of worth. In school, it is impossible for young people to feel positive self-regard when they are failing. It is also nearly impossible for students to feel good about themselves if they know they are doing much less than they are capable of. In adulthood, if we do not feel competent, productive, and needed in some sphere of life, whether at home, in the community, or in the workplace, it is very hard to maintain a positive self-image.

Behind the capacity to work is an important quality of character: the ability to delay gratification. Well-known psychoanalyst Bruno Bettelheim points out that achievement in any domain requires this self-discipline; subordinating the pleasure principle, which favors immediate gratification (e.g., watching TV instead of doing homework), to the reality principle, which forgoes present pleasure to pursue future goals (high marks, graduation, a good job). "It is this morality alone," writes Bettelheim, "that makes possible serious and consistent learning over long periods of time" (1976, p. 12).

Because many young people have not learned to postpone gratification, they have difficulty meeting the school's demands for concentration, sustained effort, and sacrifice of leisure time for study. Difficulty in delaying gratification once was considered the special vulnerability of children of poverty, but this problem now cuts across social classes.

The capacity to work is a central moral competence. That competence requires developing other traits—such as self-discipline, persistence, self-evaluation, and a sense of duty, all of which are part of good character. When people don't think work is important, don't work conscientiously at their jobs, or don't work at all, they suffer and so does the larger society.

The chief business of schools is the work of learning. From the standpoint of character education, the first step for schools is to treat work as having moral importance and the work of learning as a moral activity that contributes to character development.

The second step is to realize that schools are engaging not only in bad education but also in bad *moral* education when students are not doing the work of learning. When academic expectations are low, or when the peer culture keeps students from working hard, or when students simply don't care about the quality of their work, the fundamental purpose of schooling is corrupted. In that compromised moral environment, students are learning bad moral habits—laziness, indifference to standards, evasion of responsibility—that they will likely carry over into their adult lives.

Hard Work and a Concern for Excellence

Thomas Green implores educators to have what he calls a "conscience of craft"—a concern for excellence. The conscience of craft, Green says, calls on educators to do their jobs well (1985, pp. 25–26). To have developed the conscience of craft is to have acquired the capacity to feel satisfaction at a job well done—and to be ashamed of slovenly work. The conscience of craft motivates a mechanic to repair a car not only to our satisfaction but also to his own. It is a mark of people's character when they take care to perform their jobs and other tasks well. If people lack this kind of conscience and don't feel any obligation to do good work, something basic is missing in their moral makeup.

A considerable body of research now makes it very clear that many schools do not suffer from an environment of mediocrity. Many, even in areas where large numbers of pupils come from stressed or impoverished backgrounds, have developed academic environments that inspire responsible work attitudes and performance on the part of students (Edmonds, 1982, p. 16).

When you find good schools, you can't help being impressed. The encouraging news is there are hundreds, even thousands, of such schools all across America, along with outstanding teachers and courageous principals.

The late Ron Edmonds started the "Effective Schools Program" in the 1970s. Edmonds described the characteristics of effective schools.

Effective schools—those with high student achievement and morale—create a concern for excellence and have a moral vision. They consistently show the following characteristics:

1. Vigorous leadership: The principal works with teachers, students, parents, and community members to develop the learning environment and the school's reputation for high academic standards; incoming students know the school's reputation, and experienced students affirm the value placed on learning; faculty morale is high, and when there are openings, the principal recruits and selects teachers who share the school's goals and standards.
2. A pervasive atmosphere of caring.
3. Clear goals for both academic performance and classroom and school behavior.
4. An emphasis on fair and consistent discipline and a safe and orderly environment.
5. Teachers with the expectation that all their students can and will learn.
6. Collegial interaction among teachers in support of student learning and achievement.
7. High learning time.
8. Regular, monitored homework.
9. Frequent monitoring of students' progress in learning.
10. Recognition of student achievements (U.S. Department of Education, 1986).

Homework

More teachers will assign more homework when they discover what the research shows (U.S. Department of Education, 1986, p. 41).

- When low-ability students do just one to three hours of homework a week, their grades are usually as high as those of average ability students who do no homework.
- When average-ability students do three to five hours of homework a week, their grades usually equal those of high-ability students who do no homework.

The widespread deterioration of the work ethic reflects a long cultural slide toward self-indulgence and a get-without-giving morality. It won't be easily reversed by schools. Regardless of how tough this challenge, schools must strive to teach young people, in the words of essayist Lance Morrow, that "all life must be worked at—protected, planted, replanted, fashioned, cooked for, coaxed, diapered, formed, sustained. Work is the way we tend the world" (1988, p. 3).

Good schools will convey a balanced message about work by creating the kind of human environment where people clearly matter. At the same time, they will be diligent in teaching students a lesson they once knew better than they do now: To succeed in life and build a better world, they need more than brains and talent; they also need the capacity for working hard. Developing that capacity must be high on the agenda of our efforts to build the character of our children.

MORAL RELATIVISM IN THE CLASSROOM

Without ethical training, many teachers tend to treat moral judgment as if it were simply a matter of personal opinion. This represents the mistake of moral relativism, an error that has deep roots in contemporary culture.

Moral relativism is an outgrowth of philosophical positivism (which denies that there can be objective moral truths) and personalism (which emphasizes individual autonomy and subjective feelings). Many teachers who might not think of themselves as "moral relativists" nevertheless talk as if they were. Such teachers routinely introduce a classroom moral discussion by saying to students, "There are no right or wrong answers. . . . " In a values discussion, these teachers scrupulously avoid making any statement that could cause students to think that they might be wrong in a particular value judgment—regardless of what the students say.

Many students, unfortunately, are all too ready to believe that there are no right or wrong answers when it comes to morality. They have grown up in a society where many people think that moral values are never absolute but always relative to the individual or the society holding them. The implication of that belief is far-reaching: Nothing is objectively right or wrong; "moral" means "what's right for me."

Such thinking fails to grasp a fundamental moral truth. There are rationally grounded, nonrelative, objectively worthwhile moral values: respect and responsibility, courage, honesty, liberty, the inherent value of every individual person, and the consequent responsibility to care for each other and carry out basic responsibilities. These objectively worthwhile values require that any action by any individual, group, or state that violates these basic moral values be treated as morally wrong.

How is it possible to demonstrate rationally that moral values such as respect and responsibility have objective worth? First of all, such values serve to benefit both the individual and society. They also survive two classic ethical tests (Rath & Harmon, 1966): Reversibility (would you want to receive this kind of treatment?) and universalizability (would you want all persons to act this way in a similar situation?). Behaviors that are contrary to respect, for example, clearly fail the tests of both reversibility and universalizability. If we ourselves wouldn't want to be the victim of theft, rape, or murder (the reversibility test), and if we wouldn't want people in general to go around stealing, raping, and murdering (the universalizability test), then such behaviors are self-evidently wrong.

To the extent that a teacher thinks that all values are purely personal and relative and that there are no rights and obligations that bind everyone, the teacher is crippled as a moral educator. There are rational, objectively valid moral requirements to which all people are accountable. Society can't exist without them. One of the primary tasks of the school as moral educator is to help students understand moral facts and act accordingly. Once teachers abandon relativistic thinking and become convinced that a school has a right and a duty to teach nonrelative moral values, a major obstacle to character education is overcome.

CARING FOR AND SERVING THE COMMUNITY

Of the many things that make a person a good citizen, two stand out. One is an attitude of caring about one's fellow human beings. The other is the belief that one person can make a difference. Children are overwhelmed with all the suffering in the world, but they are usually not enabled to act.

Individuals, of course, do make a difference. Every day, people who care about more than their own comfort are doing all kinds of things to improve the lives of others. And as they help those in need, they experience a deeper fulfillment than can ever be found in a bank account. Helping young people realize that enables them to grow beyond selfishness and discover that their own capacity for doing good is a crucial part of character education.

The need for caring citizens who feel empowered to act is greater than ever before. Notes Joseph Califano, Jr., former U.S. Secretary of Health, Education and Welfare: "Government alone cannot meet and master the great social problems of our day" (*Giraffe Gazette*, 1987, p. 3). "The big ideas in this world," writes author Norman Cousins, "cannot survive unless they come to life in the individual citizen" (*Giraffe Gazette,* 1988, p. 3).

How can schools foster an "I can make a difference" sense of citizen responsibility? It starts in the classroom, where children can see the results of their actions as they work to create a caring moral community. Further, schools need to extend students' caring attitudes into larger and larger spheres so that they come to identify compassionately with the mainstream of humanity and do what they can to build a better world.

Helping students develop social conscience begins with social awareness. Facts about human want and suffering can be demoralizing, and even destructive of the will to act. Students need to know that all over the world, people are taking effective action to alleviate suffering and restore hope and dignity to the poor and oppressed.

A few years ago Ernest Boyer, former U.S. commissioner of education, made headlines with a bold proposal: Require all high school students to complete a community service term, taken for school credit (1986, pp. 10–12). Before they graduated, students would be asked to volunteer in the libraries, parks, hospitals, nursing homes, day-care centers, social agencies, or programs for the handicapped of their communities. They would learn to care about the common good by contributing to it.

Others before Boyer have argued that the way to solve the problem of youthful alienation is to give young people meaningful ways to participate in society (Kohler, 1981). But this time the idea of student community service is riding a wave of concern about national values and character. According to a 1987 Carnegie Foundation study (Working Together, p. 4), most public high schools offer some type of community service program (either voluntary or required). By the mid 1980s, one of five public high schools had some kind of service program.

Some schools have a tradition of developing social-political awareness as a source of social action. An example is Princeton, New Jersey's Stuart Country Day School. The school's principal says of their high school students:

> Our students read to the blind, work with kids in inner-city neighborhood houses, help in soup kitchens, rebuild houses, and spend two weeks in Appalachia. Many have also interviewed their congressional representatives regarding social issues. Since we believe this kind of education should ideally have an international dimension, we've also sent many students to Bogota. Our goal is to prepare our students for leadership by exposing them to the moral imperatives in the world today. (Starratt, 1989, p. 18)

Caring Beyond the Classroom

Schools can foster students' caring attitudes and active citizenship beyond the classroom if they:

1. Make students aware of the needs and suffering of others in their own country and around the world.
2. Offer examples of groups working effectively to help the poor and oppressed; organize student action projects to help.
3. Provide inspiring role models of people helping others.
4. Provide positive peer role models.
5. Give students the opportunity to render school service, especially in face-to-face helping relationships such as class buddies and in cross-age tutoring.
6. Enable students to participate in community service; where possible, integrate such service into the academic program.
7. Provide education in social justice, the politics of change, and citizen action.

CREATING A POSITIVE MORAL CULTURE IN THE SCHOOL

Six elements are important in creating a positive moral culture:

1. Moral and academic leadership from the principal.
2. Schoolwide discipline that models, promotes, and upholds the school's values in *all* school environments.
3. A schoolwide sense of community.
4. Student government that involves students in democratic self-government and fosters the feeling "This is *our* school, and we're responsible for making it the best school it can be."
5. A moral atmosphere of mutual respect, fairness, and cooperation that pervades all relationships—those among the adults in the school as well as those between adults and students.
6. Elevating the importance of morality by spending school time on moral concerns.

Progress in one element usually brings progress in another. However, a school doesn't have to be equally strong in all six dimensions to have a moral culture. It is useful to think of these elements as ideals to work toward.

SUMMARY

As the end of this century approaches, the mood of the nation is hopeful. More and more communities are recognizing the need for character education. Educational leaders are beginning to step forward also.

Enormous problems exist—a culture in which selfishness is disguised as "life-style," countless families are in crisis, and millions of children suffer from neglect of their most basic needs.

The good news is that researchers and practitioners alike know that comprehensive character education programs can make a difference.

Getting Started

1. Develop a leadership group. Form a character education council or task force that will help select target values, develop program guidelines, and take responsibility for long-range planning and program implementation. This group should be broadly representative, including the principal, teachers, a counselor or psychologist, parents, a secretary, custodian, or other member of the school's support staff, and others who can help develop, implement, and gain widespread support for the values program.

2. Do a needs analysis survey. Send a questionnaire to all school staff, parents, students, community leaders (e.g., political and business leaders, clergy, and heads of youth services), and students.

3. Develop a plan. Using the results of the needs analysis survey and the school assessment, develop a plan that includes short-range goals (e.g., for the first year) and long-range goals (e.g., for the next three years).

4. Get feedback on the plan. Present the plan to the staff, parents, and others for feedback; where desirable, incorporate suggestions for improvement; disseminate the revised plan.

5. Set up a parent committee. Ask parents serving on the values education steering committee also to establish their own parent committee and recruit members for that. This parent group then takes responsibility for keeping all parents informed about the school's values program (e.g., through a newsletter), organizing parent participation programs, and encouraging parents to foster at home the values the school is trying to teach.

6. Create special-focus subcommittees. Form one or more subcommittees focusing on a high-priority schoolwide issue or problem where there is the chance of making visible progress in the near future.

7. Provide professional development. Sponsor a series of workshops, each focusing on a particular values education strategy. Encourage *all* school staff (including secretaries, cafeteria workers, custodians, playground aides, and bus drivers) to attend at least the introductory session on the school's overall approach and reasons for undertaking values education. Allow teachers the freedom to choose those strategies they feel most comfortable implementing.

8. Set up a "partnership" system. Have teachers pair up so everyone has a "partner" with whom to compare notes on activities tried after the workshops (What worked? What didn't?). Encourage voluntary peer visitations. Make time for cross-grade sharing as well.

9. Develop or expand democratic student government. Set up a governance structure that gives students meaningful responsibilities for decision making that affects the life of the school. Establish a system of school jobs so that each class has a special task.

10. Work toward a character curriculum. Arrange for teachers to meet in grade-level groups to:
    - Identify developmentally appropriate values to emphasize at each grade level.
    - Define educational objectives for each value.
    - Develop corresponding classroom activities (Lickona, 1991).

CONCLUSION

Character education takes place least in classroom lectures (although these have a place) and is only in a limited measure a matter of developing moral reasoning. To a much greater extent, moral education is fostered through personal example and above all through fostering the proper institutional culture, from corridors and cafeteria to the parking lot and sports. In effect, the whole school should be considered as a set of experiences generating situations in which young people learn values either of compassion, honesty, sharing, and responsibility or of cheating, cutthroat competition, and total self-absorption.

Chapter VI

CREATING SMALL, CARING
SCHOOL COMMUNITIES

The crisis of confidence in American public education has a myriad of causes, one of which is the lack of confidence in large, impersonal, and uncaring schools. Creating a school climate characterized by a close, trusting relationship among students and between students and adults should be an essential characteristic of public schools, which all children deserve.

The heart of professionalism in education may be a commitment to the caring ethic. The caring ethic requires far more than bringing state-of-the-art technical knowledge to bear on one's practice. This results too often in student's being treated antiseptically, as clients or cases. The caring ethic means doing everything possible to serve the learning, developmental, and social needs of students as persons.

The probable continuing slow pace of school improvements, the deep hurt and despair of so many youth, the continuing disparagement of many caring and dedicated teachers, and the erosion of communal and national ideals leads to a compellingly different perspective about how to create schools that inspire success, rather than confirm despair.

Radical restructuring of the public schools requires that educators take into account insecurity and instability of children served by the schools. The facts about the instability of the American family are well known. Its long-term effects are not. But ask yourself what might happen to the future health of a five-year-old boy or a twelve-year-old girl living through a divorce and then in a single-parent family or a second family of stepbrothers and stepsisters, or of being a latchkey child of one of those 60% of American mothers who now work full-time or of typical fathers, who allegedly spend about ten to twenty minutes a day reading to or playing with their children, or of spending seven to eight hours a day when one, two, or three years of age in a day-care center or every day after school alone when six or seven. The limited research done on some of these questions has been neither systematic or comprehensive enough to identify honestly their long-term delayed effects, both healthy and unhealthy (Falbo, 1984).

There are, however, some sobering clues. A survey of 24,599 eighth-graders in more than one thousand public schools identified 20% as being at high risk of failing school. Two of the six best predictors of who would fail were "living in a single-parent family, and being at home alone without an adult for long periods on weekdays" (Taylor & Ellison, 1967, p. 1077). The 1988 National Health Interview Survey of Child Health independently also identified 20% of its 17,000 youngsters as having learning or emotional problems, due in large part to family disruption, single-parent upbringing, and conflicting divorcing parents. Finally, American children's poorer math performance than that of other nations' children is apparently associated more with growing up in poor single-parent families than with school (Moses, 1992).

There is one effect of such changes in parent-child relationships that cannot be denied. More children today have much less opportunity for direct emotional involvement with their mothers and fathers. They do not have the same kinds of experiences that previous generations have had by which to learn skills such as caring, cooperation, and empathy. David Bernback found that the most frequently mentioned fear of today's children of all ages is that they will lose a parent (Heath, 1994, p. 33).

Margaret Mead (1962) wisely advised that if we clearly understood our problems, their lines of solution would be prefigured. Might not a decade of frenetic but fruitless efforts to figure out how to improve our schools suggest that we have not yet clearly understood today's students, teachers, and schools? For example, consider legislator's seemingly worthwhile proposal to lengthen the school day and year, a proposal made by outsiders, not insiders, to the schools. Without an understanding of what students and teachers daily face in their classrooms, their proposal is doomed to fail, unless the organizational structure and climate of the schools changes. Coming face-to-face with youth, a growing number of whom represent the children of dysfunctional and disorganized families, requires schools to reorganize in a radical but simple way.

Vulnerable and neglected youth desperately need small schools which provide meaningful personal relationships. Such schools could become the focal point for regenerating communities and encouraging more parental support. This judgment and proposal is grounded on thirty-five years of experience in public education, most of it in poor, working-

class communities, and for the past three years researching exemplars of
school success.

SMALL SCHOOLS FOR SUCCESS

Americans have for decades prided themselves on their large comprehensive schools. The myth that bigger is better has been perpetuated by
educational leaders and school boards. Naively, the public came to
believe that a "better" school has every fashionable academic resource to
meet every need of every student. Such "shopping mall" schools that
indulge every whim and fancy provoke the question of "better for achieving what?" Research for over two decades has demonstrated no relationship between what schools buy, such as number of faculty with advanced
degrees, and any objective measure of academic achievement (Coleman,
1966; Jencks et al., 1972).

Cost

Taxpayers and critics argue that big schools are more economical:
breaking up a 2,000-student school into no fewer than four schools would
be too expensive and reduce the available resources for each school. This
is inaccurate. The argument is seriously flawed for one never accounted-
for reason. Setting aside their proportionately greater administrative,
security, discipline, and busing costs, large schools' long-term educational,
psychic, and social costs have never been estimated. What community
has determined even crudely how much its large schools may have
contributed to its miseducated and disenfranchised students' drug,
unemployment, welfare and prison costs five, ten, and fifteen years after
dropping out, if not physically, then mentally and emotionally?

Creating Caring Schools

Vulnerable children from fragmented families need a small, stable,
caring school environment that their parents know, trust, and support.
Children need to be known well by the adults in school. Impersonality
does not foster caring or understanding. To be cared for and understood
is the first, most necessary experience for one to learn how to feel for and
understand others.

Students who have low morale and are potential dropouts view their schools very differently than do students of high morale. Low student morale will prevail and programs to reduce dropout rates will fail unless schools become more caring places. Large schools make it difficult to know others so as to be able to care. Safe, caring, and "family like" schools need to be created. Schools must reintegrate with their neighboring communities to make sustained parental involvement and support possible.

Depersonalizing Large Schools

School also affects youth's interpersonal maturing. In the United States, schools commandeer about 12,000 hours of a youth's growing-up time. The facts about schools' potential effects on teachers' and students' relationships are now well established. Little other educational research has produced such consistent but such tragically and irresponsibly ignored results. We have known since the early sixties from excellent studies initiated in Kansas that abandoning small, personal schools could have numerous potentially unhealthy effects and almost no healthy effects, not even enduring academic ones, on the maturing of students (Barker & Gump, 1964).

Large schools reduce the opportunity for sustained relationships to occur between everyone in the school. Once an elementary school has more than about 200 to 350 students and middle or high school 400 to 500 or more, a host of potentially unhealthy effects become noticeable, especially for vulnerable kids (Carnegie Council of Adolescent Development, 1989). Their interpersonal climate is impersonal and bureaucratic. Teachers don't know other teachers or students as well as do those in smaller schools; they don't talk as frequently about individual students or about curricular issues in faculty meetings, do less cooperative planning and collaboration; and like students, they do not know who makes what decisions. Students see their friends less frequently, have less contact with adults other than their teachers, participate much less frequently in extracurricular activities, including athletic teams, have much less opportunity to hold leadership positions, are more aggressive and disorderly, and cheat more frequently (Carnegie Council on Adolescent Development, 1989). Parents no longer visit the school as frequently or know their children's teachers as well.

John Goodlad's (1984) thorough study of public high schools reached similar conclusions. The smallest schools in the sample were better able to solve their problems more effectively. Their atmospheres were more intellectual; their teachers cared more about students; their students and parents, as well as their teachers, were more satisfied with the school.

Only one positive educational benefit of a large high school can be found in the research literature, that being more math courses. However, computers and telecommunications may make such courses available in the future even to small schools.

Depersonalization

The research about school size in large inner-city and urban schools indicates that until these large urban "school factories" are replaced with smaller more humane schools, their students will achieve limited success, at best. Significant reform, in fact, appears unlikely unless downsizing occurs first (Heath, 1971, pp. 127–129). When asked what kind of school they wished for their children, Olson (1990, p. 12) reported that parents identified small school size as important. Teachers in small schools are, according to John Goodlad (1984), more optimistic that school improvement could succeed than those in larger ones.

Furthermore, large schools impede sustained efforts to improve them for several crucial reasons, some of which strong leaders might possibly overcome, at least temporarily. They are less likely than smaller schools to be perceived by their faculty and students as having a distinctive identity, as studies dismally show no widespread communion of value unites their faculty or students, who tend to go their own ways (Heath, 1994). Faculty agree only on the narrowest of goals, usually minimal academic ones. When faculty are not united by a commonly shared view of their goals, consensus and emotional commitment to change become frustratingly difficult to secure. Large schools represent education's dinosaurs. They need to die if students can have the caring schools they need, radical and logistically complex, yes, but absolutely necessary.

At its root, what has damaged so many children has not been lack of money but lack of a compelling vision, imagination, commitment, and will to create healthier school environments for all children. The right questions have not been asked about the steps necessary to nourish the human spirit. For example, why do school districts persist in building large schools when the evidence is so compelling that they just don't work for vulnerable kids?

The Carnegie Commission recommends that urban schools be broken up into units of no more than 450 students (Carnegie Foundation, 1986,

p. 23). Observers of New York City's honored District 4 African-American schools believe that their small sizes—fewer than 300—create the personalized learning environment that contributes to their increased achievement, a belief also shared by consultants to Philadelphia's small "schools within schools" downsizing effort.

Vulnerable youth need small, emotionally safe, personal, humane, and caring schools that their parents know, trust, and don't fear visiting. They need teachers who work with them for several years and forge a close relationship with their parents. They need older students to tutor and be friends with them. They need also, as urgently, non-age-graded, experiential and flexible classrooms and curriculum. They need more integrated school, home, and community environments.

Various studies have shown that strong positive relations between caring adults and children can have a powerful effect on the outcomes for children (Gordon & Song, 1988). According to Ann Masten, teachers can be powerful role models for children by valuing the individual, modeling competent behavior, providing information and guidance, steering children away from pitfalls, generating resources, coaching competence, engaging in advocacy, and opening doors of opportunity (Masten, 1994).

Unfortunately, the conditions in too many of our schools fail to support such possibilities, or worse, foster maladaptive behavior on the part of both teachers and students.

For example, the recent literature on our high schools describes informally struck "classroom bargains" and "treaties" between students and teachers to minimalize their mutual efforts (Powell, Farrar, & Cohen, 1988). In part, these tendencies exist because many of our schools are too large, too bureaucratic, and too impersonal to be effective at offering opportunities for adults to connect with young people.

CREATING SMALL SCHOOLS NOW

Large schools could be divided into "houses" or mini-schools to which students ride the same bus and in which they remain for most of their school years. Such houses should have their own teacher teams, student newspapers and governments, eating and recreational areas. Shared co-curricular activities, cafeteria, library, etc., dilute a house's distinctive culture. Only if houses can be granted genuine autonomy will the sharing of some common facilities not erode their ethos.

House plans which have successfully persisted are rare. If its ethos and autonomy is safely guarded, then a house plan represents a realistic, though not a fully desirable, structural way to create a school that promotes human excellence (Snider, 1989, pp. 6–7). One option which should be immediately considered by schools across the country is for school leaders to build, within the larger school, smaller communities that function as semi-autonomous schools.

We need to restructure our schools following a caring and personalization model, rather than a bureaucratic model, if we are to make them better places for making connections between adults and young people. As an antidote to the fragmentation and depersonalization of our traditional "factory model" of schooling, our big schools need to be restructured into schools within schools, with teachers and students organized into "teams" of manageable size that work together for sustained periods of time—perhaps staying together for two or three years so that strong interpersonal relationships can flourish.

CONCLUSIONS

The policy issues should be clear. School districts should no longer perpetuate a failed decision, no longer build large schools. One out of eight of today's schools needs to be replaced because of old age, structural flaws, or inadequacies, such as lack of air conditioning, that prevent their more extended use (Schmidt, 1991). Federal funding and state grants and low-interest loans should be made available to any district, especially poor ones, to recreate more humanely sized schools. Schools should no longer be mindlessly consolidated if there is the remotest possibility that creating and sustaining a caring school would be possible.

Many educational leaders and school board members argue that school districts can't afford to abandon their existing large schools. What is more practical, however, than to make a long-term investment in creating healthy learning environments for all children? School districts need to begin the transition now, creating house schools with genuine autonomy. As new schools are built, they ought to be small so that the students can receive the care they need and the success they deserve. American education can be significantly improved by permitting schools to be small, self-governed, self-renewing communities where everyone counts and everyone cares.

At its root, what has damaged so many children's spirit has not been lack of money but lack of a compelling vision and will to create healthier school environments for all children. Because educational leaders have failed in the past to create smaller schools, failed decisions should no longer be perpetuated. All children, but especially those who are at risk and disadvantaged, need small, emotionally safe, personal, and caring schools that their parents know, trust, and don't fear visiting. They need teachers who work with them for several years and forge close relationships with their parents. They need as urgently non-age-graded experiential and flexible classrooms and curriculum.

Large, bureaucratically controlling schools make mature and enduring relationships inordinately difficult. Such schools are not caring, cooperative, or sensitive to the needs of their students.

Large schools are education's dinosaurs. They must die if students can have the kind of caring schools they need. While this conclusion is radically and logistically complex, it is absolutely necessary.

Chapter VII

THE "FOSSILIZATION" OF THE
AMERICAN HIGH SCHOOL

The "fossilization" of the high school curriculum has contributed to the crisis of confidence in American public education. Despite modest tinkering (adding a course here and there—increasing the requirements for graduation), the curriculum of the American public high school remains largely unchanged over the past 50–60 years. The general studies track continues to be the most popular curriculum in most high schools. It hasn't changed much from the 1930s and 40s. The college preparatory curriculum also looks much like its 1930s ancestor. But the type of occupations available in the 1990s contrast dramatically with the job market when the American high school curriculum was first devised. Business and industrial leaders have argued persuasively for the schools to provide more flexible, highly skilled workers in an age of rapid technological change.

More and more students emerge from high school ready neither for college nor for work. This predicament becomes more acute as the fund of knowledge continues its rapid growth, the number of traditional jobs shrink, and new jobs demand additional skill and preparation. Only twenty percent of high school students complete bachelors' degrees and over fifty percent of high school graduates possess limited skills which relegate them to the lowest-paying jobs (Astin, 1982). Until this dilemma is addressed and a plan of action is developed, the confidence of the public in America's high schools will continue to decline.

MAKING WINNERS OUT OF ORDINARY STUDENTS

In today's world, a youngster who leaves school unable to read, write, and do simple arithmetic faces a bleak future. When a substantial proportion of boys and girls leave school undereducated, the rest of us face a bleak future.

Americans have always seen education as the best route to individual achievement—and as being necessary to the maintenance of democracy, the softening of class lines, and the operation of a profitable and productive economy. Today, a quality education is far more important than ever before.

In 1900, nine out of ten youngsters did not graduate from high school, but there was no high school dropout problem (Berlin, Sum, & Taggart, 1984). At mid-century, when as many dropped out as graduated, there was no reason for public concern. The avenues to self-sufficiency, indeed to prosperity, were still many and varied. A young person could become a successful adult by quitting school and going to work, as easily as remaining in school until graduation. But all that has changed in the high-tech last half century. Today there is only one way to adult self-sufficiency: the school way.

The impact on young people of not succeeding in school can be devastating. "Labor market problems of teenagers result largely from doing poorly in school" (Peng, Fetters, & Kolstad, 1983, pp. 31–32). If the American high school is incapable of changing the prospects of the 13 million teenage children currently at serious risk, says a coalition of eleven education organizations, these children will grow up to become adults who will "drain the economy in welfare and social service costs and seriously hamper the nation's ability to compete internationally (Berlin, Sum, & Taggart, 1984).

The consequences of dropping out of school are not confined to the economic sphere. Dropouts are three-and-a-half times as likely as high school graduates to be arrested and six times as likely to be unwed parents.

The school dropout's future is bleak not only because employers need better-educated workers but also because employers use the high school diploma as a screening device for almost any job—whether or not the job requires a high school education.

So it is not surprising that dropouts are seven-and-a-half times as likely as graduates to be dependent on welfare, or that dropouts are twice as likely to be unemployed and to live in poverty (Berlin, Sum, & Taggart, 1984, p. 3). The disparity in income between dropouts and graduates increases each year. Between 1973 and 1984, not completing high school meant a 42 percent reduction in what a young man in his early twenties could expect to earn (Johnson & Sum, 1987). An additional fact highlights how employers use school completion as a symbolic reassurance: The lack of a high school diploma increases the chances of being unemployed twice as much for blacks as for whites (Berlin, Sum, & Taggart, 1984).

The philosophical basis of the present high school curriculum needs to be examined against the principles of American democracy and its traditions of justice and egalitarianism. The high school curriculum needs to be evaluated in terms of effectiveness in providing opportunities for large numbers of students, especially the "underclass," to become upwardly mobile. Lastly, the instructional programs of American high schools need to be examined on the basis of how effectively students are shown why knowledge is important and how successful our high schools are in fostering a lifelong love of learning.

American education over the years has favored Plato's ideas of "classical education" over the more practical ideas of Aristotle. In fact, an important group of elitists in this country today holds that anything resembling "vocational education" has no place in the school curriculum; that the term "education" refers only to the development of the intellectual proficiencies and academic disciplines. Socrates followed this line of logic: "This is the only education which, upon our view, deserves the name; that other sort of training which aims at the acquisition of wealth or bodily strength, or mere cleverness apart from intelligence or justice, is mean and illiberal, and is not worthy to be called education at all" (Burnet, 1914).

Scholar and long-time observer of the American educational scene, Keith Goldhammer (1972, p. 26), rebuts this position:

> The establishment of a public-school system in the United States based upon the Platonic intellectual tradition has tended toward an elitist conception of its functions, has emphasized its selective characteristics, and has at least partially abrogated its responsibilities for the seventy-five to eighty percent of its students who by native ability, interest, and aspiration are identifiable with the practical affairs of our culture rather than inclined toward the more abstract and conceptual activities of the academic disciplines.

K. Patricia Cross (1984), professor at the Harvard Graduate School of Education, offers a pungent and balanced observation on this subject:

> In the final analysis, the task of the excellent teacher is to stimulate "apparently ordinary" people to unusual effort. What do the reports on school reform have to contribute to that goal? In the first place, there is surprisingly little attention given to "ordinary people" in the school reform reports. There is the clear implication that the rising tide of mediocrity is made up of embarrassing

numbers of ordinary people. Teachers' colleges are advised to select better candidates, colleges are encouraged to raise admissions standards, and the federal government is urged to offer scholarships to attract top high-school graduates into teaching. There is not a lot said in the education reports about how to stimulate unusual effort on the part of the ordinary people that we seem to be faced with in the schools and in most colleges.... The tough problem is not in identifying winners; it is in making winners out of ordinary people. That, after all, is the overwhelming purpose of education. Yet historically, in most of the periods emphasizing excellence, education has reverted to selecting winners rather than creating them.

At an international conference on higher education, David Moore, principal of Nelson and Colne College in Lancashire, England, commenting on the British educational system, said, "Our schools in England are designed to make the majority of our people feel like failures" (Moore, 1984). After reading the recent plethora of recommendations about improving American education, one might conclude that excellence in American education can only be achieved by making a majority of students feel like failures, unable to cope with modern life. Anything less than a college prep/baccalaureate degree program is viewed as somehow second-rate. Few of these national studies provide a workable solution to the problem outlined thirty years ago by John W. Gardner:

> The importance of education is not limited to the higher orders of talent. A complex society is dependent every hour of every day upon the capacity of its people at every level to read and write, to make difficult judgments, and to act in the light of extensive information.... When there isn't a many-leveled base of trained talent on which to build, modern social and economic developments are simply impossible. And if that base were to disappear suddenly in any complex society, the whole intricate interlocking mechanism would grind to a halt. (Gardner, 1984)

The Challenge of Diverse Student Needs

The current national debates, the multiple reports on how to improve the schools are symptoms of the ever-evolving nature of the American education enterprise. The diversity of individuals attending the schools is awesome. The varieties of student abilities and aspirations, of socioeconomic and cultural backgrounds, require multiple approaches in the program and in the teaching/learning process.

One of the great challenges for educators is how to meet the great range of individual differences among students while seeking the best in all people, whether rich or poor, able or disabled, destined for the university, community college, apprenticeship, military, or a specific job, including homemaking. To that end, the assumption that a baccalaureate degree is the only road to excellence, respect and dignity for all people ought to be discarded. Social and educational status should not be confused with equality of opportunity and individual achievement, regardless of the field of study. Neither should the "excellence movement" become a disguise for a retreat from equity and opportunity for all. As stated by the Commission on Pre-College Education in Mathematics, Science and Technology: "Excellence and elitism are not synonymous" (Coleman et al., 1983). Clearly, American education requires a new definition of excellence in education, a definition that will hold meaning for *all* students.

Educators and parents alike have a divided view of high schools today. Some see the high school as a sorting system separating the academically talented from the not so talented. Others see the high school as the "holding pen" for young people, keeping them off the job market until they have grown up. To see the high school as a human resource development center, a place in which to prevent the accumulation of human waste, is a vision worth adopting.

SOCIOECONOMIC INEQUITY IN THE HIGH SCHOOL

There is a continuing and widening gap between the "haves" and the "have-nots" in our society. What is disturbing in the major education reform reports is their lack of emphasis on learning incentives and learner motivation, particularly as regards underclass, blacks, Hispanics, and other minorities. Meanwhile, nearly half of the Hispanic high school students in the country drop out before graduating from high school. This is more than double the rate of black students and three times the rate of white students. Forty percent of the Hispanic dropouts never complete the tenth grade. The National Commission on Secondary Schooling for Hispanics states: " . . . the high dropout rate is a failure of the education system which has not met the aspirations and special needs of its growing Hispanic population" (*Washington Post,* 1985, p. B3). The commission blames curricula that fail to address the vocational needs of students, the lack of adequate counseling and support services, low expectations, and the strength of the work ethic among Hispanic men.

An increasing stratification seems to be taking place along economic, educational, employment, and ethnic lines. Statistics show a recent increase in the number of individuals and families in the lower-income strata and below the poverty line. There also appears to be a steadily increasing gap between low- and middle-income families and upper-income families (*Washington Post,* 1985, p. B7). When the socioeconomic circumstance of the "haves" and "have-nots" in our society is examined, some startling statistics emerge:

- Two out of three adults who currently meet the federal definition of poverty are women and more than half the poverty families are maintained by single women.
- Seventy percent of all AFDC (Aid to Families with Dependent Children) recipients are children.
- 3.1 million children, or 3,000 a day, have fallen into poverty since 1979. This is a thirty-one percent increase in the number of poverty children over a five-year period.
- There has been a fifty-two percent increase over the past eight years in working women with infants under one year of age (American Enterprise Institute for Public Policy Research, 1983).

The time is ripe for some new thinking about the technological tension and related job training. A national job skill training program which encourages and provides active help to members of the underclass who have already taken the *first steps* toward lifting themselves out of their environment ought to be developed. The most cost-effective job-training program today may be one that focuses on upward mobility. A program to identify those proven workers in dead-end jobs and offer them education and training to meet the needs of new jobs requiring new and more sophisticated skills represents a win-win situation. The employee would advance, the employer would gain a proven worker, and an entry-level job would be opened for an unskilled or less skilled worker.

Political conservatives observe these facts and aver that competition and choice are the keys to helping the poor. Political liberals look at the statistics and call for some type of federally funded job-guarantee program. While the political forces continue to debate this highly charged issue, the pool of the poor continues to grow, caught in a cycle of unemployment, loss of self-esteem, and poverty.

Other implications must be considered in reviewing the socioeconomic tensions between the "haves" and the "have-nots," but the major question to consider is what education and training can do to help. A national human resource development strategy in this country, particularly for non-baccalaureate degree individuals, has never been developed. No discussion of excellence in education in a universal education system can be complete without considering the plight of all members of society and the tensions that motivate or inhibit them. Now is the time to value our human resources as much as, if not more than, we value our natural resources of oil and gas and metals.

We tend to live somewhere between our hopes and our fears. It is possible for our age to move closer to the hopes and dreams of universal education rather than to greater social and educational inequity.

An excellent universal education system for all our citizens (in their diversity) needs to be provided. The United States has come closer than any other culture to achieving this high goal, but as yet it is still incomplete. *The nation has yet to demonstrate that it really knows how to provide a universal education for all people.* In particular, ordinary students need to be helped to become winners. The time has come to face up to the dilemma of achieving excellence in a universal education system, particularly for the ordinary student.

The Dilemma of the General Track Student

The National Commission on Excellence in Education (1983) states our present dilemma in this straightforward way: "More and more young people emerge from high school ready neither for college nor for work. This predicament becomes more acute as the knowledge base continues its rapid expansion, the number of traditional jobs shrinks, and new jobs demand greater sophistication and preparation" (Gardner et al., 1983).

Too many of the aforementioned ordinary students, termed general track students, are receiving an unfocused general education which does not prepare them for particular job skills, leads to nothing but the lowest-paying jobs, and does not prepare these students for further education. The present high school system does little to promote continuity in learning or to build personal confidence and self-esteem for general track students. Unfocused learning remains one of the major barriers to achieving excellence for a host of high school students.

The most serious educational tension in America's high schools is a self-induced program fragmentation that focuses primarily on either an academic or a vocational education track. For those students who do not fit comfortably into one or the other, an unfocused general education track leading to nowhere is offered. In recent years there has been such a significant movement of high school students from both the academic track and the vocational track into the unfocused general education track that this program has now become dominant in most high schools (Parnell, 1985, p. 25).

These general education students spend over forty percent of their high school effort outside the traditional academic courses, compared with thirty percent for the academic track students. The academic courses for these students often carry titles such as General English, General Science, General Social Studies, General Math, or Remedial English, Remedial Math. Nevertheless, more and more of these same students aspire to college and regard themselves as prepared for college attendance (Astin, 1982; Wagenaar, 1981). The high school curriculum of the general track students can best be described as a combination of general, remedial, and personal interest type courses. Even though general track students take fifteen percent of their high school credits in vocational education courses, there is little evidence of any kind of vocational focus or concentration (Adelman, 1983). Nearly half the high school time of the general education student is spent in personal interest and development courses such as physical education, arts and crafts, home economics, and work experience (Parnell, 1985). As a rule, these "general education" students receive less career counseling, have fewer marketable skills, and are unlikely to find the kinds of work that can be seen as an initial step up a career ladder, at least for several years. Their expectations are vague and unrealistic. The greatest single indicator of slippage is that nearly two out of three of the high school dropouts indicate they were enrolled in the high school general education track at the time they left school (Adelman, 1983). Is it any mystery that general track high school students are unfocused in their learning, more alienated toward school, and have a significantly higher dropout rate?

Some twenty-seven percent of high school graduates finish vocational programs. But the percentage educated as technicians is very low (1%). Almost fifty percent of high school vocational training is in agriculture, home economics, and industrial arts, areas that do not reflect the most pressing needs of the marketplace (Adelman, 1983). Nor do most high schools have the resources to mount sophisticated technical education programs that more nearly reflect the needs of the marketplace. Such training programs are usually expensive and constantly in need of update.

New high school models need to be developed to provide students with a sharper focus on their futures, to bring more structure and substance to the curricular program, to more ably prepare students for skilled jobs, and to make technical, school, community college, and baccalaureate degree programs more likely for greater numbers of students.

FOCUSING ON LIFELONG LEARNING

The rapid advances in industrial technology require a new kind of worker, one who is able to embrace change. The new worker will view changing technology and new learning as a given. High schools need to give more attention to developing life-long learners. Students who are unwilling to accept their roles as lifelong learners will be relegated to performing low-paying, low skilled jobs. If there is one thing in which the schools and colleges should excel, it is in helping the individual to develop the competencies to function in this role as a lifelong learner. The competencies that must be developed to be an effective lifelong learner include reading speed and comprehension skills, analytical skills, memory training skills, problem-solving skills, decision-making skills, synthesizing skills, human relations skills, computational skills, and computer skills.

Under our current educational practices, if an individual has not developed these competencies to a certain level by the end of eighth grade or so, he or she has been doomed forever to an educational dead end. Barriers also have been constructed for adults who need to improve their "learner" skills. Although many adults would like to improve their reading speed, analytical skills, memory skills or intergroup human relations skills and communications skills, they have no place to turn. Most high school curricula do not foster these specific competencies to become more effective lifelong learners. High schools ought to have learned a lesson, through their failure to stress lifelong learner skills. These skills need to become an area of emphasis.

Another important lesson yet to be learned by many high school educators is that the "why" of learning is more important than the "how." Those students who see no connectedness, no aim, no purpose to their education, also often see no point in continuing in school. Humans are most effective when they have hopes rather than fears, and when they are future oriented. The student who sees no future for himself or herself will make little progress in education and will devalue lifelong learning skills.

Employers indicate to us that the ability to learn is the essential hallmark of the successful employee. Yet, in most educational arenas little direct time is spent on the lifelong learner skills of human relations and intergroup relations, problem solving, synthesis, analysis, and critical thinking. Helping individuals develop the competencies to be effective lifelong learners should be a top priority of every school system.

COLLABORATIVE PLANNING AND COOPERATIVE LEARNING

Peter Drucker (1984) indicates that the greatest single barrier to improving the productivity of our nation is the consistent breakdown in the lifelong learning skills of intergroup and interpersonal communications. Employers indicate consistently that their greatest concern is with employees who fail in the human relations and intergroup relations categories. More employees are dismissed because they cannot get along with others than for any other reason and most high schools do not address this need (see also Chapter X).

The historical emphasis in American education on competition and "taking care of number one" has presented serious problems to American business. Marietta Baba, professor of anthropology at Wayne State University, argues that the self-centered mentality among American employees makes it more difficult for U.S. companies to implement new ideas, develop more efficient processes and apply better technology to compete globally (Baba, Falkenberg, & Hill, 1994).

From kindergarten through college, students are discouraged from sharing information or ideas—that's often considered cheating.

Typically in American schools, children are taught to find out what they will, excel and compete against their peers, and become Number 1. Often one student or an elite few high achievers capture the limelight, gaining more recognition than the entire group who make the task possible. In a choir, it's the soloist; in a movie, it's the leading man or woman. In the operating room, it's the surgeon.

In order to compete in the global marketplace, collaborative work groups are a necessity. In this regard American schools and colleges have been of little help. Despite the overwhelming research in support of cooperative learning (see Chapter IV) and collaborative planning (see Chapter X), as a most effective instructional strategy, few teachers or professors have the ability, training or commitment to implement collaborative processes in the classroom.

Out of frustration, A. B. Heller, Inc., a Milford, Michigan manufacturer, launched a classroom program to teach employees how to cooperate and communicate better. After five months of promoting teamwork in the classroom, the firm canceled classes. Peter Rosenkrands, president of Heller, said he was tired of hearing workers grumble, "What is this going to do for me?" (Henderson, 1994)

Baba says that American schools must change and they must change quickly. "As long as students still think it is important to get an A or B on a paper and 'to heck with everybody else,' American schools and American industry will remain in trouble" (Baba et al., 1994).

Investing in high technology and expensive information systems cannot overcome the cultural barrier of individualism facing U.S. employers. Many employers assume that technology is the best solution to the problem, not recognizing that there are human barriers that technology can't overcome. That is why American business is spending $100 billion a year on new information technology, hardware and software, without getting the payoff they expect (Henderson, 1994).

In today's global economy, every American employee must understand the need to collectively find ways for the company to reduce costs, raise quality, improve flexibility, and shorten delivery time. Students in American classrooms, cooperatively working and learning together, challenging one another, and assisting one another, must provide just the type of workers that American business needs in order to be competitive in the global marketplace.

Education for Meaning and the Continuity of Learning

Educators have a heavy responsibility to help students see meaning in their educational program. Clear goals for the curricular course or program and clear goals for the individual student are absolutely essential to achieving excellence in education. Student goals will change from time to time, indeed should change, but those changes do not invalidate the need for short-range goals. Students are better motivated when they know and understand the learning goals. It is a great disservice to allow high school or college students to wander aimlessly through the curriculum with few, if any, clearly focused goals.

If students are to be motivated to learn, they must know why they are learning, how this learning connects with other learning, and where this learning relates to real life. For teachers to be motivated to teach, administrators motivated to lead, school board members motivated to develop wise policies, and for the American public to have confidence in their schools, unrelenting attention must be paid to purposes. These purposes must be developed with such precision and with such clarity that all involved will be able to develop a sense of personal meaning and commitment.

One of the disappointing aspects of the major reports on educational reform is the scant attention given to continuity in learning. It is amazing that some students learn as much as they do, given the tremendous gaps in the substance of their learning as a result of irregular class attendance. There is a close correlation between poor attendance patterns and poor grades. In fact, irregular class attendance is an early signal of school failure and eventual dropping out of school. High school principals report that poor student attendance continues to remain one of the key problems affecting the quality of education in their schools. Yet, scant attention has been given this subject in the reform reports.

In 1982, the National Center for Education Statistics asked 571 school districts, on behalf of the National Commission on Excellence, which policies or procedures were most important for improving academic achievement. Increased daily class attendance was listed by 66 percent of the sample and 90 percent of the urban school districts as the most important (Peng et al., 1983). School leaders estimate a tremendous loss of continuity in learning and consequent school failures through absenteeism. It is one of the consistent barriers to excellence. Continuity is improved when more students experience consistent success in school. Putting into practice the reforms described in this chapter and others will significantly increase student success and continuity.

Overall student achievement test scores would likely improve significantly in most schools if student attendance patterns improved. On the skill-acquiring levels, continuity in learning is extremely important. If the students miss one or two basic steps, the next steps become increasingly difficult to achieve. As a consequence, one out of three or more students is constantly endeavoring to catch up. It is sad that most of these students spend the rest of their lives attempting to catch up and never really do (see also Chapter III on preventing school failure).

Fred Hechinger (1984), longtime observer of the American educational scene, has commented on the loss of continuity in learning:

> We are not very good at continuity . . . as a result of that, American education during the past few decades has become a collection of disjointed parts that in the main fail to connect. . . . The lack of continuity that plagues American education is something that all of education needs to address. Instead of connecting the separate levels, critics generally compound the spirit of separation by seeking scapegoats instead of remedies. . . .

If we want to reform the schools (and improve the public's confidence in them), two things are essential: continuity, all the way up the line; and understanding the "why" of every single course. As Bruno Bettelheim said: "Whatever you teach, make the children understand why they are studying it. Don't tell them: 'You'll need it later.' Later doesn't exist" (Bettleheim, 1976, p. 13). Continuity will be improved when educators set out to deliberately help students to see the meaning (the why) in every lesson, in every course in the curriculum.

NEEDED: SEAMLESS OCCUPATIONAL EDUCATION FROM PRIMARY SCHOOL THROUGH COMMUNITY COLLEGE AND BEYOND

That which is needed in today's world is neither a new brand of academicism nor a new style of vocationalism, but a fusion of the two. The emerging conception which may obliterate the false dichotomy between the academic and the vocational is that of occupational education (Goldhammer & Taylor, 1972).

The high school should help all students move with confidence from school to work and further education. Today, students are tracked into programs for those who "think" and those who "work," when, in fact, life for all of us is a blend of both. Looking beyond the year 2000, for most students, twelve years of schooling will likely be insufficient. Today's graduates will change jobs several times. New skills will be required, new citizenship obligations will be confronted. Of necessity, education requires continuity and needs to be lifelong.

Occupational education is not synonymous with vocational education, although the latter is a significant aspect of occupational education. Since the 1920s, American education has suffered from a misunderstanding of the place and value of vocational education. Unfortunately, the image in the minds of too many people is that vocational education is only specific job training. Instead, it is a way to help young people develop the competencies they need to be wage earners and producers. It is only one of several goals for schooling.

First, all of basic education should be infused with practical examples from the world of work and life roles. Even students in the primary grades ought to be able to see some relationship between what they are learning and the utility of that learning. Indeed, career awareness in the elementary schools should bring more life, more meaning, more experience, and more rigor to these early school experiences.

Second, career exploration in the middle grades can bring new purpose to those difficult adolescent years. Exploration does not mean that students will visit a little in the community or that they will talk a bit about jobs. Career exploration demands a rigorous multidisciplinary approach. Pre-vocational programs ought to explore all of the clusters and families of occupations, of which some fifteen to eighteen exist in the *Dictionary of Occupational Titles,* with such titles as health occupations and mechanics occupations. Students in the middle years should be able to explore all of the existing clusters. At the end of a three- or four-year period, students will have explored all the major clusters or families of occupations and have had actual lab experiences related to aspects of these occupations. They also will have begun to understand the relationships between economics, mathematics, communications, and other disciplines.

At the end of the tenth grade, students ought to choose one of three curricular majors:

- a college prep/baccalaureate degree major
- a 2 + 2 tech prep/associate degree major
- a vocational cluster major

All three majors would focus on preparation for the next step for the student, whatever that step might be. All three majors would also include a common core of learning, including communication skills, social sciences, physical education. Mathematics and the physical/biological sciences would be tailored for each major. Allowances for individual differences in learning speed and style would be required in the common core. Wherever possible, common-core learning would be linked with real-life examples emanating from the careers-education emphasis. The college preparatory/baccalaureate degree program would not vary much from the current grade eleven and twelve program.

The tech prep/associate degree program would include a Principles of Technology course (applied physics) and some cooperative education and/or technical lab work along with the common core of learning. (For a detailed description of this program, see Dale Parnell's excellent book, *The Neglected Majority.*)

The vocational cluster program would include the common core of learning along with any of the career clusters for specific laboratory work, i.e., accounting, agriculture, clerical-secretarial, construction, electrical, food service, graphic arts, health services, marketing, mechanical, metals, transportation, etc. The laboratory experiences would be built around the knowledge and skills common to the occupations that comprise the cluster or family of occupations.

The career-cluster program is not conceived as a means of developing a finished worker or journeyman in any given occupation. Rather, it should provide opportunities for developing entry-level skills for certain jobs and some second-level skills for others. The result of the cluster effort should be that the student will enjoy greater flexibility in occupational choice patterns. Not only will students develop some entry-level skills, but they will also have an opportunity to appraise their own abilities in relation to several levels of occupations.

For many of the two-out-of-three students now enrolled in the general education or vocational education high school tracks, the tech prep/associate degree, four-year program represents the appropriate focus. Commencing with the eleventh grade and concluding with the associate degree at the end of the sophomore year in a community, technical, or junior college, the tech prep/associate degree program is intended to run parallel to existing college prep/baccalaureate degree programs. Consisting of both vocational and liberal arts courses, the course of study rests on a solid foundation of math, science, communications, and technology courses—all in an applied setting.

High school students who select the tech prep/associate degree would do so in their junior year, just as some now elect a college prep/baccalaureate degree program; they would remain a part of the highly structured and focused program for the following four years. The tech prep students would be taught by high school teachers in the eleventh and twelfth grades but have access to the faculty and facilities of the community, technical, or junior college when needed.

But the tech prep/associate degree program can't be successful without a close and continuing interchange between the high school, college, and community college governing boards, key executive officers, and key faculty members. Such an interchange must lead to specific agreements on unified curricular programs that begin in grade eleven and continue without interruption through the associate degree.

It is crucial at this point to acknowledge that the efforts to install work-experience programs and career education just 20 years ago were utter failures. The current emphasis on including all students, not just at-risk students, provides a way to avoid the inequities often associated with occupational programs. The focus on broad clusters of related occupations—including the highest-skilled occupations and related high-level academic competencies—avoids both watering down content and tracking students away from the highest-status positions.

THE SCHOOL-TO-WORK CONNECTION

The recent federal school-to-work legislation may stimulate reform in the high schools. Norton Grubb, in his school-to-work essay (National Governors Association Report, 1994), affirms that "school to work" offers a better chance for improving high schools than any other area of reform. The school-based component requires the integration of academic and vocational education and creates bridges between secondary and postsecondary education. A work-based component provides opportunities for learning different capacities (including motivation and discipline) than schools can teach. Linkages or "connecting activities" insure that both components are consistent.

The establishment of career academies, schools with several career clusters, and magnet high schools with occupational focuses is appropriate. These efforts make the integration of academic and vocational programs easier by bringing academic and vocational teachers to gather around a common purpose. By providing an occupational focus, they make transparent the occupational purpose of high school and facilitate the connection to work-based learning.

More and more secondary schools and community colleges are recognizing the reality of shifting the curriculum to match a technological world:

> The growing pervasiveness of technology and the certainty of ongoing technical advances demand that we provide our young people with the solid

base of scientific knowledge they will require. It is not only those who create technology who should have a competency in math and science. Those who use technology should also have a degree of understanding about the tools they use. They must also be able to adapt to changes in technology and the new skill requirements they bring with them. (Young, 1985)

It is absolutely imperative that high schools and colleges, particularly community, technical, and junior colleges, become aggressive in examining, developing, and sustaining quality educational programs to serve that great host of Americans who keep this country working.

CONCLUSION

To transform American high schools into schools of purpose and hope for all students, durable partnerships between high schools, technical schools, and community colleges need to be developed. These partnerships need to produce 2 + 2 tech prep programs available to all students not pursuing the baccalaureate degree preparation program. By so doing, the confidence of the American public in its high schools will be enhanced and all students, but specifically the general track students, will realize new meaning and purpose to their schooling.

We can no longer turn our back on the general track student. The prestigious Carnegie Forum on Education and the Economy (1986) declared that the cost of our present failure to educate all American children will be "a steady erosion in the American standard of living," with a growing number of permanently unemployed people seriously straining our social fabric. The council warned that as the world economy changes shape, "it would be fatal to assume that America can succeed" if only a portion of our school children succeed (p. 11).

The prospect of a new age of American affluence will evaporate unless America's high schools can step up to the challenge to prepare a much greater proportion of this shrinking pool of young people to enter the labor market with a high level of literacy and the ability to perform sophisticated technical and managerial tasks—and with the kind of education that equips them to continue learning and relearning throughout their lives.

Once the state of technology and the state of demographics were that the economy could flourish with only a fraction of the total work force well educated and skilled. Writing off the youngsters who were least promising might not have been a moral or compassionate option, but the economy could run without them. It no longer can!

Chapter VIII

AN EPIDEMIC OF MEDIA HYPE—
THE SCHOOLS OF JAPAN

Strident criticism of American schools in the celebrated national commission reports and from individual critics has invariably compared American public schools with those of Japan. The media has portrayed Japanese education as more rigorous with an emphasis on longer school days and longer school year. The popular media, however, has failed to accurately investigate Japanese education. For that matter, many of the critics of American education and many of the references to Japanese schooling as mentioned in national commission reports contain half-truths and inaccuracies. Since unfavorable comparisons with the Japanese schools have contributed to the crisis of confidence in American public schools, the Japanese educational system should be accurately analyzed. Based on the successful experience of the Japanese, recommendations for American educational reform ought to be considered.

BRIEF HISTORY OF JAPANESE EDUCATION

In 1871, the Japanese ministry of education was created and by 1886 an outline of a national framework for education was in place. The 1870s featured extensive borrowing of educational processes from Europe and America, the building of many school facilities, and a greatly increasing number of children attending school on a regular basis (Rubinger, 1989, pp. 224–228).

By the late 1880s the Ministry of Education had created a truly national system of education. The ministry now controlled all major aspects of education, including textbook selection, establishing school hours and schedules, determining curriculum, preparing examinations, and selecting appropriate instructional methods (Rubinger, 1989). By 1900, elementary education was universal in Japan.

The end of the war in 1945 brought about a transformation in Japanese

121

education. The American occupation authorities imposed American democratic forms on all phases of Japanese government, including education. By 1950, the Japanese school system mirrored the organizational pattern of American schools. Elementary school extended from grades one to six, a middle level encompassed grades seven to nine, and a senior high school level served grades ten to twelve.

Throughout their school years Japanese children are influenced significantly by the mother. In the Japanese culture she is almost totally responsible for the education of her children. The comparatively homogeneous culture with the well-defined maternal role as nurturer, encourager and teacher of the children make comparisons with American education tenuous, at best.

SCHOOL CALENDAR

Each hour of school actually represents a forty-five- to fifty-minute lesson with a 20-minute break for student recess/exercise following every lesson. The actual number of instructional hours per year is about 800, a number comparable to actual instructional time for American school students. First grade students in Japan receive only 850 lessons, which translates to slightly more than 600 clock-hours of instruction. Even junior high school students spend only about 800 hours per year under direct classroom instruction (White, 1987). Included in these class hours is one hour per week for moral education. Activities such as assemblies, club activities, and guidance also absorb one to two hours per week of the scheduled instructional time. While Japanese students attend school for sixty more days each year than Americans, their actual number of hours of academic instruction each year is comparable to that of American students.

The legal minimum school year is 210 days, but most local school officials schedule and extra thirty days, a 240-day total, for school festivals, athletic meets, and ceremonies with nonacademic objectives, especially those encouraging cooperation and school spirit. Given that Saturday sessions last only a few hours, the actual number of equivalent full days of regular classroom academic instruction is about 195 (August, 1992, p. 142).

CLASS SIZE AND CLIMATE FOR TEACHING

Class sizes in Japanese elementary school average about forty. A teacher's primary expectation is for students to be engaged in their work, not that they will necessarily be quiet or docile. Many American teachers would find the decibel level in Japanese elementary classrooms unacceptable. These large class sizes imply expectations for pupil behavior and teacher role that would be alien to American teachers and parents. According to Tobin (In White, 1987, p. 68), "The Japanese teacher delegates more authority to children than we find in American schools; intervenes less quickly in arguments; has lower expectations for the control of noise generated by the class; gives fewer verbal clues; organizes more structured group activities, such as morning exercise; and, finally, makes more use of peer group approval and control and less of the teacher's direct influence. In general, children are less often treated on a one-to-one basis, and more often as a group" (White, 1987, p. 69).

This emphasis on the group is carried over to promotion policies and ability-grouping practices in Japanese elementary schools. Social promotion is the norm. To fail a grade or to skip a grade is unthinkable. Students are placed in mixed-ability groups in virtually all situations (Singleton, 1989). Little special attention is given to academically slow students or to the gifted student. In the upper elementary grades teachers often assign brighter students to tutor slower classmates.

By the upper years of elementary school the teacher will rely on group activities and projects as the primary instructional strategy. The class frequently divides into small groups of from four to six students known as *hans*. The leadership of each group rotates among its members with the designated leader called the *hancho*. These groups also perform the various housekeeping duties in the classroom on a rotating basis.

Japanese children, therefore, receive an early introduction to the concept of a work group, a skill that they will practice throughout their adult lives (White, 1987). These traditional work groups in Japanese schools bear a striking resemblance to cooperative learning groups found in American schools.

Elementary schools in Japan are comparatively free of the pressure and competitiveness that is characteristic of Japanese secondary schools. Children enjoy going to school and form very close social bonds with their classmates, with whom they will associate closely throughout the six years of elementary school. The emphasis on group work allows students to interact frequently with one another and to take an active part in learning activities. Frequent short breaks contribute to a relaxed pace in the school day. During the first few years of school the school day itself is comparatively short. The lack of individual attention by the teacher is more than compensated for by the intensity of the involvement of the mother in the elementary child's school experience.

Moral education is one of the compulsory subjects in Japanese schools at every grade level. One hour each week is devoted to the development of ethical and moral development, to teach ethics and morals, so that students will be able to resolve moral dilemmas.

At the elementary level, at least, Japanese academic excellence cannot be attributed to excessive pressure on students, highly disciplined and structured classrooms, or greater time allotments for academic instruction.

JAPANESE SECONDARY SCHOOLS

The junior high school years, grades seven to nine, are part of the compulsory school system. These middle school years become a time of testing for students as they begin the rigorous selection process that leads to the prestigious universities for the educational elite. Vocational training programs, or even early departure from school, await the less able or less motivated. School begins to intensify and time begins to compress for students as they reach junior high school. Additional pressure is exerted on students to conform to cultural expectations, and there is less tolerance for childlike behavior (Anderson, 1981).

The middle school years are the peak period for bullying, suicides, and violence against teachers. Such incidents illustrate the heightened pressure on Japanese students as they move through junior high school. All students in junior high schools study the same basic curriculum and continue to attend mixed-ability classes of forty or more students.

The school day is similar in length to that of the upper elementary years. The day typically begins at 8:30 a.m. and ends by 2:30–3:00 p.m. Students attend six classes each day with brief breaks between classes and about forty-five minutes for lunch. There are certain club activities that all students are expected to join. These clubs meet weekly for one hour. Students usually select one club and remain in that activity throughout their junior high school years. There are also less formally organized club activities that meet every day after school and during vacation period. Students often consider these activities as the most rewarding of their school experiences (Iwama, 1981).

By the eighth grade, ambitious Japanese students are beginning to prepare seriously for the high school entrance examinations given in the ninth grade. Great numbers of students now begin to attend remedial and tutoring schools known as *juku*. These "cram schools" are devoted to preparing students to pass the entrance examinations for the high school that the student will attempt to enter. By the ninth grade, 86 percent of Japanese students have attended juku at some point (White, 1987). Students devote two or three afternoons each week to juku lessons.

High school attendance in Japan is not compulsory. Students are not assigned to a school by geographic area, as in the United States, but instead must apply for entrance to a given school. High schools are rank-ordered according to their academic standing in the community, with vocational schools being ranked at the bottom. About 97 percent of graduates from lower secondary schools attend senior high school. Thirty percent of the students select a vocational program as they enter high school (White, 1987). Vocational training is commonly provided in specialized schools emphasizing industrial, commercial, or agricultural studies.

The 70 percent of students pursuing a general education at academic public and private high schools are very aware of the importance in Japanese society of attending the *right* university. The Japanese attach great importance to the university that the student will attend, believing that the university attended will largely determine the future success of the student. Many major corporations do indeed restrict their recruitment efforts to these select universities. This reality serves as an extrinsic motivation for many students to exert great effort in their studies.

By high school age, over 90 percent of urban students are attending juku school to enhance their chances for admission to a university. Homework will typically require three or four hours each day, with five or six hours required for the most academically ambitious students. All high schools teach the same ministry of education-approved curriculum, although the more academically elite high schools implement the curriculum at a higher level of rigor.

Currently over 30 percent of high school graduates in Japan attend some form of higher education. An additional 20 percent attend specialized short courses in vocational areas offered by private businesses. Fewer than 10 percent of the population fail to complete high school

(Shields, 1989, p. 102). Japan educates more students, at a higher level of academic achievement, than any other nation in the world.

STATUS OF TEACHERS IN JAPAN

August (1992), in his comprehensive report on Japanese education, reported that Japanese teachers have attained the highest level of professional respect and practice of all nations. Teaching is a much sought after occupation in Japan. There are as many as five to six applicants for each available teaching position in Japan. Although Japanese teachers spend twenty hours more each week at school than their American counterparts, they spend far fewer hours providing direct classroom instruction (Sato & McLaughlin, 1992). A typical Japanese teacher will spend fifteen hours each week in classroom instruction. An American teacher will spend approximately twenty-five hours each five-day week in directly teaching and supervising students (White, 1987). The Japanese teacher uses these hours of extra school time to perform a myriad of additional obligations that an American teacher, because of time and energy constraints, performs in a perfunctory fashion or not at all.

The Japanese commitment to group interaction is quite evident in the daily life of a teacher. Japanese teachers are far more involved in the governance of their schools and in collaborative planning with other teachers than are American teachers. School and teacher schedules, student assignments, and most other school matters are decided at daily and weekly teacher meetings. The meetings are held each morning as well as once per week after school for about one hour. The teachers chair these meetings on a rotating basis (Iwama, 1989). Japanese schools each have one large room where each teacher has a desk. Here teachers devote their noninstructional time to grading papers, preparing lessons, collaborative planning, and discussing teaching techniques. Teachers use this space for faculty or department meetings to resolve both administrative and instructional issues. Much of the nonteaching time available to Japanese teachers during the school week is devoted to these group meetings.

There are also regular meetings planned by the principal to allow experienced professionals to advise and guide their younger colleagues. Meetings are organized among groups of teachers to discuss teaching techniques and to devise lesson plans and teaching materials.

What is the effect in the classroom of this attention to lesson construction, the honing of teaching skills, and the free flow of ideas and strategies among teachers? To begin with, Japanese teachers appear to be filled with zest and enthusiasm. Lessons are presented with great energy and the teachers succeed in engaging students in the lessons, in spite of average classes of about forty students. Japanese teachers can draw on greater energy reserves because of their lighter teaching schedule compared to American teachers. Japanese teachers have considerably more available time during the day to collaborate, to prepare lessons, grade papers, work with individual students, and perform other job-related tasks (Stevenson, 1989).

Lessons at these levels emphasize problem solving rather than rote mastery of facts and procedures. The teacher is a discussion leader who tries to stimulate students to explain and evaluate solutions to problems. In whole-class discussions and through working in their small groups, Japanese students are active participants in the learning process. Teachers design the lessons to fill a forty-five to fifty-minute period with sustained attention and the development of a concept or skill. Lessons have an introduction, a conclusion, and a unifying theme (Stigler, 1991).

The economic status of teachers in Japan matches their high social status. In 1984, teachers earned 1.77 times the average salary of a manufacturing worker in Japan. This differential far exceeds that for teachers in any other country (Nelson, 1991). On an international comparison of teacher salaries, however, Japanese teachers earn just 95 percent as much as American teachers (Stevenson, 1989). To ensure a steady supply of suitable teachers in Japan, a law was enacted in 1973 setting teacher salaries at a higher level than that of other national public service personnel (Nelson, 1991).

Prior to World War II, teachers in Japan were considered to be *obedient servants of the state.* A Japanese union for teachers, known as *Nikkyoso,* was formed at the end of the war. This union is socialistic in political orientation and has for forty years vigorously opposed most of the initiatives of the conservative Ministry of Education. Japanese teachers do not have the right to bargain collectively or to strike (Ota, 1989).

A national personnel authority makes recommendations to the cabinet, the ruling party in the government, regarding salary scales necessary to keep teacher salaries competitive with those of private industry. The cabinet may accept, modify, or ignore these recommendations. The cabinet does, however, ultimately set a national wage scale for public employees.

There are several aspects of a Japanese teacher's life-style that make teaching an attractive alternative to corporate life in Japan. Unlike corporate workers, teachers can live out their professional lives in one region and not be forced to uproot their families for frequent transfers. Further, Japanese teachers are not expected to engage in long evenings of business-related socializing that are so much a part of the Japanese corporate culture. Lastly, the teacher in Japan enjoys a greater degree of autonomy than many other professions permit (White, 1987).

CULTURAL DIFFERENCES

In comparing Japan to America, Imamura identifies three major differences between the two cultures. "(1) The Japanese middle-class mother is more solely responsible for children's education than the American; (2) the Japanese mother-child (especially mother-son) tie is more intensive than the American; (3) the Japanese individual is bound by the family for life and learns to consider the effect of all his actions on the family. The American child makes more distinctions between family-controlled areas and those outside the family" (Imamura, 1989, p. 17).

Mothers in Japan guide their children away from negative behaviors and toward positive behavior. They accomplish this through mild disapproval rather than through harsh disciplinary measures. To Western observers, child-rearing practices in Japan appear to be laissez-faire, or even permissive. The closer emotional bond between mother and child in Japan probably allows the mother to exercise a more powerful influence over her child than is common in the West.

The Japanese mother's orientation is primarily toward the rearing and educating of her children, rather than toward her own career or personal fulfillment, as if often true with the American mother. The Japanese husband remains willing to work from early morning to late at night as the primary, if not sole, breadwinner for his family. This attitude contrasts with that of both American men and women that the woman will be a partner in providing an income for the family. The primary emotional tie for the Japanese woman is her children, rather than her husband. An American parent is more likely to subordinate the parent-child relationship to the demands of the spousal relationship. The Japanese lack of emphasis on husband-wife relationships may partially account for the extremely low divorce rate in Japan in comparison to the United States.

Japanese students mature in a culture where elders are respected, if not venerated. Three-generation households are still commonplace in Japan. The youth subculture in Japan is but a mere shadow of the strength and influence of the teenage subculture in the United States. Japanese adolescents accept greater academic accountability than their American peers but are given less social freedom than American teen-agers (Shields, 1989). Not surprisingly, Japan's problems with teenage pregnancy, drug and alcohol abuse among youth, and delinquency are minuscule compared to those of the United States.

In America we think of education primarily in terms of cognitive development and academic achievement. A review of the goals of the America 2000 education plan, with the narrow emphasis on academic dimensions, is testimony to this limited concept of schooling. Americans tend to concentrate on technical explanations for achievement differences between American and Japanese students, such as "time on task" or "time in school." A more productive approach might be to accept a basic cultural explanation for the differences. The Japanese simply think about education differently than Americans do (Singleton, 1989).

Group identity is maintained in Japanese classrooms by total mixed-ability grouping and virtually 100 percent promotion rates from grade to grade. The students remain in one classroom for the full day, except for special subjects such as industrial arts, science, or physical education. This common classroom system continues through the secondary school years, where the teachers move from room to room and the students remain in their own classroom for most of the day (Iwama, 1989).

Communal responsibility and service to others are taught through the Japanese practice of four or five students from a class, on a rotating basis, serving hot lunches to their fellow classmates in the classroom.

Several characteristic Japanese cultural traits are plainly evident in the educational system. These traits include *gambaru* (persistence), a strong identity with the group rather than the individual, and a deep respect for their cultural heritage and traditional ways of life.

Because citizens in Japan must be eighteen to apply for a driver's license, high school students are not distracted from their studies by the use of the automobile. Very few young people have access to cars and in many cases school rules prohibit students from driving cars, or motorbikes, to school (McAdams, 1993, p. 214).

Life for the Japanese students revolves around the school. The entire culture appears mobilized to reinforce the importance and primacy of education in the life of its youth. The family, the school, and the wider community cooperate closely in a shared responsibility for educating the next generation of citizens. The distractions of jobs, sports, cars, sexual activity, and drug and alcohol use, so prominent in the lives of America's students, are virtually absent in the Japanese culture.

LOCAL AND STATE ADMINISTRATION

American administrators are trained to take a management approach to their teachers, with an emphasis on supervision and evaluation of practice. The Japanese principal, however, views his/her function as protecting teachers from external pressures and managing the school in a manner that will allow teachers the greatest latitude in performing their duties. The principal views his/her main duty as providing advice and guidance to teachers, rather than supervising directly, and formally evaluating their work (Anderson, 1981).

The Ministry of Education exercises strict control over the curriculum by publishing courses of study for every subject and by dictating the amount of time to be allocated to each subject. Local officials select textbooks from a published list of acceptable titles prepared by the national Ministry of Education. The ministry also allocates financial aid to prefectures and municipalities and provides prefectural and municipal school boards with advice and guidance.

Finances

Critics of American education often cite international cost comparisons for public education to insist that Japan is able to produce a highly educated citizenry at a lower cost than the United States. This cost advantage is often attributed to the very large class sizes in Japan. The assumption that Japanese schools save vast sums of money on staffing because of large class size, however, represents a distortion. Although the Japanese teacher has very large classes, he or she also has fewer student contact hours compared to American teachers. Thus the actual student-to-teacher ratio in Japan is similar to that in the United States. In 1987 there were 20.7 students per teacher in Japan compared to 18.4 students per teacher in the United States (Nelson, 1991, p. 33).

The major reason for lower public educational expenditures in Japan versus the United States is that universal public support for education in

Japan ends after ninth grade. There are insufficient public high schools in Japan to accommodate all high school students. Even those students admitted to these highly competitive public high schools must pay part of their educational costs. Twenty-eight percent of Japanese high school students attend private high school where there is a small state subsidy, but where the major cost burden falls to the parents. Additionally, the almost universal practice of students attending juku tutoring schools is an educational cost borne solely by the parents. Thus the private contribution to upper secondary school education in Japan, through tuition and fee payments by parents, far exceeds the direct contribution of American parents of high school students toward educational costs.

A major distortion in comparing international educational expenditures occurs when data on higher education costs are included in the comparisons. Since the United States supports a comparatively high proportion of students in higher education, this factor alone substantially raises the level of public spending on education in the United States compared to other countries (Rasell & Mishel, 1990). Critics of American elementary and secondary schooling consistently used data that includes our large expenditures on higher education to demonstrate that America spends more than almost every other country on education.

A second source of distortion is the fact that the United States has a relatively large school-age population compared to most other industrialized countries. This fact also raises the proportion of national income dedicated to education. By adjusting for the relative size of each country's K–12 enrollment, a recent sixteen-country comparison of educational spending shows that the United States spends less on pre-college education than all but two of the countries in the study. The data from this study indicates that in 1985 Japan spent 4.8 percent of the gross domestic product on K–12 education compared to 4.1 percent of the gross domestic product in the United States (Rasell & Mishel, 1990, pp. 1–5).

The successes of the Japanese educational system have not produced self-satisfaction or complacency among the Japanese. While foreign observers are quick to praise Japanese schools, the Japanese themselves are highly critical of their education system. The Japanese National Council of Educational Reform captures the intensity of this internal criticism in its conclusion that "Japanese education currently suffers from a 'grave state of desolation' caused by pathological conditions of society and schools" (Shimhahara, 1989). Interestingly enough, the council's concerns relate to perceived failings in the area of moral education more than in the academic areas. Indeed, Japan appears to have their own unique crisis of confidence in public education.

CONCLUSIONS

The most significant difference between American schools and the Japanese relates to the pace of the school day. An American secondary school typically has a seven- or eight-period school day with only three or four minutes between classes and thirty minutes for lunch. Japanese schools allow more time between class periods or schedule ten- to fifteen-minute breaks for both students and teachers every few class periods.

This dual burden on American teachers of more classroom instructional time, with heavier out-of-class supervisory responsibilities, ensures both high frustration and low job satisfaction. American teachers must prepare for approximately 50 percent more instructional hours within a workweek, with about 50 percent less preparation time, than is common in many of the other survey countries. This unreasonably heavy work load creates exhaustion and morale problems. It also produces a superficiality in the teaching of those unwilling or unable to devote the hours and effort to excel, and is not in the best interest of the students. Significant reductions in teacher work loads will, however, require either more teachers (an expensive proposition) or increases in class sizes.

An increase in average class size of three students would allow each teacher in many schools to have an additional forty-five minute planning period each day, with a corresponding decrease in one teaching period each day. These relatively modest changes in the size of groups could dramatically improve the work life and productivity of the typical teacher.

The opening up of the daily schedule for teachers provides both the time and the opportunity for collaborative staff development by teachers with their school colleagues. Strong peer coaching relationships can be fostered among teachers who teach the same subjects to similar students in a common work environment. Many such sessions could be planned and conducted by the teachers themselves, while others could be led by curriculum and instruction specialists.

Japanese schools schedule less time each day for purely academic instruction than is common in America, however, they do schedule a longer school year, 226 days. American schools should move toward a 200-day school year. This extra time could be used to adopt a more humane daily schedule for teachers and students and to provide the necessary time to implement an effective student assessment program. Such changes in the school day and school year would also have a positive impact on student behavior and teacher and student morale. Taken together, these school calendar and daily scheduling changes would of themselves lead to improved student achievement.

American schools should follow Japan's lead in promoting collaborative learning among both elementary and secondary students. Students in Japan often are assigned to the same group of peers throughout the school day, often over a period of several years. Teachers and students work together to prepare students to pass the external exams or meet other goals common to all class members. The students perceive the teacher more as a mentor or coach to help them prepare for the external evaluation. Students in such an environment feel a sense of group identity that serves to motivate them to attend school and contribute to the academic achievements of the group.

Schools in Japan consider the moral development of students as an educational priority. The Japanese concept of ningen, referring to the development of full human beings, forms the basis for their one hour per week of required moral education at every grade level. Opinion leaders, the media and the Japanese schools are outspoken in attacking irresponsible behaviors, such as drug and alcohol abuse, family desertion, and sexual promiscuity. As a result of such strong social stigma, the impact of these behaviors on Japanese families and children is not significant.

In America, the damage done to children by these individual life-style choices has devastating effects. Furthermore, the harm done to these innocent children will reflect itself in the dysfunction and dissolution of the larger society as these children reach adulthood. American political, media and other opinion leaders need to become far more outspoken on these issues than is presently the case.

Chapter IX

RUSSIAN ROULETTE AND
MARKET-DRIVEN SCHOOLS

The public's growing infatuation with the deregulation of public schools, private school vouchers, and market-driven schools represents additional evidence that a crisis of confidence in America's public schools does exist. The decline in confidence in the public schools has been accompanied by the rise in status of private schools (Coleman & Hoffer, 1987; Coleman, Hoffer, & Kilgore, 1982). Chubb and Moe (1990) have argued strongly that private-sector schools are market driven and thus more competitive than public-sector schools. To this date, however, it is still unclear whether or not private-sector schools are more academically effective than public schools, once the family backgrounds of students are taken into account. From a political point of view, the differences that distinguish public and private schools in terms of causing differences in student achievement are less significant than the fact that these differences can be used effectively in the larger political struggle to break the so-called public school "monopoly." In the view of market-driven reformers, education should be treated as a consumer item like any other consumer item.

POLITICAL AND ECONOMIC FACTORS

In response to the economic crisis of the late 1970s and early 1980s, groups and individuals within the business community mobilized their formidable political resources behind demands for high-quality academic education—thus focusing in on, and, in effect, serving as a vanguard for the broader, more diffuse constituency for reform at the grass roots. This combination was politically effective, and, by the early 1980s, politicians and educational professionals were exclaiming their genuine interest in educational reform. The same problem, however, persisted: What exactly could be done to promote academic excellence? The reformers had achieved enough power, it appeared, to pressure successfully for change, but they did not know what changes to pressure for.

This situation gave rise, over just a few years, to literally hundreds of official commissions empowered to study America's schools and to explore and suggest ideas for reform. Some of these commissions were set up by the state and federal governments. Some were funded by private foundations, whose enthusiastic participation in educational reform both reflected and reinforced the highly charged political atmosphere.

The commissions' findings were on the whole critical of the public schools. But as often happens in politics, a single event proved to be a watershed. In this case it was the April, 1983 report of the National Commission on Excellence in Education, which almost immediately came to symbolize the nation's lack of confidence in public education and its commitment to meaningful reform. The eighteen-member panel, appointed some two years earlier by Secretary of Education, Terrel H. Bell, painted a grim picture of *A Nation at Risk.*

Critics have charged that *A Nation at Risk* (1983) was a prime example of making the economy's needs paramount in judging and reforming education. The market-driven school proponents' belief that competition is the best organizing principle for almost any collective endeavor is another such example.

Two illustrations will suggest just how market competition can govern a conception of educational purpose and organization. The U.S. Chamber of Commerce position on "Choice in Education" (1991, p. 3) reads: "Incorporating competitive forces into our nation's schools can lead to a higher caliber work force and increase productivity and economic growth." A second example comes from a Select Committee on Educational Reform named by Arizona's business community. Its report, *Better Schools for Arizona* (1990), suggests the extent of the guidance the business market analogy can yield in recommending school structure. Although the report backs school-based management as well as choice, it qualifies its recommendation for the former in this way:

> We take exception to one practice prevalent in school-based management—giving parents who serve on site councils equal participation in making educational decisions ... we would not let customers set our budget, determine our manufacturing or service-deliver processes, or determine which employees we should hire—and we don't think the schools should either. (p. 15)

These illustrations suggest an economics-driven perspective, in that economic concerns supply the ends and means of schooling. But there is a separate sense in which some perspectives on educational choice appear to be economics driven: It consists of the acceptance of the basic concepts of the discipline of economics as a guide to understanding and perceiving human affairs. Thus, some have applied those same concepts to interpret individual human motivation, and some have applied it to interpret the behavior of the role takers who operate organizations and institutions. Accordingly, some attribute public schools' shortcomings to their noncompetitive, monopolistic, and no-incentives status and look to market solutions to cure these ills (Kearns & Doyle, 1988; Kolderie, 1985). This chapter will examine the validity of the claims made by the advocates of market-driven schools and those who insist that the deregulation of public education would have a harmful effect on the quality and effectiveness of the public schools.

Probably no educational issue stimulates a more emotional response among educators, the business and political communities than school choice. The arguments are mainly theoretical and ideological. The examination of both the pro-choice and anti-choice arguments will therefore tend to be of a theoretical and ideological nature. Meager empirical data is available.

ISSUES IN EDUCATION CHOICE

Opposing sides in the debate over educational choice come to opposite conclusions on what would result from a choice system. The arguments are summarized in Table I. The arguments outlined in the table are not empirical in nature; that is, they emphasize what theorists believe would result from an educational choice system. Theorists, however, also differ greatly in the values they place on different outcomes.

As these positions illustrate, the choice debate evokes deep-rooted values and raises controversial issues that education policymakers have grappled with for generations.

Even if any of these arguments is accepted at face value, however, it is unclear what to make of the debate. Proponents of choice stress the primary value of liberty, a more equitable dispersion of that liberty, and pluralistic diversity. Opponents of choice stress equality, an integrated society, and common school traditions. Philosophers have been debating these value differences for years. It is no wonder that these arguments divide well-intentioned parents, education providers, and policy experts.

Table I
PRO- AND ANTI-CHOICE ARGUMENTS

Pro-Choice Arguments:

1. Choice would require less bureaucracy and more school-level autonomy.
2. Staff motivation, leadership, and morale would improve with educational choice.
3. Parental involvement will be greater under choice.
4. Schools will be more diverse, innovative, and flexible.
5. As a result of 1 through 4, student achievement will increase under choice.
6. Competition and market forces will reduce costs and increase efficiency under choice.

Anti-Choice Arguments:

1. Selectivity of students will increase inequality between schools.
2. Geographic distribution of students by race and class will produce inequitable choices and increase school segregation.
3. Special needs of students with learning disabilities and handicaps will not be met as well under a choice system.
4. Accountability will be considerably reduced and minimum standards will not be maintained under choice.
5. Information on schools will be costly, inadequate, and more readily available to families of higher socioeconomic status.
6. The common school tradition will be lost as educational diversity increases (Witte, 1992).

A MARKET SYSTEM

Under a market system, say the choice supporters, the children of uncritical and uncaring parents would often benefit from the school choices of parents who were deeply concerned about schools. Automobile manufacturers, for example, often incorporate safety features to attract a minority of careful buyers. As a result, all automobile buyers benefit from improvements stimulated by discriminating buyers. The same process could take place in the school situation. Choice advocates insist that children of the most indifferent parents would probably be better served by a highly competitive system of schools than by the public school monopoly.

Generally speaking, parents in a choice system would have more opportunity to evaluate schools than any other major product or service they buy. Information about schools, say choice advocates, would be readily available from neighbors, church members, fellow employees, and other sources. An increase in private information and advisory services not beholden to any particular school could benefit all parents. Even in the absence of such possibilities, parents would not be required to enroll their children for more than a year at a time. A poor school for a year is always undesirable, but it is not an irremediable catastrophe, according to choice advocates.

According to those who advocate a market system, the educational world is divided into good schools and bad schools; good schools are choice schools and bad schools are bureaucratic (Chubb & Moe, 1990; Paulu, 1989).

> Choice is a self-contained reform with its own rationale and justification. It has the capacity *all by itself* to bring about the kind of transformation that, for years, reformers have been seeking to engineer in myriad other ways. Indeed, if choice is to work to greatest advantage, it must be adopted *without* these other reforms, since the latter are predicated on democratic control and are implemented by bureaucratic means. (Chubb & Moe, 1990, p. 217)

The essence of a market-driven system is the belief that the best protection that parents could possibly get would be perfect competition among schools. Choice proponents say competition will force schools to offer similar services at similar prices. Assume there are three schools, for example, competing intensively for students. If one gets a reputation for poor-quality instruction, it loses market share. Why would any parents enroll their child in such a school, knowing that its services and prices were no better than those of two other available schools? Competition that involves repeat customers is an excellent consumer safeguard, say the market advocates. The danger would not be competition but the absence of it, they argue.

EQUALITY OF EDUCATIONAL OPPORTUNITY

Although often overlooked, there is a basic conflict between liberty and government efforts to foster equality of educational opportunity. The resolution of this conflict depends partly on the answer to this question: To what extent should government eliminate or reduce inequalities of educational opportunity resulting from parental interests, family resources, geographical location, cultural influences, and other nonschool factors affecting educational achievement? Herein exists a great debate which polarizes people along political, economic and ideo-logical fault lines. John Chubb and Terry Moe (1990) argue that government has made little progress in eliminating inequalities in educational opportunity. They assert that government has not solved the equity or quality problem because government is the problem. They contend that the political institutions that govern America's schools function natu-rally and routinely, despite everyone's best intentions, to burden the schools with excessive bureaucracy, to inhibit effective organization, and to stifle student achievement.

Myron Lieberman (1993) argues that a change to a market system of education will come about because the conditions that gave rise to public education no longer exist and its rationale is no longer viable. Here exists a choice. On the producer side, a system exists in which 4.5 million school district employees advance their interests by political action (p. 316). The policy alternative is a system in which their interests are served by providing better service at a lower price. On the consumer side, consumers lack information about the system, lack incentives to get information, and must attempt to achieve their educational objectives through political processes in which the cards are often stacked against them. The policy alternative is represented by a system in which con-sumers can act individually with reasonable prospects for success if their views are shared by even a relatively small number of others.

The equity argument will not be resolved easily nor will it go away. The question is: Will a market system ameliorate or exacerbate inequal-ity in American society? Both pro and anti-market proponents agree that education is an investment in human capital. The anti-market argument is that if the level of such investment is resolved by market forces, the affluent will invest more and receive more from their investment than the poor. This would exacerbate inequality in American society. The objection does overlook an important consideration, that is, the extent to which public education has always favored its upper-middle-class clientele. Because of its so-called monopoly status, however, public education must resist avoiding responsibility for the education of the disadvantaged. Its recent efforts to address the problem have by necessity emerged from concern over the political consequences of continued failure to consistently address it.

SCHOOL AUTONOMY

The advocates of market-driven schools argue that public school forces to resist reform and autonomy are powerful. Autonomy turns out to be heavily dependent on the institutional structure of school control. In the private sector, where schools are controlled by markets—indirectly and from the bottom up—autonomy is generally high. In the public sector, where schools are controlled by politics—directly and from the top down—autonomy is generally low. Deregulation of the public schools holds promise of giving parents and school personnel more autonomy and control. Offering choices is important, so that students and parents feel they have, and in fact do exert, some autonomy and control over their schooling or their child's education, say the advocates of market-driven schools.

The issues and structures over which choices can be offered are numerous: schedule, teachers, counselors, courses, activities, public service involvement, school subunit membership, unique educational and work-related programs, and so on. It is often easier not to offer choices, to treat students as cases being integrated, lockstep, into the existing school program. But generating choices gives students, parents, and teachers reason to come together to discuss the children's best interests. It gives the important adults in each child's life occasions to express visible interest, the importance they attach to education, concern, and affection for the child. It can give the student, parents, and teachers a better understanding of each other's needs, hopes, and limitations.

While many public school systems have experimented with magnet schools and creatively tinkered with other in-district choice programs, proponents of deregulation argue that public school choice is not an alternative in smaller school systems, and that larger systems often terminate or alter magnet programs without parent consultation.

The union movement, while significantly improving the economic status of teachers, has served to increase bureaucracy, slowed the school-reform process, and resisted local school autonomy. Collective bargaining leads to formal contracts that specify, usually in excruciating detail and at spectacular length, the formal rights and obligations of both parties and the formal machinery by which these rights are to be implemented and enforced. This translates directly into bureaucracy: rules governing organizational incentives, rules governing what teachers do, and rules governing how basic education decisions must get made and who gets to make them. Unions use their power in collective bargaining to formalize public education and to reduce collaborative decision making at the local school level. Whether in politics or collective bargaining, unions do not favor school autonomy.

Social Status and the Education Market

The opponents of a market-driven system argue that a deregulated, free-market system in which the government gives all parents a set per-pupil amount to spend in public or private schools of choice—a system in which every family fends for itself—will lead to greater racial, ethnic, and economic segregation and stratification.

Many educators argue the anti-market forces are faced with more difficult choices than others—choices that are mired in the reality of discrimination and domination (Bridge & Blackman, 1978). Many black parents who have sent their children to desegregated schools often tell of the trade-off between the pain of exposing their sons or daughters to racism and thereby possibly destroying their self-esteem and the desire to enroll them in a higher-status school. White parents, in their search for whiter, wealthier schools, usually do not have to make such trade-offs. In a society steeped in status group conflict and stratified according to race and class, a decision to keep a black child in a low-status, all-black school to spare him or her the pain of racism may be a perfectly rational choice (Elmore, 1986).

Unfortunately, exploring various social science perspectives of how parents and students choose schools is politically unpopular. Those who raise such issues are accused of calling poor and minority parents too uninformed or uncaring to choose a school. To examine the social context of decision makers, however, and consider the different ways in which they are constrained by a view of where they fit into the large social structure is not an attempt to judge the rationality or irrationality—and certainly not the wisdom—of their decisions. Rather, it is a way of looking more carefully at the social framework of those decisions and asking what variables may cause people to make educational choices in which academic quality plays a role secondary to issues of dominance and resistance.

School-status perceptions do affect parents' school choices. Wells (1991) presents clear evidence that some poor and minority parents fear that their children cannot compete with whiter and wealthier students in high-status schools. In her study of urban black students' willingness to participate in a voluntary transfer program that would enroll them in predominantly white, upper-middle- and middle-class high schools, she found that isolated poor and minority students often maximize on the comfort and familiarity of the neighborhood school when making a choice despite their stated beliefs that the faraway suburban schools—the whiter and more affluent schools—are *"better."* The parents of these students, many of whom expressed feelings of powerlessness and alienation from their children's school, deferred to the wishes of their children and did not involve themselves in the school choice process at all (Wells, 1991).

In a comprehensive study of parental choices in a voucher demonstration project in Alum Rock, California, Bridge and Blackman (1978) found that providing the least-educated parents with vouchers to spend at the school of their choice did not lower their high level of alienation. Instead, the researchers found that these parents were inhibited from gathering information that would allow them to make decisions based on school-quality factors as opposed to school location and convenience.

The problem, therefore, in discussing objective goal-oriented, economic behavior in the context of school choice is that people do not make choices in social and economic vacuums. Decisions about symbolic social institutions such as schools are strongly affected by where the choosers see themselves fitting into a stratified society.

Indeed, an argument can be made that maximizing on the socioeconomic power of a given school is rational, especially for an upwardly mobile family. Similarly, one could argue that maximizing on the comfort, familiarity, and convenience of a same-race school is an equally rational choice for an isolated and alienated black family. But will choices based on such nonacademic factors lead to any real and meaningful educational improvement? Will these "rational choosers" place pressure on schools to provide better services to all children?

The anti-market advocates argue convincingly that members of dominant status groups—that is, the white and wealthy—will have greater market resources, including time, money, information, educational background, political clout, and personal connections and far fewer market constraints (Elmore, 1986). This will give them a definite advantage in the competition against members of subordinate status groups for seats in the most demanded schools (Bourdieu & Passeron, 1977). When parents of the dominant class are able to transmit high-status culture that is greatly valued and generously rewarded in the educational system to their children, the children of lower-status groups are likely to have a disadvantage in the competitive educational market.

Market-driven schools are scarce. The effort to privatize selected school districts through such firms as Whittle Communications' Edison Project or the emergence of charter schools in some states (Minnesota, California, Colorado, Michigan) provide insufficient examples or data from which valid conclusions can be drawn regarding the social or educational effectiveness implications of school choice (see also Appendix A on charter schools).

There are, however, cross-cultural comparisons from the Netherlands, Australia, and Canada which can provide some insight into the influence which market-driven factors have had on the school systems in those nations.

SCHOOL CHOICE IN OTHER COUNTRIES

The Netherlands, Canada, and Australia represent countries with nationwide school choice programs involving public and private schools supported with public funds.

Holland is unique in that education and most other social services are financed by the government but are generally operated by private non-profit organizations, often religious in nature. A small fraction of social services are delivered by the government (James, 1986; Louis & Van Veizen, 1991). This delivery system is derived from a special feature of the Dutch society, "pillarization," which is the tendency for Catholics, Protestants, and other groups to exist separately in every aspect of Dutch life, including residence, jobs, friends, and politics (James, 1986; Louis & Van Veizen, 1991).

In 1917, a coalition between Catholics and Protestants produced a national constitution that provided public support for religious schools. In 1920, a national education law was enacted to implement this education policy. In the Netherlands today, there are 4,000 independent governing school boards for 8,050 elementary schools and 2,000 secondary schools. Approximately 69% of all elementary pupils attend privately operated, publicly funded schools and 31% attend public schools. At the secondary level, 72% attend privately operated schools and 28% attend public schools. The average enrollment for an elementary school is 175 and is 545 for a secondary school. Most, 95%, of the privately operated schools are church related (James, 1986). Choice has existed in Holland for 85 years but has not been replicated in any other European country.

What can be learned from school choice in the Netherlands? Parents may choose any school for their child, but private schools may select from among applicants. There is less social conflict over education, and experimentation is possible but is rarely found in Dutch schools (James, 1986). Curriculum, pedagogy, and school organization are generally uniform throughout the country. The Dutch schools conform to the desire for pillarization in Dutch society. Religious affiliation and residence are the strongest factors influencing school choice. Less popular schools do not disappear, as market incentives would dictate. Pedagogy is in the hands of professional educators, with almost no parent participation. Parents determine a school's quality more on the visible social-economic mixture of students and less on a school's academic performance. All schools, public and private, must follow rigid central government regulations on the curriculum, but pedagogy is left to teachers. All students must take a national exam at the end of elementary school and at the end of high school. Teacher salaries, teacher credentials, and working conditions are regulated by the central government.

Catholic schools are generally located in Catholic neighborhoods; teachers are affiliated with the Catholic church and have been trained in privately operated Catholic teacher education colleges. Students may engage in religiously related curricular activities. The same is true for the Protestant and other religiously oriented schools.

What are some of the negatives? Private schools may select from among student and teacher applicants. With choice, schools with high immigrant enrollments are experiencing "white flight." Dutch parents use choice to desert "black schools" (Louis & Van Veizen, 1990–1992, p. 69). In recent years, there has been a tendency for Muslim residents to establish their own schools. More than ten Muslim elementary schools have been established (Louis & Van Veizen, 1990–1992, p. 70). The children of most "guest workers" are enrolled in public schools. "Tracking" takes place at age 12 via a required national examination, which results in academic sorting for subsequent schooling (James, 1986).

In Canada, Erickson (1986, p. 104) found that citizen dissatisfaction with publicly funded private education in British Columbia compares with negative feelings by former Dutch citizens living in Canada toward Dutch publicly funded Calvinist schools. These ex-Dutch citizens felt that the schools were private in name only and were public schools in reality. They expressed a strong desire for private schools without public support. One must also remember that, in Holland and in Canada, there is no constitutional separation of church and state. Therefore, one would expect public schools also to engage in religious activities. With a uniform state-mandated curriculum, the distinction between public and private schools may be minor. Unlike those in the Netherlands, however, Canadian private schools may not use religious affiliation as criterion for accepting students or for hiring teachers.

Erickson (1986) also found that the most active choosers of private education in Canada were the better-educated and wealthier parents; this was also true for parents who selected public schools. He also found that protected private schools with full state funding were significantly "deprivatized" and de facto public schools. The terms *Catholic* or *private* are rarely used in referring to Catholic schools. These schools are in every way public schools. Residents in Toronto refer to their schools in terms of the public school district and the "separate" school district (Catholic). Constitutionally protected private schools and public schools in Canada receive equal public funding.

The Australians have also experimented with school choice (Birch & Smart, 1990; Boyd, 1987). Beginning in 1973, the national government initiated the funding of private elementary and secondary schools on a need basis. Today in Australia, 30% of all students attend private schools, of which 75% are Catholic schools and 70% attend public schools. The schools are funded on a need basis with the poorest private schools receiving approximately $3,200 per pupil from the national and state government and the wealthiest schools receiving approximately $1,000 per pupil (Birch & Smart, 1990, p. 49). This support accounts for about 75% of the operating expenses for the poorest private schools, which are mainly Catholic schools. Boyd and Stuart (1987) sum up the impact of choice on education in Australia:

> What is critical is who goes to private schools. In Australia, three-quarters of the students still go to government schools. But the prestige and career advantages of attending the elite private schools (which charge substantial fees despite receiving state aid) foster a creaming-off process that drains government high schools of most of upper-middle-class students. The creaming-off process reduces the reputation of state schools and sets in motion a dual school system by race and class. (p. 3)

School choice in Holland, Canada, and Australia that allows the use of public funds to support privately operated schools is derived from each country's dominant political ideology. Review of the experience with school choice in the three countries discussed supports the following conclusions: Choice has not resulted in market incentives to improve education. Choice has not improved educational opportunities for the poor. Choice has promoted traditional schools, but not innovative ones. Choice has not altered the influence of professional educators or increased the influence of parents in the schooling process. Private choice schools have become de facto public schools. Parents continue to use a school's social class mix of students and the neighborhood where the school is located to select schools for their children, and not the school's academic performance.

Cross-cultural comparison needs to be treated with caution. The mores, traditions and beliefs unique to a given culture make generalization from one culture to another somewhat dangerous. Nevertheless, the lessons of school deregulation in the Netherlands, Canada, and Australia should be carefully studied.

CONCLUSION

Not all school-choice policies imply the deregulation of the American school system. Controlled choice, for instance, does not rely on deregulating assumptions or on arguments against democratic control and state regulations (Alves & Willie, 1990). Free-market school choice, however, if it is to succeed as an educational reform, must lead to the deregulation of the public school system, because state control is antithetical to the operations of a free market. If public schools are deregulated, a chapter in American history will be closed. Despite the crisis of confidence and despite all of the criticisms directed at them (and the criticisms are legion), public schools have survived because they fulfill a basic requirement of democracy. In principle, free public education promises every child an equal opportunity. This promise has been abrogated repeatedly, but not because the idea is flawed. It has been abrogated because, in a highly stratified society, schools have limited capacities to bring about greater social equity. If the public school system was to lose its authority and mission, it would probably wither and become less effective serving mostly the poor and the powerless.

Most professional educational groups have expressed opposition to choice involving private schools. Some supporters of choice are now beginning to call for a go-slow approach by conducting experiments with choice before full implementation. For example, Owen B. Butler (1991), chair of the Committee for Economic Development and former chair of Proctor and Gamble Corporation, feels there are too many questions to be answered before choice programs are implemented. Butler adds that, under a voucher plan, all students will qualify for public support for their schooling, and publicly funded private schools will have to meet the same accountability standards in the use of public funds as private schools. The question of who will pay for the added cost of educating all students currently enrolled in private schools needs to be answered.

This chapter has attempted to outline the arguments about whether educational choice would wreak havoc on our current education system, produce great improvement, or generate results somewhere in between. There are no clear and definitive answers based on theory, practice, or inferences drawn from research undertaken in existing public and private schools. Because we know little, however, does not mean that we should not experiment with choice; indeed, that may be one of the strongest arguments for experimenting. But experimentation does not mean that a state should contemplate completely overturning its existing systems and adopting a deregulated system of choice, such as Chubb and Moe (1990, p. 219) advocate. In a democracy, that is up to the citizens and officials of each state. Given the limited knowledge and evidence available to date, great caution should be exercised and prior assessment of educational problems throughout the state should be studied before experimentation is begun. Choice is not without risk or potential significant damage to education systems that may be functioning adequately.

Chapter X

HARNESSING THE CHANGE PROCESS

There are two basic reasons for the decline in confidence in public education. One is that the problems are complex and intractable. Workable, powerful solutions are hard to conceive and even harder to put into practice. The other reason is that the strategies that are used do not focus on things that will really make a difference. They fail to address fundamental instructional reform and associated development of new collaborative cultures among educators.

Significant numbers of adults still retain images of the way schools "used to be," images of the schools they attended. But the economic, social, and political world has changed immensely, and many of these adults have not come to terms with these changes.

The Phenomena of Change

A trip back just fifteen years or so reminds us that some parts of life have changed more than would have been dreamed possible, technology being the main catalyst. In 1978, *U.S. News and World Report* ran an article titled "New Gadgets Give TV a Run for Its Money" (p. 41). Video discs, cable TV, and videotape recorders (selling then for around $1,000) would, predicted the magazine, change the face of home entertainment—especially "if and when the price (of videotape recorders) falls to $300 or $400, as many expect."

A glance at the 1978 issue of *Reader's Guide to Periodical Literature*, which indexes most popular magazines, reveals that articles about microcomputers appeared in hobbyist magazines like *Popular Electronics*, but only one article was listed in a general-interest magazine. *Mechanics Illustrated* was amazed that year by a "Copier that Does It In Color." Compact discs were not mentioned fifteen years ago; but in 1993, a list of articles about the CD's and CD players filled nearly 3 full pages in *Reader's Guide*.

Other changes have not been so wondrous. Fifteen years ago, *Reader's*

Guide listed ten articles on cocaine, most of them reports of research. Crack was not mentioned at all in the 1978 index. AIDS was not mentioned, nor was Alzheimer's disease. References to "Aged" and "Aging" accounted for about two pages of entries fifteen years ago. By 1993, those headings took up more than ten pages plus more than 90 cross-references. Little was written in 1978 about children committing suicide. Unless you lived in New York, Chicago, or Los Angeles, you didn't hear much about children joining gangs.

Never has there been such an outpouring of creativity in all fields of endeavor—the arts, the humanities, medicine, technology, the sciences. Never has there been so much money or such a wealth of things to buy with that money. And never, in this nation (except perhaps during the depression years), have there been so many people living in poverty, homeless, hungry, jobless.

As the twenty-first century approaches, it brings with it the realization that technology and scientific discoveries don't, in themselves, solve problems—in fact, they create more choices, compromises, and dilemmas.

Whatever can't be predicted about the future, there are two things which can be said, one with a high level of certainty and the other with an even higher level of certainty. The future will surely continue to bring more change, and if the immediate past is any indication, that change will come faster and faster.

Making Change Work Positively

American public schools cannot slow social and technological change, nor can the schools effectively resist these powerful change forces. There are, however, three things educators can do to bring about fundamental systemic school improvement. First of all, educators must view change as a fact of life, embrace it and nurture it as a positive force. Secondly, educators need to abandon their isolation.

The culture of most schools is characterized by norms of privatism and isolation, which keep teachers apart. Furthermore, although administrators often talk about the value of collegiality, their actions sometimes encourage teachers to compete, rather than cooperate. Personal growth and improvement doesn't occur in a vacuum. Teachers and administrators must function as teams of educators, collaboratively planning, questioning, and challenging each other every day. Thirdly, educators must reclaim moral purpose as their heritage, believing that they can indeed make positive differences in the lives of their students.

EMBRACING CHANGE

As the reader will readily understand, quick fixes won't work, innovations have been tried and found wanting. As the public confidence in its schools wanes, time grows short. Educators from coast to coast have heard the cry for better schools. Yet educators are commonly perceived as keepers of the status quo.

Educators resist change for all sorts of reasons. Fear is a major reason. Educators may or may not like the way things are, but at least they're used to it and they know how to function. Some resist because they have turf to protect, whether that turf consists of power or security. Change, however, is mandatory; growth is optional (Laing, 1992). We do not have a choice between change and non-change, but we do have a choice about how we respond. Education, far from being an incubator for nurturing people to deal with change in basic ways, is just the opposite. To break through this impasse, educators need to see themselves and be seen as experts in the dynamics of change. To become expert in the dynamics of change, educators—administrators and teachers alike—must become skilled change agents. If they do become skilled change agents and possess moral purpose, educators will make a difference in the lives of students from all backgrounds and, by so doing, help produce greater capacity in society to cope with change.

This is not one of these goals that educational leaders can tinker with, that can vaguely or obliquely be expected to happen or that can be accomplished by playing it safe. The goal of greater change capacity must become explicit and its pursuit must become all out and sustained.

Leadership for the Change Process

Every organization has three kinds of people, according to California-based education consultant Richard L. Foster, who has helped many school districts across the nation meet change head on. Foster's recommendations are supported by leading scholars of the change process (Fullan, 1991; Senge, 1990).

About 15 percent of educators are innovators. They want to introduce changes and aren't afraid to depart from established precedent. Foster calls them "15 percenters." Another 75 percent are followers. They are dependable; they do what is asked of them without much complaint. He calls them dynamic conservatives. The remaining 10 percent are resisters. They are injustice collectors whose goal is to discourage innovators and followers. Foster calls them "stones" and adds that as they get older they become "boulders." "For an organization to effectively change, the 15 percenters must be encouraged" (In Billings, 1989, p. 82).

For those who do want to support the innovators in their organizations, Foster offers several suggestions drawn from his experience working with dozens of school districts.

- Hire them, acknowledge them, give them space and protect them from the rest of the staff. "Learn how to live with mavericks. Yes, they'll make some mistakes but so do the stones." (Billings, 1989, p. 82)
- Stress cooperation over competition. Cooperation promotes "the intelligent exchange of ideas, motivates energetic people to become more interested in their work and creates a more humane environment. Collaboration and consensus building are unique to the best of America's corporate society and almost nonexistent in the political arena" (Fullan, 1991).
- Solicit ideas rather than reports. When people are sent to a meeting or conference, "don't ask them to come back and give a report because nobody listens. Have them come back with one or two ideas that can be put to use" (In Billings, 1989, p. 81).
- Allow the person who has the idea to put it in place and train others. This concept, already employed by innovative corporations, "creates a meaningful reward system, releases ideas into the system and lets people flow with them. Ideas don't just fall by the wayside, but get carried out" (Billings, 1989, p. 83).
- Don't allow the resisters to gain control. They will bog down meetings with complaints and, on the job, will be "organizing to keep leadership busy so they won't have time to think about change" (Billings, 1989, p. 83).
- Leaders should see how long they can go without holding meetings. Reducing the frequency of meetings encourages people to consider long-term as well as short-term solutions to problems, according to Foster, because they won't be under as much pressure to produce immediate results.

Life isn't easy for the 15 percenters, Foster warns. If they try to create change by putting new ideas into practice, "the system will attack them." In fact, he keeps saying to people that "if you have not been attacked, then you're not in a leadership role." "Every creative person places a stable world in peril" (Billings, 1989, p. 82).

Real change requires educators to resist tinkering with innovations. Taking on one innovation at a time is fire fighting and faddism. Institutional development of schools and districts increases coherence and capacity for sorting out and integrating the myriad of choices, acting on them, assessing progress and re-directing energies. The greatest problem faced by school systems is not resistance to innovation but taking on too many changes indiscriminately.

Rather than grasping the latest innovation, meaningful systemic change can only be achieved through teamwork and collaboration. The problem of change, then, is turning the educational system into a learning organization—expert at dealing with change as a normal part of its work, not just in relation to the latest policy, but as a way of life.

COLLABORATION AND TEAMWORK

Teaching has long been called "a lonely profession," always in pejorative terms. The professional isolation of teachers limits access to new ideas and better solutions, drives stress inward to fester and accumulate, fails to recognize and praise success, and permits incompetence to exist and persist to the detriment of students, colleagues, and the teachers themselves (Lortie, 1975). Isolation allows, even if it does not always produce, conservatism and resistance to innovation in teaching.

Isolation and privatism have many causes. Often they produce a kind of personality weakness revealed in competitiveness, defensiveness about criticism, and a tendency to stockpile resources. But people are creatures of circumstance, and when isolation is widespread, we have to ask what it is about our schools that creates so much of it.

Isolation is a problem because it imposes a ceiling affect on inquiry and learning. Solutions are limited to the experiences of the individual. For complex change many people are needed, working insightfully on the solution and committing themselves to concentrated action together. In the words of Konosuke Matsushita, founder of Matsushita Electric Ltd.

Business, we know, is now so complex and difficult, the survival of firms hazardous in an environment increasingly unpredictable, competitive and fraught with danger, that their continued existence depends on the day-to-day mobilization of every ounce of intelligence. (Pascale, 1990, p. 27)

Educational problems are all the more complex, and collaborative, "learning enriched" schools do better than those lingering with the isolationist traditions of teaching (Rosenholtz, 1989; Fullan & Stiegelbauer, 1991). To enable teachers to plan and team with one another is imperative. Many teachers will not be effective collaborators at first. Through their undergraduate academic course work and during their field experiences and student teaching most teachers have had little experience in professional collaboration. Goodlad (1990) and his associates in a comprehensive investigation of twenty-nine university teacher training programs was critical. Among their main findings:

The preparation programs in our sample made relatively little use of the peer socialization processes employed in some other fields of professional preparation. There were few efforts to organize incoming candidates into cohort groups or to do so at some later stage. Consequently, students' interactions about their experiences were confined for the most part to formal classes. (p. 698)

From the experiences of working with local school collaborative planning teams, Maeroff (1993, p. 517) has gleaned some of the main ways that collaborative groups can get change started in their schools.

- Collaborative teams can set priorities so that all of the collaboration teams' ideas are not just dumped on the school with no sense of what is most important.
- Collaborative planning teams can model the kinds of behavior that they would like to elicit from colleagues.
- Collaborative planning teams can try to anticipate objections so that the answers are provided before some of the negative reactions are registered.
- Collaborative planning teams should remember that each member is only part of the team and does not speak for the entire group unless delegated to do so.
- Collaborative planning teams can make certain that team members interact with their colleagues.
- Collaborative planning teams should take every opportunity to spread ownership through the school community.

- Collaborative planning teams should strive to get time in the school's schedule to work on the change process with colleagues.
- Collaborative planning teams should keep the school community informed about their plans/progress.
- And finally, collaborative planning teams should maintain a sense of humor about the serious work at hand.

Developing collaborative work cultures is also clearly central to this theme. It helps reduce the professional isolation of teachers, allowing the codification and sharing of successful practices and the provision of support (see Fullan, 1990, and Little, 1987, for a discussion of the pros and cons of collaboration). Working together has the potential of raising morale and enthusiasm, opening the door to experimentation and an increased sense of efficacy (Cohen, 1988; Rosenholtz, 1989). Constant communication and joint work provide the continuous pressure and support necessary for getting things done.

Intrinsic Motivation

Through collaboration the best ideas, the most creative thoughts, and the most effective planning is fostered. Time to team, to collaborate together improves morale and increases intrinsic motivation.

"What gets rewarded gets done," an opposing rule based primarily on bureaucratic authority, relies heavily on extrinsic gain to get people to do something.

Incidentally, alliances, partnerships, consortia and collaboration all connote joint agreements and action over a period of time in which all parties learn to work differently and achieve qualitatively different results. Cooperation, communication, coordination all have their place, but may not go deeply enough. Schrage's (1990, p. 40) definition of collaboration captures the idea nicely:

> Collaboration is the process of *shared creation:* two or more individuals with complementary skills interacting to create a shared understanding that none had previously possessed or could have come to on their own.

One of the strongest and most likely outcomes of collaborative planning and team building at the local school building level is its favorable effect on individual members of the team. It is safe to say that those who participate in collaborative planning are usually changed by the experience.

Individual team members of collaborative planning groups are girded by a greater sense of self esteem, tend to be more willing to speak out in their schools and to talk about what is needed for change to take place and flourish. Teachers involved in collaborative planning recognize as a group that the mantle of shared authority is accompanied by many responsibilities that extend beyond one's classroom. "The big thing that happens," said one principal, "is teachers stop using excuses for why they can't do it and start controlling their own destiny. It has been wonderful this year. I haven't heard the staff say 'They won't let us.' They don't talk that way anymore" (Maeroff, 1953, p. 519).

The "what gets rewarded gets done" approach provokes a short-term response, in the sense that someone externally gives something, or promises not to take away something, in return for compliance. It is little more than a trade. People are likely to continue participating in this trade as long as they are getting what they want. Otherwise, people seek either to renegotiate the trade or to back out; involvement in work is calculated. The negative but unanticipated consequences of overemphasizing this rule are summarized by W. Edwards Deming: "People have innate intrinsic motivation, dignity, curiosity to learn, joy in learning. The forces of destruction begin with toddlers—a prize for the best Halloween costume, grades in school, gold stars and on up through the university. On the job, people, teams, divisions are ranked—reward for the one at the top, punishments at the bottom. MBO [management by objectives], quotas, incentive pay, business plans, put together separately, division by division, cause further loss, unknown and unknowable" (In Senge, 1990, p. 7). Commenting on Deming's analysis, Senge (1990) points out that "by focusing on performing for someone else's approval, corporations create the very conditions that predestine them to mediocre performance" (p. 9). Senge believes that superior performance depends on individual and organizational learning, and that both are discouraged by the rule that what gets rewarded gets done.

"What is good gets done" is a rule that asks us to respond because of obligations, duties, a sense of righteousness, loyalty to the group, felt commitments, and other reasons with moral overtones. This is the approach that emerges when community norms are in place in the school and when people are committed to the professional ideal. People respond to work for internal reasons and not because someone out there is "leading" them.

Vision Building

A vision isn't a plan or a document. It isn't a goal. A vision is a vivid image of an intense desire, the ability to conceive of an improved future. It comes from within and has little to do with what is practical or possible. Yet without vision, very little is possible. Vision is the flame that energizes, motivates and provides the will to persevere even during the inevitable letdown that comes when it's time to start translating the vision into reality (Kouzes & Posner, 1987).

A vision needs to be expressed, written down, and detailed in describing what is to be accomplished. It also needs to be a cooperative venture, because too often educational visions are someone else's visions, and the "someone else" is not part of the group that will put the system into operation, or live with the results. Only when all parts of the school community come to believe that the vision for an effective educational system is their own, and will fulfill their needs—needs which will change from time to time, and require adjusting as they change—will the educational system become truly responsive to the people it serves, the children of the future.

Starting with personal vision-building is advisable because it connects so well with moral purpose in contending with the forces of change. Shared vision is important in the long run, but for it to be effective leaders must have vision. Working on vision means examining and reexamining, and making explicit to ourselves why we came into education. Asking "What difference am I trying to make personally?" is a good place to start. For most educators it will not be trying to create something out of nothing. The reasons are there, but possibly buried under other demands or through years of disuse, or for the beginning teacher still underdeveloped. Vision should not be thought of as something only for leaders. It arises when educators determine to articulate what is important to them. Block (1987) emphasizes that "creating a vision forces educators to take a stand for a preferred future"; it signifies disappointment with what exists now (p. 102). To articulate a vision of the future "is to come out of the closet with our doubts about the organization and the way it operates" (Block, 1987, p. 105).

Says Block writing more generally about organizations: "We all have strong values about doing work that has meaning, being of real service to our customers, treating other people well, and maintaining integrity in the way we work" (p. 123). Teachers are in one of the most "natural" occupations for working on purpose and vision, because underneath that is what teaching is all about.

Moral Purpose

A compelling moral purpose distinguishes the education profession from many other professions. The moral purpose is to make a difference in the lives of students regardless of background and to help produce citizens who can live and work productively in increasingly dynamically complex societies. This is not new either, but what is new is the realization that to do this puts teachers precisely in the business of continuous innovation and change. Teachers are, in other words, in the business of making improvements, and to make improvements in an ever-changing world is to contend with and manage the forces of change on an ongoing basis.

We are a society addicted to plans, systems, lists, how-to's. Review the magazines on the newsstand or the professional literature you receive. They are dominated by bare bones, no-nonsense ways to get things done. Unfortunately, all those lists and systems and how-to's often don't get the job done. If they do, why aren't thin thighs, exquisitely ordered desks, and buckets of huge financial rewards the prevailing norm? Why, after managing by objectives, strategically planning, and interfacing at management retreats, don't contemporary organizations run like clockwork? Why, instead, do educational and business leaders feel guilty because they can't even follow a simple system that would lead them straight to the desired goal? It is because the plans and systems are somebody's abstract idea of what "should" work. And they may work—but only if they are fired with the energy of a vision.

Newsweek found 50 "everyday heroes" to highlight (July 10, 1989). These heroes are simply people with moral purpose who are doing something concrete to make the world a better place. They include: a man in Alaska who organized a wildlife-rescue effort after the Exxon tanker spill. A New Orleans woman who has created and is enforcing a drug-free zone in the housing project where she lives. A North Dakota woman who founded the Incest Awareness Project and works to prevent child abuse and help victims. A Harvard senior who returned to her working-class Boston neighborhood to create a tutoring program for welfare mothers and children. Two Kentucky teachers who gave up their retirement benefits and took 20 percent cuts in salary to keep their preschool open, hoping that they can break the grim cycle that results in 71 percent of their county's adults dropping out of high school. A former heroin addict whose first husband died from drugs, who counsels wives of prison inmates, listening, accompanying them to court, and helping them to find work.

We can learn some things from these accounts. For example, it is true of all the people mentioned that:

1. They didn't take on the world. Each chose one well-defined objective and gave it everything.

Author Wendell Berry, in a commencement address reported in *Harper's Magazine* (September, 1989, p. 31), observes that there are "no national, state, or county problems, and no national, state, or county solutions. . . . The problems, if we describe them accurately, are all private and small."

2. They don't wait for organizations and bureaucracies to respond to a need. Each has taken the initiative and done what needs to be done. In some cases, they have had to circumvent organizations.

Consultant Bill Banach, in the 1988 edition of his annual *Top Ten Educational Issues*, observes that:

> While the context in which change is occurring is large, the means to accommodating change is small. School problems are not solved by governments or business or the educational community. Problems are solved by people, teams of educators talking things over. In fact, it has been estimated that well over 90 percent of all problems are solved by people working in groups of two or three—sifting through solutions, laughing off mistakes, coming to consensus. (In Billings, 1989, p. 53).

3. Each has chosen a cause near to his or her heart. What shines through their stories is a sense that they aren't doing something they felt they "ought" to do, but something they were compelled from within to do. In short, they have vision.

CONCLUSION

Genuine school reform and restored confidence in American public education can be achieved when thousands of educators exercise the kind of moral purpose *Newsweek* highlighted. The human spirit is the only hope the public schools have for change. And the human spirit does rise up, often when and where it is least expected. People often are way ahead of their self-styled leaders and the institutions that support the hierarchy of leadership.

First, teachers of the future must make their commitment to moral purpose — making a difference in the lives of children — more prominent, more active, more visible, more problematic. Many teachers have moral purpose now, but they do not conceptualize it that way. They do not give themselves the stature they deserve. They must push moral purpose to the forefront as never before.

Finally, educators must stop using vast amounts of energy, fruitlessly resisting change. It is not as if change can be avoided, since it pursues us in every way. We might as well, then, make the best of it. The answer is not in avoiding change but in facing it head-on, in embracing it. The most effective approach is to exploit change before it victimizes us. Change is more likely to be an ally than an adversary, if it is confronted. In this way, we can learn to reject unwanted change more effectively while at the same time becoming more effective at accomplishing desired improvements.

The educational system is killing itself because it is more designed for the status quo while facing societal expectations of major reform. If teachers and other educators want to make a difference (and this is what drives the best of them), interacting with other like-minded individuals and groups to form the critical mass is necessary to bring about continuous improvement.

EPILOGUE

The reader will note that this book is not about how schools can do a better job of public relations. The present crisis of confidence transcends public relations' efforts. The best public relations experts on "Madison Avenue" can't repair the damages to the public confidence in America's schools.

As good as the data is in supporting arguments that the public schools are doing a good job of educating the young, defensive posturing today is greeted by cynicism. It behooves educators and citizens alike to attend to the recommendations set forth in this book. Public schools can and must improve. Improvement is well within the grasp of most public schools today.

There are no panaceas. The most serious problems in American education exist in the same place they have for several generations: in our inner cities. The problems are multifaceted. They include, but are not limited to, a lack of basic skills, poor or nonexistent study habits and skills, low educational expectations, low self-esteem, poor language skills, dropping out, and concentration on nonacademic distractions that range from drugs to the violence of the streets. These problems are not simple; they cannot even be catalogued easily. They certainly are not all captured, or even approximated, by standardized test results, contrary to what some critics seem to imply. And they will not be solved quickly or easily by implementing some single policy.

As concern grows about the number of young people leaving school without the skills and motivation to work, about a shrinking pool of youngsters available for today's hi-tech economy, about the growing costs of prisons and welfare, and about the prospect of a permanent underclass, it is becoming clear the effective interventions put forward in this book provide some powerful answers to these concerns. The will to implement solutions is gaining momentum. School leaders, teachers, boards of education, politicians, business leaders, and citizens are reexamining outmoded practices and boundaries and are joining hands to promote and to provide intensive, comprehensive and flexible changes in America's public schools, changes which profoundly have the potential to restore the public confidence in the schools of the nation.

Appendix A

CHARTER SCHOOLS

C harter schools represent a growing phenomena. The movement is too new, and empirical data is virtually nonexistent. Ted Kolderie, director of the Center for Policy Studies, is a credible national expert and advocate for charter schools. Kolderie's essay appeared in *Enterprising Educators as School Partners, A Manual for Educator Entrepreneurs and School Officials,* Watertown, Wisconsin, American Educators in Private Practice. Kolderie's essay appears in full.

It is included to provide the reader with balance and the most up-to-date information which may influence future public confidence in American public education.

Ted Kolderie, Center for Policy Studies, Saint Paul, Minnesota

The charter schools idea, enacted in Minnesota in 1991 and in California in 1992, spread rapidly in 1993. It was introduced in some form in 16 states. By December, 1993, bills had passed in Georgia, New Mexico, Colorado, Massachusetts, Michigan, and Wisconsin, and the idea was under active discussion in Illinois and several other states.

The essential idea is worth re-stating: **It is to offer change-oriented educators or others the opportunity to go either to the local school board or to some other public body for a contract under which they would set up an autonomous (and therefore performance-based) public school which students could choose to attend without charge.** The intent is not simply to produce a few new and hopefully better schools. It is to create dynamics that will cause the main-line system to change so as to improve education for all students.

Legislation passed in 1993 increases those dynamics by enlarging significantly the role of the state. Originally, in Minnesota, for example, a proposal died without the approval of "a school board." In 1992, California provided an appeal to the county school board. Colorado became the first state to allow an appeal to the state board of education in its original legislation, and Minnesota added the state board appeal. New Mexico and Massachusetts made chartering a state decision.

Legislative activity continues to be conspicuously bipartisan, and governors and legislators continue to show remarkable political courage as they push the charter idea. Governor Roy Romer's intervention in Colorado was the most determined advocacy seen so far from a governor. Second-order effects of charter school legislation are beginning to appear. Districts are responding quickly to the prospect that some other public body might offer public education in the community. Boards are moving to make changes they resisted before. Legislatively, some are seeking authority to charter existing schools.

So the idea itself continues to evolve. Initially, it was a way to create a new autonomous public school. People saw quickly that it could also be used to convert an existing school from administered to autonomous status. Initially, too, people assumed that teachers would be employees. But they quickly began to think about offering teachers a professional opportunity to own the learning program in which they teach. For governors and legislators, the charter idea has been liberating; a strategy for change that offers them real leverage while minimizing additional taxes and avoiding the political quicksand of the voucher idea.

Essentials of the Charter Idea

Because the charter idea challenges most of the conventional ideas about how to organize and how to change public education, there is a growing need for understanding the idea itself and where it fits in the national discussion about strategy.

A state interested in charter schools probably ought not to begin with what has come out of the legislative process in other states. Here is an uncompromised charter school model:

First, the state says it is okay for more than one organization to offer public education in a community. Today, in most states, only the local board may start a public school. With a charter law, the state says it is okay for somebody other than the local board to run a public school, sponsored, if necessary, by some public body other than the local board. Generally, anyone may make a proposal. Nobody can actually start a school without the approval of a sponsor. The sponsor might be (as originally in Minnesota) only "a school board." But proponents should be able to approach either a local board or some other responsible public body: the state board of education, the board of a public college or university, a city council, or a county board.

Second, it is *public* education. The test of what is public is in the principles on which the activity operates, not in the legal character of the agent. A road is a public road because it is commissioned by the public, to serve a public purpose, paid for by the public, and open to the public. Nobody thinks the test is in who built it. A charter school follows principles of *public* education. It is commissioned by the public to serve a public purpose. It is paid for by the public and may not charge tuition. It is open to the public: no picking and choosing "nice kids" and no elite academies. It may not discriminate. It may not teach religion. It must follow health and safety requirements. It is accountable to its public sponsor for meeting the objectives that it and its sponsors agree on.

Third, the school becomes a legal entity. Today, the school does not exist, legally. The district exists; a school is a *non*-entity. A school cannot act; the district acts. The school may advise; the district decides. This reality means that most so-called site management is mainly rhetoric. The charter idea changes the rhetoric into reality. It makes site management real. A charter school becomes a legal entity. Some states let it choose any form of organization available under state law. Minnesota specifies that the organization be a nonprofit or a cooperative. The school has the power to hire employees, hold property, make agreements, etc. It is governed as provided in the charter school law.

Fourth, accountability shifts from process to performance. Today, the district's "deal" with its school is this: "We don't give you autonomy; in return, you don't give us accountability." Control is focused on process: the district worries more about how the school does things than about what students learn. The charter idea turns this around. In return for accepting the accountability represented by (a) the requirement to meet student performance objectives it agrees with its sponsor it will meet, and (b) the obligation to attract and to hold its student and parent community, the school is waived clear of state regulations and statute law. Control shifts to performance: the school decides how things will be done; it goes at risk for student performance. The charter is granted for a term: it may be not renewed or it may be revoked for cause during its term.

Fifth, "charter" can be combined with choice. Strictly speaking, the charter idea has to do with who gets to offer public education in the community. How students get to school is a second and separate question. The old system of assigning kids to schools could continue if a state were willing for students to be assigned to innovations. In practice, most states provide for charter schools to be schools of choice.

Sixth, the state pays the school. The idea is for the charter schools to get basically the same amount of funding per student available to regular schools in the district or in the state. Typically, in a district, some students are fully paid from local sources; the rest are fully paid by the state. The student who moves is treated as state-paid and essentially is an accounting transfer on the books of the state department. In the charter school, the state pays the school directly.

Seventh, the teachers have the professional option to be the owners. Teachers may choose to be employees, in which case they would be employees of the school. They could elect to organize and bargain collectively, in a bargaining unit at the school, separate from other bargaining units. Teachers also should have the option not to be employees but to work in a professional partnership. They might well join the union. For example, one of the first acts of teachers at the first charter school in St. Paul, Minnesota was to join the Minnesota Education Association. But when they have no employer, no question of bargaining arises: teachers are working for themselves.

Eighth, the state lists questions the school/sponsor must answer. Normally, the state will simply ask the school and its sponsor to say what the school will be and do: what ages/grades, what curricular focus, what admission procedures, what the teachers will be legally, where the school will locate, what the outcomes and method of assessment will be, who will buy the insurance, etc. The idea, says Senator Gary Hart, chairman of the State Education Committee in California, is for the state to be " 'open,' to list the questions and not to dictate answers."

Distinguishing Charter Features in the Seven Charter States

In **Minnesota**, all schools authorized in 1991 were approved by early 1993. Legislation in 1993 raised the "cap" on the number of charters available from eight to 20 and let proponents appeal to the state board if they get at least two votes in a local board. The law is geared more toward new schools than to conversions. Most approvals so far are for "non-traditional" students. Boards resist proposals for "main-line" students. Charter contact is Ted Kolderie, Center for Policy Studies: 612-224-9703.

In **California**, the law gives a lot of flexibility to schools and sponsors. The requirement that teachers sign on to a proposal (half the teachers in a school or 10 percent in the district) means the law may be used to convert existing schools from administered status to charter status. Up to 100 schools are allowed. Subject to the limit of 10 in any district, a board may itself propose to convert all its schools to charter status. There is much interest up and down the state and high visibility, partly because of voucher plan plans voted on during the 1993 election. Charter contact for California is Merrill Vargo, Department of Education: 916-657-2516; Senator Gary Hart: 916-445-5405; and Eric Premack, B & W Associates: 510-843-8574.

In **Georgia**, the law is a variation on the school-improvement program. School does not become a legal entity. There is a blanket waiver in return for performance. School applies; local board approves; state board charters. No limit on the number of charters. Specifics, including everything about finance, remain to be worked out. Charter contact is John Rhodes, Department of Education: 414-656-0644.

In **New Mexico**, there is a small pilot program intended only for the conversion of existing schools to charter status. The legislative author, seeing district boards had no incentive, provided for state chartering. Local boards may attach advisory recommendations. Charter contact for New Mexico is Richard LaPan, New Mexico Department of Education: 505-827-6625.

In **Colorado**, legislation provides for up to 50 charters with 13 reserved for "at-risk" kids. New schools and conversions are possible. The appeal process is complicated. Intense opposition produced complicated provisions about financing, the waiver from regulations, and the status of teachers. The first school has opened. Interest from parents and community, after the bill was signed, surprised most everyone. Charter contact is Bill Porter: 303-466-4666. Barbara O'Brien, Colorado Children's Campaign: 303-839-1580.

In **Massachusetts**, charter legislation offers what may be the closest to the real charter model. It is keyed to new schools, up to 25 initially. School is clearly a separate entity. Open as to applicant. No local board role: State Secretary of Education issues charters. Preference for low-performing areas. Contact Linda Brown, Pioneer Institute: 617-723-2277.

In **Wisconsin**, legislation is unusual in having support from the Wisconsin Association of School Boards (WASB). Charters are granted on the condition that the local board be the sponsor, but in Wisconsin, ten charters were allowed in the state and in 23 days ten applications came in (from Milwaukee, Madison and other districts). Law provides that teachers will be employees of the district, so in the strict sense, this is a district-site-management program. Contact is Senn Brown, WASB: 608-257-2622.

In **Michigan**, new legislation permits local and intermediate school boards, public community colleges and universities to charter schools. The law permits new schools and conversions. Ten schools are expected to be operational in 1994–1995. Contact Joel Galloway, Office of the Governor: 517-335-0561.

Emerging Dimensions of the Charter Idea

The charter idea is changing as it spreads. Two new features have come into the discussion. One opens a new opportunity for school boards. The other opens new opportunities for teachers.

First, charters change existing public schools from administered to autonomous status. Not surprisingly, parents and teachers (even school boards), frustrated with bureaucratic resistance and disappointed with conventional "site management," ask: "Why can't we 'go charter'?" That makes sense.

Once the legislature has opened the way for new charter schools to appear, it should give existing schools the opportunity to have that freedom, too.

The idea of having all schools on a contract with the board seems to be the only effective solution for urban districts in this country. New charter schools may enroll only a small number of students, but their presence can stimulate the district to change. But in big cities, action needs to happen at scale and quickly. That will happen best if existing schools convert from administered to charter status.

Conversion to charter status would work the same way it works when a new charter school is created: the school becomes a legal entity and the board gets accountability, controlling through performance rather than through process. Clearly, in converting an existing school, there has to be some way to get consent of teachers and parents and there has to be alternate arrangements for those teachers and parents who choose not to remain after the school changes.

Basically, the idea of changing schools to autonomous status means that boards become buyers of instruction. This has three important implications.

• First, divestiture offers a way to "break up" big-city districts without creating unacceptable problems of equity. In city after city, from New York to Los Angeles, people want to reduce the size of school systems. But some people assume that "breakup" must be territorial; boards cut up along with the bureaucracy. The effort fails because dividing large districts into smaller districts separates majority and minority neighborhoods, rich tax bases and poor tax bases. Where boards no longer own the schools, boards can become buyers of instruction. Boards continue to represent whole communities. The operating side, the bureaucracy, is broken up into schools or into groups of schools.

• Second, opening up choice for school boards greatly increases system capacity for change. Boards can do little today to change the educational program. Districts are single, unitary organizations. They cannot be changed one part, one school, or one department at a time. Boards can change only one person at a time, and then usually only as individuals resign or retire. Mainly, they try to improve the skills and attitudes of the people they have, but they are in a situation where these people know they really do not have to change at all. If boards could "buy in" parts of the educational program, they could change and improve their offerings as fast as new methods and technology appear.

• Third, developing a capacity really to change and improve the learning program might save the American school board. This is a troubled institution. More and more, boards are trying to run the system they own; less and less are they inclined to leave that to their administration. This brings them more and more into conflict with their superintendents: boards now are turning over these positions about every four years on the average. This makes meaningful restructuring impossible. Never-ending pressure for more money builds resistance in the public. Resistance is compounded when programs are cut to fund salary settlements. The effort to run everything distracts the board from the job of education. In Los Angeles, for example, the district owns the second-largest law enforcement organization in the state. Problems with its police are the district's legal obligation as an employer.

As board effectiveness grows weaker, the state role grows stronger and so does the idea that more decisions should be made at the learning site. What is emerging is the concept of a two-tier system: state and school. Boards resist this. But people are now wondering openly if we really need that layer in the middle. If the school board is to survive, it must find a useful role.

In Colorado, the appearance of the charter idea and an alliance between a Democratic governor and a Republican state senator that the Colorado Association of School Boards (CASB) and the Colorado Education Association together could not overcome led CASB Executive Director Randy Quinn to write about the board's role. "It can be an opportunity to do something creatively different," Quinn says. "School boards have been the providers (producers) of public education, hiring teachers, administrators and other staff. . . . Under charter schools that role will change. Schools granted charter status will become substantially self-governing. . . . This is a dramatic difference that forces the board to re-examine its role. The board has an opportunity to become the purchaser of education services on behalf of the community," says Quinn.

"This opens up all kinds of possibilities. Viewed one way the principle underlying charter schools is not new. School boards now contract with (others) to do some things, including transportation, food, cleaning, and maintenance services. Extending that concept to academic areas is a leap, but not unimaginable. . . . In my view, Colorado school boards would be well advised to examine how this new concept can serve their communities. . . . Moving away from the role of exclusive (producer) of education may be a blessing in disguise," says Quinn.

Which leads to another intriguing question: "If the board did not own the learning program, who might?"

Second, charters open a professional opportunity for teachers. Initially, the thinking about teachers assumed that teachers would be employees. This complicates the design of a charter law and of a charter school. In July, 1992, discussions in Minnesota focused on giving teachers the choice to work as members of or as partners in a professional group which they would own collectively. Minnesota law permits a school to organize as a cooperative. In July, 1992, Dan Mott, whose work has taken him into education, law, politics, and cooperatives, made these suggestions:

• Set up a two-part structure. Form the school as a nonprofit so it is eligible for tax-exempt gifts. Form a cooperative as a vehicle for teachers.

• The nonprofit could be organized by parents or teachers or by some institution (a science museum, the zoo, the Smithsonian in the District of Columbia) or some individual; with the approval of a public sponsor, of course. The nonprofit would hold the charter. It would handle noninstructional functions. It would make agreements with the teacher group.

• The teacher group, formed as a cooperative or a partnership, would organize and run the instructional program. Within the framework of what the school has decided to be, teachers would organize the courses, pick the materials and methods, make the work assignments, select and evaluate their own colleagues, and settle their own compensation in the same manner as other professional groups.

The worker's cooperative is a well-established (if not well-known) way of organizing. In Philadelphia, Pennsylvania, there is a child day-care organization, Childspace, set up on the two-part model that Dan Mott advocates for schools. The people who work there are not servants of owners. They are owners. They make the decisions, receive the revenue, and run the operation. They keep at the end of the year what they do not spend; they build up equity. It makes a difference: people behave differently when they are owners. This, too, has big implications.

The teacher group would be capitalized, given a fixed number of dollars per student, at the existing level of expenditure. It would have the freedom the charter law provides to change and improve the program. Because teachers could keep for use in their program or as personal income what they did not need to spend, they would have both a reason and an opportunity to bring in new methods and technologies and to re-allocate existing patterns of expenditure. This could be important for teachers, for technology, and for taxpayers.

The technologies for transmitting, sorting, manipulating, and displaying information now are all coming together in digital form. Business firms are moving quickly to buy up rights to "intellectual property" all over the world: film and photo archives, art museums, science museums, libraries, etc. Commercial applications will soon follow. Soon it will be possible, school by school or department by department, to design and to assemble the learning program in the form of high-quality, full-motion video or (with the parallel improvements in printing technology) as hard copy delivered in color and at high speed.

None of this has to happen in school. Most of the learning system is outside school. Businesses can market these new technologies direct to families able to pay with their own money, providing programs that enable kids to move at their own pace. They also can design and market tests and diplomas, demonstrations and certificates of competence, validated by colleges' and employers' acceptance.

Think about the applications of electronic technology already in entertainment, and think about how students respond. It is hard to believe that the potential for learning in these technologies is not going to come together with the interests of students and the educational needs of the nation. They will come together around the institution of school, if necessary, in something like the way the automobile went around the streetcar. They may create serious problems in equity, but this will not stop what is happening.

Technology *would* move into schools if the teacher group rather than the board or the superintendent were the buyers in the marketplace. Teachers favor improvements that make their work easier, more successful, and financially more rewarding.

If the decisions were theirs to make, technologies ranging from digital electronics to cooperative learning, raising the quality both of teachers' practice and of students' performance, would be adopted as rapidly in schools as new technologies were taken up on the family farm where workers were the owners.

"Management cannot do it," says Jim Walker, superintendent at North Branch, Minnesota. "Only the teachers can do it." Unless change is in the teachers' interest, there is no way to change existing patterns of expenditure in public education. So long as teachers' interest is entirely in salary, they will push endlessly for more to be spent on the same. Boards will neither be able to reallocate nor to raise and spend significant amounts of new money for anything but salaries.

Early discussions with union leadership are not negative. Responses are pragmatic. They ask: "How would we grow our compensation under that arrangement?"

What Next?

With charter bill introductions in 16 states and enactments now in seven, "charter schools" is becoming a visible option on the national policy scene. The idea is appearing not only in the education press and in discussions about education policy but also now in newspapers and on television, as on ABC's "This Week With David Brinkley." The National Conference of State Legislatures, the Education Commission of the States, and the National Governors Association are beginning to track the idea and its spread so they can answer queries. As the idea spreads, the people involved are getting acquainted, at least by phone and fax. A national network is developing.

Three challenges lie ahead:

• **The first challenge is to get new schools set up.** This is not easy. Forming a new organization is difficult if you have never done it before. It is especially difficult if the opposition continues to undercut implementation. The job can be made tougher by a well-meaning bureaucracy which, shaped by its experience of trying to control schools they cannot get rid of, is slow to understand the possibilities of a new approach which focuses on students' performances. On the positive side, efforts are appearing to help move charter schools up the learning curve. In California, organizations are helping schools through the process of approval and start-up. In Colorado, where foundations understand the potential, the concept of a larger-scale "charter schools network" is emerging. The network will provide support services to new schools once in operation. Setup skills are developing rapidly.

• **The second challenge is legislative and political.** Bills are likely to be back in 1994, an election year. Opponents will fight hard to remove all the dynamics: to limit sponsorship to the local board and to require teachers to be employees of the sponsoring district. Proponents will work to introduce a "somebody else" clause, understanding that to give districts an exclusive is to give these organizations the power to control the state.

The growing aggressiveness of elected officials is very striking: Governor Romer in Colorado, Kathleen Brown in California, Representative Mark Roosevelt in Massachusetts, Governor John Engler in Michigan.

• **The third challenge is to distinguish the charter idea from other ideas now crowding in around it.**

Vouchers — This idea lets people start schools if they meet certain criteria. The state pays the parents, who pay (all or part of) the school's charges. Schools may be religious schools. Accountability is to parents: there is no performance contract with a board or other public body. It is a consumer market, not as with the charter idea, which is a social market.

Contract management — Here the idea is for a commercial organization to sell instructional or noninstructional services, or just the management of those services, to the district. It remains a district model: there may be no concept of autonomy either for the school or for the teachers. Vendors are likely to want to deal with large districts to minimize management and marketing costs.

Contract schools — In this case an organization does propose to run one or more discrete schools. The school probably would be built to the vendor's design, however, and operated not as an autonomous and locally controlled organization but as a unit of the vendor's larger organization.

The "charter district" — Districts sometimes ask to be waived clear of "the rules" themselves. They do not necessarily intend to pass the freedom on to their schools, and certainly, they do not intend that anyone else might offer public school within the district. Governors and legislators are likely to be cool to the proposal for an unregulated public utility, but in some states, districts will give "charter districts" a try.

It will be a challenge to distinguish the charter idea from other strategies proposed to improve K–12 education.

The "Charter" Idea and System Change

For governors and legislatures, the charter idea is important because it goes to the heart of the problem in our system of education. At its heart, the problem is simple: the reward structure is backward. School is supposed to be about learning, about the interests of students and about the needs of the nation. But for districts and adults in them, systems pay off whether the objective is accomplished or not.

This is true. The current system givens . . . mandatory attendance, districting, the rule that only one organization may offer public education, and tax financing appropriated per pupil . . . interact to create an arrangement in which the state assures the district its customers, its revenues, its jobs, and its existence whether or not it changes and improves and whether or not students learn.

This is important. It is not smart to expect performance from an institution in which the rewards are provided whether the mission has been accomplished or not. Why would an organization do the hard things that excellence requires, take risks, upset adults' comfortable routines, challenge powerful interests, put customers first, when this is not required?

This explains why the K–12 system behaves as it does. It explains why good teachers and administrators describe change, and the effort to put students first, as a risk. It explains why standards are not set for student and teacher performance. It explains why performance is not measured. It explains why rewards are unrelated to performance. It explains why senior teachers get to teach where they want to teach rather than where they may be most needed. It explains why so much money is spent for training driven more by teachers' personal interests than by the needs of the organization. It explains why the system does not incorporate new technologies, hard and soft. It explains why leadership does not intervene decisively when students are not learning. Why create controversy when the rewards are provided anyway?

"I'm convinced that we in education are not going to do the hard things needed to change the schools unless we have to," Albert Shanker, president of the American Federation of Teachers, told teachers in St. Paul, Minnesota. "Something has to be at stake. There is, in other fields: your organization could fail. People in these fields dislike change, too. But they have to do it. We in education don't (have to change) because for us nothing is at stake. If our kids do brilliantly, nothing good happens. And if we don't push, we can count on remaining popular with our colleagues. We have got to deal with this question of consequences for adults. We do need something to happen that is truly revolutionary."

Strategies approved by educators since the *Nation at Risk* report accept the basic system givens and accept perverse reward structures. This means they cannot succeed. However earnestly people profess their intentions, however hard or long they work at it, these strategies cannot succeed. It is beyond the capacity of administration, regulation, and the political process to secure basic changes in powerful organizations when nothing makes it necessary. And it is silly to try to force improvement into systems built not to need improvement.

The sensible course is obvious: give districts a reason, a need and an opportunity to make required changes and improvements and re-align the reward structure so that performance is followed by consequences, if the mission is accomplished and if it is not, for districts and for the adults in them.

Governors and legislators understand this. They want improvement to move faster. Increasingly, they see how the reward structure they have created works against their own interests. They realize that what they have done to themselves, they cannot undo. They have discovered that, confronted by a district that they cannot "make" perform, they can say: "We will get somebody else who will perform," and they can do this within the principles of public education.

Done skillfully, charter schools can be made to work in the interests of school boards and of teachers at the same time.

Ted Kolderie is director of the Center for Policy Studies. You can contact him at 59 West Fourth Street, Saint Paul, MN 55102, or at 612-224-9703.

Appendix B

EDUCATIONAL SPENDING INCREASES

S chool critics have weakened the public's confidence in the schools by focusing on spending increases which allegedly have failed to produce gains in academic achievement. To provide a balanced perspective on school funding, a recent article in the *Illinois School Board Journal* is included.

School Funding, Another Perspective (January/February 1994, Illinois School Board Journal)

Irving Kristol recently attached Clinton's social spending plans by asserting: "Look at the spending on public schools. It goes up and up, and the results go down and down, and down."

When Benno Schmidt resigned Yale's presidency in 1992, he denounced public education to justify a new national for-profit private school chain:

> We have roughly doubled per-pupil spending (after inflation) in public schools since 1965. . . . Yet dropout rates remain distressingly high . . . overall, high school students today are posting lower SAT score than a generation ago. The nation's investment in educational improvement has produced very little return.

In 1990, the U.S. spent $5,521 per pupil on public schools, more than double the $2,611 (in 1990 dollars) spent 25 years earlier. More money for schools won't do any good, critics assert; it's just pouring good money after bad.

But spending more hasn't failed. The truth is that little new money has been invested in regular educational improvements since 1965. How has the money been used?

Special education. Nearly 30 percent of new education money has gone for "special education" of children with disabilities. Since 1975, federal law has required public schools to provide a "free appropriate education" to each child, no matter how seriously handicapped. The services for handicapped children distinguish America as the world's most caring society. The cost of these services provides comprehensive high-quality educational services. Mention of the cost of special education is in no way meant to imply that funding on services should be reduced, only to explain how increased financial allocations to schools have been spent. Schools must design an "individualized education program" for each child with a specific disability. Publicly financed medical diagnoses, special transportation arrangements, personalized instruction, reduced class sizes, specially trained teachers, and the purchase of special equipment may be required to place a child in the "least restrictive environment." Parents dissatisfied with their child's program are entitled

173

to a hearing. The Supreme Court has ruled that cost cannot be an excuse for failing to design an appropriate program. If a handicap is too severe for a public setting, schools must pay the child's private tuition so the child's needs can be appropriately met.

Education of the handicapped is very worthwhile, but it is incorrect to imply that special education funds should produce academic gains for regular students and, when they do not, argue that money spent on public schools is wasted.

Nutrition programs. School breakfast and lunch programs have absorbed nearly 10 percent of increased cost. In 1951, nutrition programs were mostly self-supporting, selling milk and ice cream their main function. Today, 35 percent of all students get free or reduced price meals, costing over $6 billion a year.

Fourteen percent of Americans lived in poverty in 1992, the highest rate since 1964. Growth of overall poverty masks more drastic growth in child poverty. In 1990, nearly 25 percent of American children under age six were poor, an increase from 18 percent in 1979. With a probable deterioration in the nutritional condition of children when they come to school, it is questionable whether educational improvement can be expected from today's breakfast and lunch programs. Nor is it appropriate to suggest that maintenance of such expenditures would, from an educational point of view, be throwing good money after bad.

Smaller classes. Nearly one-third of new school money has gone for smaller classes. Pupil-teacher ratios have declined by about 30 percent since 1965 and average class size is now about 24, requiring more teachers and extra classrooms. It seems reasonable that this investment should produce academic gains. Yet while reducing class size to 24 creates better teacher working conditions and may improve classroom management — as education becomes more universal and society's authority norms weaken — unless class sizes get small enough (around 15) so that the method of teaching can change to individualized instruction, smaller classes have no measurable academic effect.

Salary increases. Teacher salaries have grown 21 percent — less than 4 percent a year — from an average of $27,221 in 1965 (1990 dollars) to $32,977 in 1990. This increase is responsible for another 8 percent of increased education costs. This added expenditure should result in improved student achievement if higher salaries attract more highly qualified graduates to teaching. But if other professional salaries grew at the same rate or at a higher rate, higher teacher pay would not enable school districts to maintain teacher quality in the face of greater competition from other professions.

Since 1975, starting teacher pay increases have lagged behind pay increases of some other beginning professionals with bachelors' degrees. Starting teacher salaries have grown by 149 percent since 1975, less than the rate of inflation. For beginning engineers, the increase was 153 percent; for marketing reps, 169 percent; for business administration grads, 171 percent; for mathematicians and statisticians, 163 percent; for economists and finance personnel, 161 percent; for liberal arts graduates, 183 percent. Teachers did better than chemists (144%) and accountants (130%).

Teacher salaries increased faster from 1965 to 1975 than after. But over 25 years the overall increase in real teacher pay at best maintained schools' ability to attract candidates. The increase has been barely adequate to maintain teaching's competitive standing, since more professions have welcomed women since 1975. Highly qualified female college graduates have many options available to them today. All told, teachers' pay gains since 1965 can't reasonably be expected to produce higher student achievement.

Transportation. Transportation has consumed 5 percent of increased costs. In 1965, 40 percent of public school students were bused at an average cost of $214 (1990 dollars). By 1989, 59 percent were bused, and the cost jumped to $390.

Fewer dropouts. About 3 percent of new spending stems from keeping more students in school. The oft-repeated worry that more students are dropping out has no factual basis. Since a student dropping out of one school may move to a new community and enroll there, the most accurate measurement of dropouts is not schools' own records but census information on young adults who have completed 12 years of school.

In 1970, 75 percent of youths between ages 25 and 29 had completed high school. By 1990, 86 percent had done so. Minority dropout rates have steadily declined—in 1940, only 12 percent of 25- to 29-year-old blacks had completed high school. In 1950, the black completion rate rose to 24 percent; in 1960, to 39 percent; in 1970, to 58 percent; in 1980, to 77 percent. The rate continued to rise in the 1980s, to 83 percent in 1990.

Hispanic dropout rates are less accessible because the 1980 decennial census was the first with separate data on Hispanics and because many so-called Hispanic dropouts (young adults who have not completed high school) are immigrants, some of whom came to the U.S. too old to enroll in school.

In 1990, only 58 percent of Hispanic 25- to 29-year-olds had completed high school. But for Hispanics in their forties (who were in their twenties in 1950), the rate was only 38 percent. Thus, it seems, Hispanic dropout rates are declining as well.

The typical dropout completes 10.5 years of school. This higher completion rate has increased per-pupil costs 1.3 percent since 1965. The added spending does not improve overall high school graduates' average academic achievement. While preventing dropouts is important, lower dropout rates reduce average test scores, since a broader base is now tested, including those less academically motivated than earlier groups that did not include potential dropouts. Fewer dropouts will also generate more anecdotes about high school graduates who don't read or compute well. So, paradoxically, expenditures for more schooling can seem to reduce academic achievement while contributing to an improved education level for society.

In sum, special education, smaller classes, school lunches, better teacher pay, more buses, and fewer dropouts account for over 80 percent of new education money since 1965. These expenditures are not the kind which would be expected to cause an increase in school achievement.

Appendix C

THE SANDIA REPORT

The congressional testimony, presenting some of the major findings of the Sandia Report, are included as Appendix C. The report contains data of a fair and accurate nature regarding the performance of public school students and the condition of the public schools.

The Sandia Report

Joining the cabinet-level ground swell in support of President Bush's call for the overhaul of the American public schools, Adm. James Watkins, the secretary of energy, announced in February, 1990 that he had instructed the Sandia National Laboratories to undertake a study of American education.

Historically, the Sandia National Laboratories had been involved in higher education, but the charge by Secretary Watkins to study our K–12 public schooling was distinctly different from anything the organization had previously undertaken. The Sandia researchers undertook their work with no a priori premises to prove.

The following report reviews some of the major findings of the Sandia Report, as presented in congressional testimony in July, 1991 by Michael A. Wartell and Robert M. Huelskamp, Sandia National Laboratories, before the Subcommittee on Elementary, Secondary, and Vocational Education Committee on Education and Labor U.S. House of Representatives.

When President Bush and America's governors set forth national education goals in October, 1989, Sandia National Laboratories in New Mexico took notice. We listened further to a challenge from the Secretary of Energy, Admiral James Watkins, that the national laboratories become more involved in education. Because Sandia conducts scientific research for the U.S. government, we have a keen interest in the educational system that develops future scientists, engineers and mathematicians. We decided to rise to this challenge by initiating several new programs. In the past, much of Sandia's thrust has been directed toward programs at the post-secondary level, but a significant portion of the new emphasis is directed toward elementary and secondary education. All told, Sandia is investing $12 million in its numerous projects.

In support of these new efforts, the New Initiatives Division of Sandia's Systems Analysis Department is conducting a wide-ranging analysis of local, state and national educational systems to determine where Sandia can maximize its contribution. Sandia is located in Albuquerque, New Mexico and is one of the largest employers in the region with over 7,000 employees; so, in addition to focusing on education in

176

the nation generally, the study looks at education in New Mexico. A group of three systems analysts is focusing on the following areas:

HISTORICAL PERFORMANCE
    Dropout–Retention Rates
    Standardized Tests
    College and University Data
    Expenditures for K–12 Education
    International Comparisons
    Status of Educators
FUTURE REQUIREMENTS
    Work Force Skills
    Changing Demographics
    Education Goals

The study is producing interesting results. It has greatly changed Sandia's initial perceptions in several of the areas and reinforced others. Overall, it provides an objective "outsider" perspective on the status of education in the United States.

To ensure the accuracy of their findings, the analysts are subjecting their lengthy report to critical peer review with representatives from the U.S. Departments of Education and Energy, the National Science Foundation, the Office of Technology Assessment, and numerous state and local educators and researchers. The following is a brief summary of the major findings in the report.

Dropout–Retention Rates

America's on-time high school graduation rate has been steady for 20 years at roughly 75% to 80%. However, some students require more than 4 years to complete high school and many dropouts avail themselves of opportunities to reenter (GED, night school, etc.), resulting in an overall high school completion rate for young adults of over 85%. This rate is improving and is among the best in the world.

The analysts note, however, that merely reporting gross national numbers can mask underlying problems. The "fine structure" indicates that the most significant dropout problems are among minority youth and students in urban schools. Nearly 80% of white students complete high school on time, and roughly 88% do so by age 25. Minorities do not fare as well. Only 70% of black students and 50% of Hispanic students graduate on time. By age 25 roughly 82% of blacks complete high school (only 6% less than whites), but only 60% of Hispanics do so. Finally, dropout reports indicate that urban students, regardless of race, drop out at very high rates.

The report shows that recent immigration of undereducated Hispanic young adults who are beyond high school age is significantly inflating dropout figures for that population. Further analysis of this phenomenon is essential to properly understand the educational needs of this growing population.

Standardized Tests

The analysts evaluated student performance on both the National Assessment of Education Progress (NAEP) and the Scholastic Aptitude Test (SAT). They found that performance has been steady or improving on the NAEP with the greatest gains in basic skills. Furthermore, these gains have not been at the expense of advanced skills.

The analysts also discovered that the much publicized "decline" in average SAT scores misrepresents the true story about student SAT performance. Although it is true that the average SAT score has been declining since the 1960s, the reason for the decline is not decreasing student performance. They found that the decline arises from the fact that more students in the bottom half of the class are taking the SAT today than in years past. Since 1971 the median test taker has dropped from the 79th percentile in class rank to the 73rd percentile. Additionally, every ethnic group taking the test is performing better today than it did 15 years ago. More people in America are aspiring to achieve a college education than ever before, so the national SAT average is lowered as more high school seniors in the 3rd and 4th quartiles take the test. However, as in the dropout data, analysis of the "fine structure" indicates that minority youth continue to lag far behind their white peers on the standardized tests. For example, in spite of a 50-point improvement over the past decade in average SAT scores, black students still average nearly 200 points lower than whites. Similarly, Hispanic and Native-American scores lag white scores by more than 100 points.

College and University

Nearly 60% of today's youth attempt post-secondary studies at accredited institutions, and two-thirds of these (40% of all youth) enroll in four-year institutions. Eventually, one in four of today's youth will obtain at least a bachelor's. These rates are the highest in the world.

Of significant importance is the changing population on today's college campuses. The number of women enrolled in college has been increasing steadily for thirty years while male enrollment has remained steady. Female enrollment surpassed male enrollment in the mid seventies. College populations are aging as more people enroll in post-secondary studies later in life. Additionally, four out of five college students nationwide are commuters, and over 25% hold full-time jobs while in school. As a result of these and other changes in student demographics, many universities are evolving from traditional, residential four-year institutions to a more flexible environment which better meets the needs of today's population.

As a National Laboratory, Sandia is particularly interested in possible shortages in technical degree attainment. The analysts found that roughly 200,000 U.S. students earn technical bachelor's degrees in the Natural Sciences and Engineering each year, up significantly from 20 years ago but representing a fairly steady rate of 4%–5% of U.S. youth. The United States grants a large number of advanced technical degrees to non-U.S. citizens. Nearly 50% of engineering Ph.D.'s and 25% of science Ph.D.'s are awarded to non-U.S. citizens annually. However, statistics show that about half of these recipients remain in the United States.

The analysts also point out that female and minority technical degree attainment continues to lag far behind their white male peers. This is in spite of impressive growth in technical degrees for women and minorities in the past two decades.

Expenditures for Education

In their investigation of educational expenditures, the analysts learned that most of the increase over the past twenty years has been in special education. According to their calculations, roughly 20%–35% of all K–12 expenditures today are directed to the 10% of the student population who qualify for special education.

Real increases in K–12 "regular" education expenditures during this time period have been modest and are the result of decreased pupil-to-teacher ratios and modest salary increases for teachers. The salary increases consistently follow increases in average household income in the U.S.

Compared to sixteen other industrialized countries, the analysts found that U.S. spending for "regular" education is about average when adjusted for purchasing-power parity, though how it ranks with specific countries is heavily dependent on the method of accounting.

International Comparisons

As was the case in other areas investigated, the analysts found little credible data regarding international comparisons. The most complete data are found in the International Assessment of Educational Progress (IAEP) report. The results of most international studies indicate that average U.S. student performance continues to be low in both math and science compared to other participants. However, the analysts discovered that many educators discount the value of an international assessment of 13-year-olds. Quite often the major differences in educational systems across countries render such single-point comparisons invalid. Additionally, many educators question the utility of the IAEP for instructional improvement. Reporting only the average performance of a large heterogeneous population provides little insight into the quality of educational services provided to various subpopulations (urban students, ethnic groups, etc.).

Other international indicators of education system performance reflect well on the U.S. Only Belgium and Finland exceed the U.S. in the percentage of 17-year-olds enrolled in school. The U.S. continues to lead the world in the percentage of young people obtaining bachelor's degrees and the percentage of degrees obtained by women and minorities. This is true for both technical and non-technical degrees.

The analysts' comparison of technical work forces also reflected well on the U.S. educational system. Although the U.S. lags behind other countries in certain specialties (such as industrial engineering), the overall technical degree attainment by the work force and population as a whole is unparalleled in the world.

Status of Educators

Our analysts found that direct, quantitative measures of teacher status are very difficult to obtain.

Indirect measures (e.g. interviews, opinion polls, etc.) indicate that the status of educators is low both within and outside the profession. The analysts have interviewed nearly 400 individuals to date, and low self esteem among teachers is a common theme. The analysts believe that the foundation for this low self-opinion and poor public perception is based on misinterpretations of simplistic data such as average SAT scores and international comparisons. This unfortunate cycle of low self-esteem followed by unfounded criticism from the public raises the specter for a downward spiral in future educational quality.

Work Force Skills

Of late, much of the education debate has focused on the system's inability to produce students with adequate "skills" for the work force. According to many, this is a primary cause for a perceived decline in U.S. international economic competitiveness.

However, the analysts' review of the limited research in business education and training practices found that very few companies point to inadequate academic preparation of new employees but rather focus on social "skills" such as punctuality and personal appearance. They found that much of the negative data circulating in New Mexico is anecdotal, and they suspect that the same is true on the national level. The business community is not uniformly responding to any forecasted "crisis" in work force skills. Nationally, nearly 90% of business training dollars go to college-educated employees (managers, professional sales, etc.) and skilled laborers, and very few business training dollars are dedicated to academic remediation. Finally, the analysts emphasize that much of the current "basic skills" training is directed at older workers and immigrants, not recent graduates.

Additionally, the analysts emphasize that even if the K–12 educational system markedly improves the "skills" of its students, this reform will not impact the workplace for 10–20 years. Thus, Sandia believes that improvements in K–12 pedagogy will only make a limited contribution, even in the long term, to improving the economic competitiveness of U.S. businesses.

Changing Demographics

Perhaps the dominant influence on future education requirements is the changing demographic makeup of the student body. Immigration was higher in the 1980s than any other decade this century except the 1920s. Coupled with slow native-born birth rates, this is creating significant changes in the demographic makeup of today's classroom. It is estimated that up to 5 million children of immigrants will be entering the K–12 education in the 1990s. More than 150 languages are represented in schools nationwide, and figures nearing this number occur in single large districts.

Also, the American family structure is changing, and teachers are encountering more children from single-parent homes and homes where both parents work. These demographic changes are real, persistent, and accelerating. They will drive change in education, and other social institutions as well, especially since we continue to accept the challenge to educate all of our youth. More and more, society is turning to the schools to be engineers of social change by becoming increasingly involved in meeting students' nonacademic needs.

Education Goals

With respect to leadership in educational improvement, the analysts found that the call for educational reform is truly widespread and includes many new voices. The president and governors have articulated goals for education by the year 2000. However, the analysts believe that some suggested initiatives to achieve these goals may be in conflict. They believe that implementation of several programs without proper coordination or a clear understanding of desired outcomes could result in little or no gain and possibly even set back the impressive gains of the past two decades.

The analysts believe that American society has not clearly articulated the changes required to meet future goals. In fact, they assert that forming a consensus on required changes may be the greatest challenge facing education today. However, the concept of a national consensus is itself debatable. The analysts point out that the U.S. educational system was built on the foundation of local control, state influence, and federal interest. The nearly sixteen thousand independent school districts nationwide attest to this concept. Forming a national consensus will be difficult and may even be undesirable.

Summary of Issues

Based on their work to date, the analysts believe the following issues are the greatest challenges to education in the 1990s:

- Forming a national consensus and finding leadership in educational improvement.
- Improving the performance of minority and urban students.
- Adjusting to demographic changes and immigration.
- Improving the status of elementary and secondary educators.
- Upgrading the quality of educational data.

The analysts also believe that the following impediments to educational improvement must be overcome:

- "System-wide crisis" rhetoric.
- Misuse of simplistic measures with dubious value.
- Preoccupation with the link to economic competitiveness.
- Focus on forecasted "shortfalls" in technical degrees.

Sandia National Laboratories is using these challenges as the foundation for its increasing involvement in education at local, state, and national levels.

REFERENCES

Achilles, C. M., and Lintz, M. N.: *Information and Communication Tools for Increasing Confidence in the Schools.* New Orleans, American Educational Research Association, ERIC, ED 376700.

Adelman, C.: *Devaluation, Diffusion, and the College Connection.* Unpublished paper for the National Commission on Excellence in Education. Washington, D.C., 1985.

Albritton, M.: *DeZavala Elementary School: A Committed Community. Case Study.* Department of Education, Trinity University, 1991.

Alves, M. J., and Willie, C. Y.: Controlled choice assignments: A new and more effective approach to school desegregation. *The Urban Review,* 1967, 1990.

American Association for the Advancement of Science. *Science for All Americans: A Project 2061 Report on Literacy Goals in Science.* Washington, D.C., American Association for the Advancement of Science, 1989.

American Educators in Private Practice. *Enterprising Educators as School Partners: A Manual for Educational Entrepreneurs and School Officials.* Waterstown, WI, American Educators in Private Practice, 1994.

American Enterprise Institute for Public Policy Research. *Women, Welfare, and Enterprise.* Washington, D.C., American Enterprise Institute for Public Policy Research, 1983.

Anderson, R. C., Elfrieda, H. H., Scott, J., and Wilkinson, I. A. G.: *Becoming a Nation of Readers: The Report of the Commission on Reading.* Washington, D.C., National Institute of Education, 1985.

Anderson, R. S.: *Japanese Education, Comparative Educational Systems.* Itasca, IL., F.E. Peacock Publishers, 1981, p. 264.

Astin, A.: *The American College Freshman, 1966-1981.* Commissioned paper, The National Commission on Excellence in Education, Washington, D.C., 1982.

August, R. L.: *Education in Japan: A Country Study.* Washington, D.C., Department of the Army, 1992, pp. 68–142.

Baba, M., Falkenburg, D., and Hill, D.: *The Cultural Dimensions of Technology — Enabled Corporate Transformation.* Detroit, Wayne State University, 1994.

Bain, H., Achilles, C.M., Dennis, B., Parks, M. and Hooper, R.: Class size reduction in Metro Nashville: A three year cohort study. *ERS Spectrum,* 6:30–36.

Banach, W.: Futurevisions. In Billings, J.C.: *Creating Schools for the Twenty-first Century.* Illinois Association of School Boards, Springfield, 1989, pp. 10–12.

Banach, W.: How to parent proof a school. *Education Digest,* December, 1980, p. 46.

Banerji, M.: *Longitudinal Effects of a Two Year Developmental Kindergarten Program on*

Academic Achievement. Unpublished paper, American Educational Research Association, Boston, 1983.

Barker, R. G., and Gump, P. V.: *Big School, Small School: High School Size and Student Behavior.* Palo Alto, CA., Stanford University Press, 1964.

Barnett, W. S., and Escobar, C. M.: The economics of early intervention, a review. *Review of Educational Research, 57:*387–414, 1977.

Benne, K. D.: Democratic ethics and social engineering. *Progressive Education, 7:*201–206, 1949.

Berlin, G., Sum, A., and Taggart, R.: Consequences of dropping out of school. In *Cutting Through.* Washington, D.C., U. S. Department of Education, Government Printing Office, 1984.

Berrueta-Clement, J. R., Scheveinhard, L. J., Barnett, W. S., Epstein, A. S., and Weikert, D. P.: *Changed Lives.* Ypsilanti, MI, High Scope, 1984.

Berry, W.: The futility of global thinking. *Harpers Magazine,* September, 1989, pp. 16–19.

Bettleheim, B.: Education and the reality principle. *American Educator, 12:*14, 1976.

Billings, J.: *New Horizons for Local School Leaders: Creating Schools for the Twenty-first Century.* Springfield, IL., Illinois Association of School Boards, 1989.

Birch, I., and Smart, D.: Economic rationalism and politics of education in Australia. In Mitchell, D. E., and Goertz, M. E.: *Education Politics for the New Century.* New York, Falmer, 1990.

Bliss, J. R., and Firestone, W. A.: *Rethinking Effective Schools: Research and Practice.* Englewood Cliffs, N.J., Prentice-Hall, 1991.

Block, P.: *The Empowered Manager.* San Francisco, Jossey-Bass, 1987.

Bok, D.: Ethics, the university and society. *Harvard Magazine,* May–June, 1988, p. 22.

Bourdieu, P., and Passeron, J.: *The Inheritors: French Students and Their Relation to Culture.* Chicago, University of Chicago Press, 1964.

Bourdieu, P., and Passeron, J.: Reproduction in Education, Society, and Culture. R. Nice, Trans. London, Sage, 1977.

Boyd, W. L., and Stuart, D.: *Educational Policy in Australia and America: Comparative Perspectives.* London, Falmer, 1987.

Boyer, E.: Education today and tomorrow: What we need to do. *PTA Today.* October, 1986, pp. 10–12.

Boyer, R., and Savageau, D.: *Places Rated Almanac: Your Guide to Finding the Best Places to Live in America.* Chicago, Rand McNally, 1985, p. 3.

Bracey, G. W.: Test data distorted. *Chicago Tribune,* March 8, 1994, p. B6.

Bracey, G. W.: The Third Bracey Report. *Phi Delta Kappan,* October, 1993, p. 16.

Bradley, A.: New York City to create small theme-oriented high school. *Education Week.* April 1, 1992, p. 5.

Bremer, N.: First grade achievement under different plans of grouping. *Elementary English, 35:*324–326, 1958.

Bridge, R. G., and Blackman, J.: A study of alternatives in American education. In Vol. 4: *Family Choice in Schooling* (Report No. R-217014-NIE). Santa Monica, CA, Rand Corporation, 1978.

Brookover, W.: *School Social Systems and Student Achievement: Schools Can Make a Difference.* New York, Praeger, 1979.

Brown v. Board of Education. State of Kansas. 1954.

Burnet, J.: *Greek Philosophy, Thales to Plato.* London, Reeves, 1914.

Burnham, W.: *Critical Elections and the Mainstreams of American Politics.* New York, W. W. Norton, 1970.

Butler, O. B.: Some doubts on school vouchers. *The New York Times,* July 5, 1991, p. A11.

Butts, R. F., and Cremin, L.: *A History of Education in American Culture.* New York, Henry Holt & Co., 1953, p. 433.

Bybee, R.: *Science and Technology Education, the Elementary Years: Frameworks for Curriculum and Instruction.* Andover, MA, National Education, 1989.

Cahen, L. S., Filby, N., McCutcheon, G., and Kyle, D.: *Class Size and Instruction.* New York, Longman, 1983.

Callahan, R. E.: *Education and the Cult of Efficiency.* Chicago: Knopf, 1960, p. 240.

Carnegie Council on Adolescent Development. *Turning Points: Preparing Youth for the 21st Century.* New York, Carnegie Foundation, 1989.

Carnegie Council on Community Service. *Working Together.* New York, Carnegie Foundation, 1987.

Carnegie Forum on Education and the Economy, Task Force on Teaching as a Profession. *A Nation Prepared: Teachers for the 21st Century.* New York, Carnegie Foundation, 1986.

Carroll, J. B.: The national assessments in reading: Are we misreading the findings? *Phi Delta Kappan,* June, 1987, pp. 424–428.

Chase, A.: *The Legacy of Malthus.* New York, Alfred A. Knopf, 1947.

Choice in education, Media sheet, U.S. Chamber of Commerce, Washington, D.C., 1991, p. 3.

Chubb, J. E., and Moe, T. M.: *Politics Markets and America's Schools.* Brookings Institution, Washington, D. C., 1990.

Cohen, D., and Spillane, J.: Policy and practice: The relations between governance and instruction. In Grant, G.: *Review of Research in Education.* American Education Research Association, Washington, D.C., AERA, 1988, pp. 3–49.

Coleman, J. S.: *Equality of Educational Opportunity.* Washington, D.C., M.S. Office of Education, 1966.

Coleman, J. S., Hoffer, T., and Kilgore, S.: *High School Achievement: Public, Catholic, and Private School Compared.* New York: Basic Books, 1982.

Coleman, J. S., and Hoffer, T.: Public and Private High Schools: *The Impact on Communities.* New York, Basic Books, 1987.

Coleman, W.: *Educating Americans for the 21st Century,* National Science Board, Commission on Pre-College Education in Mathematics, Science and Technology. Washington, D.C., Government Printing Office, 1983.

Coles, R.: *The Moral Life of Children.* Boston, The Atlantic Monthly Press, 1986.

Comer, J.: Educating poor minority children. *Scientific American, 259:*42–48, 1988.

Comer, J. P.: *Academic and Affective Gains from the School Development Program.* 1986, ERIC, ED 274750.

Comer, J. P.: *Stress, distress and educational outcomes: Toward ensuring the emotional well-being of our children.* Transcripts of invitational roundtable, October 18, 1988. Philadelphia, School District of Philadelphia.

Counts, G. S.: *Education and American Education.* New York, Teachers College Press, 1952.

Counts, G. S.: *The American Road to Culture.* New York, John Day, 1930.

Cremin, L.: *American Education: The Colonial Experience, 1607–1783.* New York, Harper and Row, 1970, p. 152.

Cross, K. P.: *Societal Imperatives: Need for an Educational Democracy.* Unpublished paper, National Conference on Teaching and Excellence, Austin, TX, 1984.

Cuban, L.: Reforming again, again, and again. *Educational Research, 19:*107, 1990.

Cummins, J.: Empowering minority students: A framework for intervention. *Harborg Educational Review, 56:*18–36, 1986.

Dahl, R. A.: *Who Governs.* New Haven, Yale University Press, 1961.

Damon, W.: *The Moral Child.* New York, The Free Press, 1988.

Day, J. D., Cordon, L. A., and Kerwin, M. L.: Informal instruction and development of cognitive skills: A review and critique of research. In McCormick, C. B., Miller, G. E., and Pressley, M.: *Cognitive Strategy Research: From Basic Research to Educational Aspirations.* New York, Springer Verlag, 1989.

Deci, E. L., and Ryan, R. M.: *Intrinsic Motivation and Self Determination in Human Behavior.* New York, Plenum Press, 1985.

Dewey, J.: *Human Nature and Conduct.* Troy, MO, Holt, Rinehart and Winston, 1922.

Dewey, J.: The need for a philosophy of education. *The New Era in the Home and School, 15:*211–41, 1934.

Dictionary of Occupational Titles. Washington, D.C., Government Printing Office. 1985.

Dominguez, A.: Schools return to neglected subject-values. *Detroit News,* January 27, 1994, p. B6.

Doyle, D., and Bernbach, I.: Youthful worries. *Wall Street Journal,* December 4, 1985, p. 33.

Drucker, P.: *Management: Tasks, Responsibilities, Practices.* New York, The Free Press, 1984.

Durkheim, E.: *Moral Education.* New York, The Free Press, 1973.

Dyer, P.: Reading recovery: A cost-effectiveness and educational outcomes analysis. *ERS Spectrum, 10:*10–19, 1992.

Eastman, G.: *Family Involvement in Education.* 1988, ERIC, ED 316802.

Edmonds, R. R.: Effective schools for the urban poor. *Education Leadership, 37:*15–27, 1972.

Elam, S. M., Rose, L. C., & Gallup, A. M.: The 25th Annual Phi Delta Kappa/Gallup Poll of the public's attitudes toward the public schools. *Phi Delta Kappan,* September, 1993, pp. 137–140.

Elam, S. M., Rose, L. C., & Gallup, A. M.: The 26th Annual Phi Delta Kappa/Gallup Poll of the public's attitudes toward the public schools. *Phi Delta Kappan,* September, 1994, pp. 41–56.

Ellson, D. G., Barber, L., Engle, T. L., and Kempwerth, L.: Programmed tutoring: A teaching aid and a research tool. *Reading Research Quarterly, 1:*77–127, 1965.

Elmore, R. F.: *Restructuring Schools.* San Francisco, Jossey-Bass, 1990.

Elmore, R. F.: *Choice in Public Education.* Santa Monica, CA, Rand Corporation, 1986. Report No. JNE-01.

Entwistle, D., and Hayduk, L.: Academic expectations and the school achievement of young children. *Sociology of Education, 54:*34–50, 1981.

Epstein, J. L., and Dauber, S. L.: *Teacher Attitude and Practices of Parent Involvement in Inner-City Elementary and Middle Schools.* Baltimore, Center for Research on Elementary and Middle Schools, the Johns Hopkins University, 1989. Report No. 32.

Epstein, J. L.: Effective schools or effective students: Dealing with diversity. In Haskins, R., and MacRae, D.: *Policies for America's Public Schools.* Norwood, NJ, Ablex, 1988.

Erickson, D. A.: Choice and private schools: Dynamics of supply and demand. In Levy, D. C.: *Private Education: Studies in Choice and Public Policy.* New York, Oxford University Press, 1986, pp. 82–109.

Esternacht, G. J.: Characteristics distinguishing vocational education students from general academic students. *Multivariate Behavior Research, 11:*477–490, 1982.

Etzioni, A.: *The Spirit of Community.* New York, Crown, 1993.

Falbo, T.: *The Single Child Family.* New York, Guilford Press, 1984.

Farr, B., Quilling, M., Bessel, R., and Johnson, W.: *Evaluation of Prime Time: 1986-87 Final Report.* Indianapolis, Advanced Technology, 1987.

Federal Bureau of Investigation. *Age-Specific Arrest Rates and Race-Specific Arrest Rates for Selected Offenses, 1965-88.* Washington, D.C., Federal Bureau of Investigation, 1990.

Florio, R. S.: Social organization of classes and schools. In Reynolds, M. C.: *Knowledge Base for the Beginning Teacher.* New York, Pergamon, 1989, pp. 163–172.

Fordham, S.: Racelessness as a factor in black students' school success: Pragmatic strategy or psychic victory? *Harvard Educational Review, 58:*54–58, 1986.

Fuerst, J. S., and Fuerst, O.: *Chicago Experience With Early Childhood Programs: The Special Case of the Child Parent Center Programs.* Unpublished manuscript, Loyola University, Chicago, 1991.

Fuerst, J. S.: Why Head Start is not enough. *Newsweek,* April, 1992, p. 51.

Fullan, M., Bennett, B., and Rolheiser-Bennett, C.: Linking classroom and school improvements. *Educational Leadership, 47:*13–19, 1991.

Fullan, M., and Stiegebauer, S.: *The New Meaning of Educational Change.* New York, Teachers College Press, 1975.

Garber, H. L.: *The Milwaukee Project: Preventing Mental Retardation in Children at Risk.* Washington, D.C., American Association of Mental Retardation, 1989.

Gardner, D. P.: *A Nation at Risk: The Imperative for Educational Reform,* The National Commission on Excellence in Education, Washington, D.C., Government Printing Office, 1983.

Gardner, J.: *Excellence.* New York, Norton, 1984.

Giffin, M. E., and Felsenthal, C. A.: *A Cry for Help.* Garden City, NY, Doubleday, 1983.

Giraffe Gazette, Fall, 1987, p. 3.

Giraffe Gazette, Fall, 1988, p. 2.

Goldhammer, K., and Taylor, R.: *Career Education, Perspective and Promise.* New York, Charles Merrill, 1972.

Good, H. G.: *A History of Western Education.* New York, MacMillan, 1960, p. 421.

Good, T. L.: Classroom research: A decade of progress. *Educational Psychologist,* *3:*127–44, 1983.

Goodlad, J.: *A Place Called School: Prospects for the Future.* New York: McGraw-Hill, 1984.

Goodlad, J., and Klein, M.: *Behind the Classroom Door.* Worthington, Ohio, Charles A. Jones, 1970, p. 36.

Goodlad, J.: Studying the education of educators: From conception to findings. *Phi Delta Kappan,* September, 1990, pp. 689–701.

Goodlad, J.: Understanding schools is basic to improving them. *National Forum of Applied Educational Research Journal,* March, 1988.

Goodlad, J., and Anderson, R. H.: *The Non-Graded Elementary School.* New York, Harcourt and Brace, 1963.

Gordon, E. W., and Song, L. D.: Variations in the experience of resilience. In Wang, M., and Gordon, E. W.: *Educational Resilience in Inner-City America: Challenges and Prospects.* Hillsdale, N.J., Erlbaum, 1994.

Gould, S.: *The Mismeasure of Man.* New York, Norton, 1981.

Grant, G.: Schools that make an imprint: Creating a strong positive ethos. In Bunzel, J. H.: *The Case for Standards and Values.* New York, Oxford University Press, 1985.

Green, T.: The formation of conscience in an age of technology. *American Journal of Education,* November, 1985, pp. 1–38.

Greenleaf, R. K.: *Servant Leadership.* New York, Paulist Press, 1977.

Gregory, T. R., and Smith, G. R.: *High Schools as Communities: The Small School Reconsidered.* Bloomington, IN. Phi Delta Kappa Educational Foundation, 1987.

Gross, N., Gianquinta, J., and Bernstein, M.: *Implementing Organizational Innovations: Sociological Analysis of Planned Educational Change.* New York, Basic Books, 1971.

Grubb, N.: *School to Work.* Washington, D.C., The National Governance Association, 1994.

Gutierrez, R., and Slavin, R.: Achievement effects of the non-graded elementary school: A best evidence synthesis. *Review of Educational Research, 62:*333–376, 1992.

Hagerty, R., and Howard, T.: *How to Make Federal Mandatory Special Education Work for You.* Springfield, Charles C Thomas, 1978, pp. 29–81.

Hampel, J.: *The Administrator as Servant: A Model for Leadership Development.* Unpublished manuscript, Department of Education, San Diego State University, 1988.

Handbook for Developing Public Confidence in Schools. Bloomington, IN, Phi Delta Kappa Commission on Developing Confidence in Schools, 1988.

Harbaugh, M.: Small schools with big ideas. *Instructor and Teacher.* September 1985, pp. 20–22.

Harste, J. C.: *New Policy Guidelines for Reading: Connecting Research and Practice.* Urbana, IL, National Council of Teachers of English, 1989.

Hassett, G.: But that would be wrong. *Psychology Today,* November, 1981, pp. 34–50.

Haxby, B., and Madden, N. A.: *Success for All Family Support Manual.* Baltimore, Johns Hopkins University, 1991.

Heath, D. D.: *School Size: The Effect on Adjustment and Social Contact of High School Seniors.* Unpublished doctoral dissertation. University of Pennsylvania, 1971.

Heath, D. H.: *Humanizing Schools: New Decisions.* Rochelle, Park, NJ, Hayden Press, 1971.

Heath, D. H.: *Schools of Hope.* San Francisco, Jossey-Bass Publishers, 1994.

Hechinger, F. M.: School-college collaboration—an essential to improved public education. *NASSP Bulletin,* October, 1984, pp. 66–69.

Henderson, A. B.: Making teamwork work. *Detroit News,* September 5, 1994, p. C1–2.

Herzberg, F.: *Work and the Nature of Man.* New York, World, 1966.

Hicks, J.S.: *Early Identificiation Program.* 1976. ERIC, ED 141 479.

Hill, P. T., Foster, G. E., and Gendler, T.: *High Schools with Character.* Santa Monica, CA, The Rand Corporation, 1990.

Hill, P. T., Wise, A. E., and Shapiro, L.: *Educational Progress: Cities Mobilize to Improve Their Schools.* Santa Monica, CA, Center for the Study of the Teaching Profession, Rand Corporation, 1989.

Hillocks, G.: *Research on Written Composition.* Urbana, IL, National Council of Teachers of English, 1989.

Hodgkinson, H. L.: The right schools for the right kids. *Educational Leadership, 45:*10–14, 1990.

Hoffer, T. B., and Coleman, J. S.: Changing families and communities: Implications for schools. In Mitchel, B., and Cunningham, L. L.: *Educational Leadership and Changing Contexts of Families, Communities, and Schools.* Eighty-ninth Yearbook of the National Society for the Study of Education, Part II. Chicago, University of Chicago Press, 1990.

Honig, B.: *Last Chance for Our Children.* Reading, MA, Addison-Wesley, 1991, p. 95.

Hudson, L.: Commentary: Singularity of talent. In Messick, S.: *Individuality in Learning: Implications of Cognitive Styles and Creativity for Human Development.* San Francisco, Jossey-Bass, 1976.

Iwama, H. F.: Japan's group orientation in secondary schools. In Shields, J. J. Jr.: *Japanese Schooling.* University Park, PA, The Pennsylvania State University Press, 1989, pp. 76–81.

Iannaccone, L.: Callahan's contributions in the context of American realignment politics. In Eaton, W. E.: *Shaping the Superintendency.* New York, Teachers College Press, 1990.

Imamura, A. E.: Interdependence of family and education: Reactions of Japanese to the school system. In Shields, J. J. Jr.: *Japanese Schooling.* University Park, PA, The Pennsylvania State University Press, 1989, p. 17.

James, E.: Public subsidies for private and public education: The Dutch case. In Levy, D. C.: *Private Education: Studies of Choice and Public Policy.* New York, Oxford University Press, 1986, pp. 113–137.

James, L. R., and Jones, A. P.: Organizational climate: A review theory and research. *Psychological Bulletin, 2:*1096–1112, 1974.

Jellison, J.: The ethics of American youth. *Cortland Standard,* November 5, 1988, p. 1.

Jencks, C., Smith, M., Aciano, H., Bane, M. J., Cohen, D., Gentis, H., Heyns, B., and Michelson, S.: *Inequality: A Reassessment of the Effect of Family and Schooling in America.* New York, Basic Books, 1972.

Johnson, C., and Sum, A.: *Declining Earnings of Young Men: Their Relation to Poverty, Teen Pregnancy, and Family Formation.* Washington, D.C., Children's Defense Fund, Adolescent Pregnancy Prevention Clearinghouse, 1987.

Johnson, L. M., and Garcia-Quintana, R. A.: *South Carolina First Grade Pilot Project, 1976–77: The Effects of Class Size on Reading and Mathematics Achievement.* Columbus, South Carolina, South Carolina Department of Education, 1978.

Johnson, D. W., Johnson, R. T., Holubic, E., and Roy, P.: *Circles of Learning: Cooperation in the Classroom.* Alexandria, VA, Association for Supervision and Curriculum Development, 1984.

Karweit, N.: *Effective Kindergarten Programs and Practices for Students at Risk.* Boston, Allyn and Bacon, 1989.

Karweit, N. L., Coleman, M. A., Waclawiw, I., and Petza, R.: *Story Telling and Retelling: Teachers Manual.* Baltimore, Johns Hopkins University, 1990.

Katz, M. B.: *The Irony of Early School Reform: Educational Innovation in Mid-Nineteenth Century Massachusetts.* Cambridge, MA, Harvard University Press, 1968.

Kearns, D. T., and Doyle, D. P.: *Winning the Brain Race: A Bold Plan to Make Our Schools Competitive.* San Francisco, Institute for Contemporary Studies, 1988.

Kelly, F. J., Veldman, D. J., and McGuire, C.: Multiple discriminant prediction of delinquency and school dropouts. *Educational and Psychological Measurement, 24:*535–544, 1964.

Kennedy, M. M., Berman, B. E., and Demaline, R. E.: *The Effectiveness of Chapter I Services.* Washington, D.C., Office of Education Research and Improvement, 1986.

Kidder, R. M.: Public concern for ethics rises. *The Christian Science Monitor,* January 2, 1990, p. 13.

Kirk, R.: *Beyond the Dreams of Avarice.* Chicago, Henry Regnery Co., 1956.

Kirk, R.: *The Roots of American Order.* LaSalle, IL, Open Court, 1974.

Kirst, M. W., McLaughlin, M., and Massell, D.: Rethinking policy for children: Implications for educational administration. In Mitchel, B., and Cunningham, L. L.: *Educational Leadership and Changing Contexts of Families and Communities and Schools.* Eighty-ninth Yearbook of the National Society for the Study of Education, Part II. Chicago, University of Chicago Press, 1990.

Kohler, M. C.: Youth participation, the key to responsibility. *Phi Delta Kappan,* February, 1981, pp. 70–72.

Kolderie, T.: Charter schools: The states withdraw the "exclusive." In *A Manual for Educator Entrepreneurs and School Officials.* Watertown, WI, American Association of Educators in Private Practice, 1994.

Kolderie, T.: *Competition as a Strategy for Public School Improvement.* Unpublished memo, Humphrey Institute, University of Minnesota, Minneapolis, 1985.

Kouzes, J., and Posner, B.: *The Leadership Challenge.* San Francisco, Jossey-Bass, 1985.

Kyle, R., and Allen, E. J. Jr.: *Parental Choice of Education: A Literature Review of Significant Research.* Washington, D.C., E. H. White, 1982.

Kyle, R. M. J.: *Reaching for Excellence: An Effective School Sourcebook.* Washington, D.C., National Institute of Education, 1985.

Laing, P.: *Change Process.* Unpublished paper, Administrative Workshop, Durham Board of Education, Oshawa, Ontario, 1992.

Lazar, I., and Darlington, R.: Lasting effects of early education. *Monograph of the Society for Research in Child Development, 47:*2–3, 1982.

Levin, H. M.: *Accelerated Schools for At-Risk Students.* New Brunswick, Center for Policy Research in Education, 1988.

Levine, D., and Havighurst, R. J.: Social systems of a metropolitan area. In Havighurst, R. J.: *Metropolitanism: Its Challenge to Education.* Sixty-seventh Yearbook of the National Society for the Study of Education. Chicago, University of Chicago Press, 1968, pp. 37–70.

Levine, D. U., Levine, R. F., and Eubanks, E. E.: Successful implementation of instruction at inner-city schools. In Lane, J. J., and Walberg, H. J.: *Effective Schools Leadership: Policy and Process.* Berkeley, CA, McCutcham, pp. 65–88.

Lewis, A.: Another generation lost? *Phi Delta Kappan,* July, 1986, pp. 555–556.

Lickona, T.: *Educating for Character.* New York, Bantam, 1991.

Lieberman, A.: Expanding the leadership team. *Educational Leadership,* February, 1988.

Lieberman, A., and Miller, L.: Restructuring schools: What matters and what works. *Phi Delta Kappan,* June, 1990.

Lieberman, A., and Miller, L.: Restructuring schools: What matters and what works. *Phi Delta Kappan,* June, 1990, p. 260.

Lieberman, M.: *Public Education: An Autopsy.* Cambridge, Harvard University Press, 1993.

Little, J. W.: Teachers as colleagues. In Richardson, K.: *Educator's Handbook: A Research Perspective.* White Plains, NY, Longman, 1987.

Lloyd, D. N.: Prediction of school failure from third grade data. *Educational and Psychological Measurement, 38:*1193–1200, 1978.

London, P.: Character education and clinical intervention: A paradigm shift for U.S. schools. *Phi Delta Kappan,* May, 1987, pp. 667–673.

Lortie, D.: *School Teacher: A Sociological Study.* Chicago, University of Chicago Press, 1975.

Louis, K. S., and Van Veizen, B. A. M.: A look at choice in the Netherlands. *Educational Leadership, 48:*66–72, 1990–1991.

Madden, N.A., Slavin, R. E., Karweit, N. L., and Livermon, B. J.: Restructuring the urban elementary school. *Educational Leadership, 46:*14–18, 1989.

Maehr, M. L.: Meaning and motivation: Toward a theory of personal investment. In Ames, C., and Ames, K.: *Research on Motivation in Education,* Vol. 1, *Student Motivation.* San Diego, CA: Academic Press, 1984.

Maehr, M. L., Midgley, C., and Urdan, T.: School leader as a motivator. *Education Administration Quarterly, 28:*410–429, 1992.

Maeroff, G. I.: Building Teams to Rebuild Schools. *Phi Delta Kappan.* March, 1993, p. 517.

Manning, J. B.: *Roles and Activities of Special Education Elementary Support Team Members: Perceptions of Philadelphia School Principals.* Doctoral dissertation, Temple University, 1987.

Masten, A.: Resilience in individual development: Successful adaptation despite risk and adversity. In Wang, M., and Gordon, E.: *Educational Resilience in Inner-City America: Challenges and Prospects.* Hillsdale, N.J., Erlbaum, 1994.

McAdams, R. P.: *Lessons from Abroad.* Lancaster, PA, Technomic Publishing Co., Inc., 1993, p. 214.

McCollum v. Board of Education. State of Illinois. 1948.

Mead, M.: *Coming of Age in Samoa.* New York, Bantam, 1952.

Moline, J.: Classical ideas about moral education. In Wynn, E.: *Character Policy: An Emerging Issue.* Lanham, MD, University Press of America, 1982.

Moore, D.: *The English Educational System.* Unpublished paper, Regional and Community College, An International Symposium, Negev, Israel, 1984.

Morrow, L.: Children. *Time,* August 8, 1988, pp. 3–8.

Moses, S.: Schools' rough seas due to social factors. *APA Monitor,* July, 1992, pp. 40–41.

Mullis, I. V. S., and Jenkins, L. B.: *The Reading Report Card, 1971-78.* Washington, D.C., U.S. Department of Education, 1990.

Murphy, J.: *Restructuring Schools.* New York, Teachers College Press, 1991.

Nash, P.: History and Education: *The Education Uses of the Past.* New York, Random House, 1970, pp. 127–131.

National Center for Education Statistics. *Two Years After High School: A Capsule Description of 1980 Seniors. High School and Beyond:* A National Longitudinal Study for the 1980's. National Center for Education Statistics. Washington, D.C., Government Printing Office. 1984.

National Center for Health Statistics, 1988.

National Commission on Excellence in Education. *A Nation at Risk: The Imperative for Educational Reform.* Washington, D.C., Government Printing Office, 1983.

National Commission on the Social Studies. *The Tool Kit.* Washington, D.C., National Council for the Social Studies, 1985.

National Council of Teachers of Mathematics, Commission on Standards for School Mathematics. *Curriculum and Evaluation Standards for School Mathematics.* Reston, VA, National Council of Teachers of Mathematics, 1989.

National Governors Association. *Report on Education: A Time for Results.* Washington, D.C., Carnegie Forum on Education and the Economy, 1987.

National School Public Relations Association. *School Public Relations: The Complete Book.* Arlington, VA, 1986.

National Science Teachers Association. *Position Statements on Preschool and Elementary Level Science Education for Middle and Junior High Students.* Washington, D.C., National Science Teachers Association, 1985.

Nelson, F. H.: *International Comparisons of Public Spending on Education.* Washington, D.C., American Federation of Teachers, 1991, pp. 33–37.

Nettles, S. M.: Community involvement and disadvantaged students: A review. *Review of Educational Research, 61:*379–406, 1991.

Newman, M.: Finance system for New Jersey schools is struck down. *Education Week,* March 3, 1990, p. 1.

Newsweek. America's Unsung Heroes. July 10, 1989, pp. 54–56.

Newsweek. So long wonder years. June 26, 1992, p. 8.

Norman, C., and Zigmond, N.: Characteristics of children labeled and served as learning disabled in school systems affiliated with child service and demonstration centers. *Journal of Learning Disabilities, 13:*542–547, 1980.

Novak, M.: Crime and character. *This World,* Spring-Summer, 1986, p. 1.

Oakes, J.: *Keeping Track: How Schools Structure Inequality.* New Haven, Yale University Press, 1985.

Oakley, H. T.: *Parental Choice of Elementary Schooling Alternatives in an Affluent Suburban Community.* Doctoral dissertation, Ohio State University, 1985.

Ogbu, J. U.: Class stratification, racial stratification, and schooling. In Weiss, L.: *Class, Race and Gender in American Education.* Albany, NY, State University of New York Press, 1988a.

Ogbu, J. U.: Diversity and equity in public education. In Haskins, R., and MacRae, D.: *Policies for America's Public Schools.* Norwood, NJ, Ablex, 1988b.

Ogbu, J. U.: Origins of human competance: A culture ecological perspective. *Child Development, 52:*413–429, 1981.

Ogbu, J. U.: The individual in collective adaptation: A framewood for focusing on academic underperformance and dropping out among involuntary minorities. In Weis, L., Farrar, E., and Petrie, H. G.: *Dropouts from School: Issues Dilemmas, and Solutions.* Albany, NY, State University of New York Press, 1981.

Olson, L.: Gallup poll finds doubts goals can be met by 2000. *Education Week,* September 5, 1990, p. 12.

Ota, H.: Political teacher unionism in Japan. In Shields, J. J. Jr.: *Japanese Schooling.* University Park, PA, The Pennsylvania State University Press, 1989, pp. 243–245.

Painton, P.: Shrugging off the homeless. *Time,* April 16, 1990, pp. 14–16.

Parnell, D.: *The Neglected Majority.* Washington, D.C., The Community College Press, 1985.

Pascale, P.: *Managing on the Edge.* New York, Touchstone, 1990.

Patterson, G. R., and Dision, T. J.: Contributions of families and peers to delinquency. *Criminology, 23:*63–69, 1985.

Paulu, N.: *Improving Schools and Empowering Parents: Choice in America Education.* Washington, D.C.: Government Printing Office, 1989.

Peng, S. S., Fetters, W. B., and Kolstad, A. J.: *A Capsule Description of High School Students: High School and Beyond, A National Longitudinal Study for the 1980s.* National Center for Education Statistics. Washington, D.C., Government Printing Office, 1983.

Pinnel, G. S.: Reading recovery: Helping at-risk children learn to read. *Elementary School Journal, 90:*161–182, 1989.

Plank, D. N.: The eyes of Texas: Rhetoric, reality, and school reform. *Politics of Education Bulletin, 13:*2, 1986.

Phoenix Select Committee on Educational Reform. *Better Schools for Arizona.* Phoenix, Arizona Business Leaders for Education, 1990.

Powell, A. G., Farrar, E., and Cohen, D. K.: *The Shopping Mall Hill School: Winners and Losers in the Educational Marketplace.* Boston, Houghton, Mifflin, 1985.

Proctor, R. E.: *Education's Great Amnesia: Reconsidering the Humanities from Petrarch to Freud.* Bloomington, Indiana University Press, 1988.

Psychology Today. Survey of Sexual Behavior, April, 1969, pp. 28–33.

Psychology Today. Survey of Sexual Behavior, May, 1981, pp. 34–50.

Ramey, C. T., and Campbell, F. A.: Preventive education for high-risk children: Cognitive consequences of the Carolina Abecedian Project. *American Journal of Mental Deficiency, 88:*515–523, 1984.

Rasell, M. E., and Mishel, L.: *How U.S. Spending on Grades K-12 Lags Behind Other Industrial Nations.* Washington, D.C., Economic Policy Institute, 1990, pp. 1–5.

Rath, L., Harmon, M., and Simon, S.: *Values and Teaching.* Columbus, Merrill, 1966.

Readers' Guide to Periodical Literature. New York, H. W. Wilson, 1978, 1993.

Roseholtz, S.: *Teachers' Workplace: The Social Organization of Schools.* New York, Longman, 1989.

Rhine, W. R.: *Making School More Effective: New Directions from Follow Through.* New York, Academic Press.

Rosenshine, B., and Meister, C.: The use of scaffolds for teaching higher-level cognitive strategies. *Educational Leadership, 49:*26–33, 1992.

Rubinger, R.: *Continuity and Change in Mid-Nineteenth Century Japanese Education.* University Park, PA, The Pennsylvania State University Press, 1989, pp. 224–232.

Ryan, K., and Wynne, E.: *Reclaiming Our Schools: A Handbook on Teaching Character, Academics and Discipline.* Columbus, Merrill, 1994.

Sarason, S.: *The Culture of the School and the Problem of Change.* Boston, Allyn and Bacon, 1982.

Sarason, S. B.: *The Culture of the School and the Problem of Change.* Boston, Allyn and Bacon, 1982.

Sato, N., and McLaughlin, M. W.: Context matters: Teaching in Japan and the United States. *Phi Delta Kappan,* May, 1992, pp. 362–363.

Sawhill, I. V.: Anti-poverty strategies for the next decade. In *Work and Welfare: The Case for New Directions in National Policy.* Washington, D.C., Center for National Policy, 1987.

Sawhill, I. V.: *Poverty and the Underclass, An American Agenda: Report to the Forty-First President of the United States.* Washington, D.C., Government Printing Office, 1988, pp. 27–28.

Schattschneider, E.: *The Semi-Sovereign People.* New York, Teachers College Press, 1952.

Schuetz, P.: *The Instructional Effectiveness of Classroom Aides.* Pittsburgh, University of Pittsburgh, Learning Research and Development Center, 1980.

Schmidt, P.: School building inventory finds 1 in 8 inadequate. *Education Week.* November 27, 1991, p. 1.

Schmuck, R., and Schmuck, P.: *Group Processes in the Classroom.* Dubuque, IA, William C. Prawn, 1988.

Schmuck, R. A., and Runkel, P. J.: *The Handbook of Organization Development in Schools.* Palo Alto, CA, Mayfield, 1985.

Schrage, M.: *Shared Minds.* New York, Random House, 1990.

Schorr, L. B., and Schorr, D.: *Within Our Reach: Breaking the Cycle of Disadvantage.* New York, Anchor, 1989.

Select Committee on Educational Reform. *Better Schools for Arizona.* Phoenix, Select Committee on Educational Reform, 1990, p. 15.

Senge, P. M.: *The Leader's New Work: Building a Learning Organization.* New York, Doubleday, 1990.

Sharon, S., and Sharon, Y.: Changing instructional methods in the culture of the school. In Wyner, N.: *Current Perspectives on School Culture.* Cambridge, MA: Brookline Books, 1990.

Shields, J. J. Jr., ed.: *Japanese Schooling: Patterns of Socialization, Equality and Political Control.* University Park, PA, The Pennsylvania State University Press, 1989, p. 102.

Shimhahara, N. K.: Japanese educational reforms in the 1980s: A political commitment. In Shields, J. J. Jr.: *Japanese Schooling.* University Park, PA, The Pennsylvania State University Press, 1989.

Silver, A. A., and Hagin, R. H.: *Disorders of Learning in Childhood.* New York, Wiley, 1990.

Singleton, J.: Gamburu: A Japanese cultural theory of learning. In Shields, J. J. Jr.: *Japanese Schooling.* University Park, PA, The Pennsylvania State University Press, 1989.

Slavin, R. E.: A theory of school and classroom organization. *Educational Psychologist, 22,* 89–108, 1987.

Slavin, R. E., Karweit, N. L., and Madden, N. A.: *Effective Programs for Students of Risk.* Boston, Allyn and Bacon, 1989.

Slavin, R. E., Madden, N. A., Karweit, N. L., Dolan, L., and Wasik, B. A.: *Success for All: A Relentless Approach to Prevention and Early Intervention in Elementary Schools.* Arlington, VA, Educational Research Service, 1992.

Slavin, R. E.: Reading effects of IBM's Writing to Read program: A review of the evaluations. *Educational Evaluation and Policy Analysis, 13:*1–11, 1991.

Slavin, R. E., Schlomos, S., Spencer, K., Webb, C., and Schmuck, R.: *Learning to Cooperate, Cooperating to Learn.* New York, Plenum Press, 1985.

Smith, L., and Keith, P.: *Anatomy of an Educational Innovation: An Organizational Analysis of an Elementary School.* New York, Wiley, 1971, p. 289.

Snider, W.: Personalizing high schools. *Education Week,* March 1, 1989, pp. 6–7.

Spring, J.: *American Education: An Introduction to Social and Political Aspects.* New York, Longman, 1989, p. 28.

Spring, J.: *Education and the Rise of the Corporate State.* Boston, Beacon Press, 1972.

Spring, J.: *The American School, 1642–1985.* New York, Longman, 1986.

Starratt, R. J.: *Sowing Seeds of Faith and Justice.* Washington, D.C., Jesuit Secondary Education Association, 1989, p. 18.

Stedman, L. C.: A new look at effective schools literature. *Urban Education. 20:*295–326, 1985.

Stevenson, H. W.: The Asian advantage, the case of mathematics. In Shields, J. J. Jr.: *Japanese Schooling.* University Park, PA, The Pennsylvania State University Press, 1989, pp. 94–95.

Stigler, J. W., and Stevenson, H. W.: How Asian teachers polish each lesson to perfection. *American Educator, 15:*1, 1991.

Strom, M. S.: Facing history and ourselves: Holocaust and human behavior. In Mosher, R.: *Moral Education: A First Generation of Research and Development.* New York, Praeger, 1980.

Taylor, C. W., and Ellison, R. L.: Biographical predicators of scientific performance. *Science, 155:*1075–1080, March 3, 1967.

Taylor, F. W.: *Scientific Management.* New York, Harper and Row, 1947.

Testa, M., Astone, N. M., Krogh, M., and Neckerman, K. M.: Employment and marriage among inner-city fathers. In *Annals of the Academy of Political and Social Science, 501:*79–91, 1989.

Tocqueville, A. de: *Democracy in America.* New York, Knopf, 1945, p. 132.

Tom, A. R.: *Teaching as a Moral Craft.* White PLains, NY, Longman, 1984.

Touflexis, A.: Our violent kids. *Times,* June 12, 1989, p. 55.

Tyack, D., and Hansot, E.: *Managers of Virtue: Public Leadership in America, 1820-1980.* New York, Basic Books, 1982.

U.S. Constitution, Amendment I.

U.S. Department of Education. *What Works: Research About Teaching and Learning.* Pueblo, CO, U.S. Department of Education, Consumer Information Center, 1986.

U.S. General Accounting Office. *Labor Market Problems of Teenagers Result Largely from Doing Poorly in School.* Washington, D.C., U.S. Government Printing Office, 1982.

U.S. News and World Report. New gadgets give TV a run for its money. June 4, 1978, p. 41.

U.S. Supreme Court. *Engle v. Vitale* (1962).

Vygotsky, L. S.: *Mind in Society: The Development of Higher Psychological Processes.* Cambridge, MA, Harvard University Press, 1978.

Wagenaar, T.: High school seniors' view of themselves and their schools: A trend analysis. *Phi Delta Kappan,* September, 1981, pp. 629–632.

Wagstaff, L. H., and Gallagher, K. S.: Schools, families, and communities: Idealized images and new realities. In Mitchel B., and Cunningham, L. L.: *Educational Leadership and Changing Contexts of Families, Communities, and School.* Eighty-ninth Yearbook of the National Society for Study of Education, Part II. Chicago, University of Chicago Press, 1990.

Wallach, M. A., and Wallach, L.: *Teaching All Children to Read.* Chicago, University of Chicago Press, 1976.

Wallerstein, J.: *Second Chances: Men, Women, and Children a Decade After Divorce.* New York, Ticknor and Fields, 1989.

Wang, M. C., and Peverly, S. T.: The self-instructive process in classroom learning contexts. *Contemporary Educational Psychology, 2:*370–404, 1986.

Washington Post. Flaw in education of Hispanics cited. January 29, 1985, p. B3.

Watkins, B. T.: Boston U. and Chelsea are optimistic but wary as they start second year of school-reform project. *The Chronicle of Higher Education,* October 10, 1990, p. A14.

Wayson, W. W., Mitchel, B., Pinnel, G. S., and Landis, D.: *Up From Excellence: The Impact of the Excellence Movement on Schools.* Bloomington, IN, Phi Delta Kappa Educational Foundation, 1988, p. 143.

Wehrwein, A. C.: School size related to test scores, study finds. *Education Week,* May 14, 1986, p. 9.

Weller, H. H.: Education, public confidence and the legitimacy of the modern state: Do we have a crisis? *Phi Delta Kappan,* September, 1982, pp. 9–14.

Wellins, R. S., Byham, W. C., & Wilson, J. M.: *Empowered Teams.* San Francisco, Jossey-Bass, 1991.

Wells, A. S.: *The Sociology of School Choice: A Study of Black Students Participation in a Voluntary Transfer Plan.* Doctoral dissertation, Columbia University, Teachers College, 1991.

Williams, M. F., Hancher, K. S., and Hutner, A.: *Parents and School Choice: A Household Survey.* Washington, D.C., U.S. Department of Education, 1983.

Word, E., Johnson, J., Bair, H. P., Fulton, B. D., Zaharias, J. B., Lintz, M. N., Achilles, C. M., Folger, J., and Breda, C.: *Student/Teacher Achievement Ratio: Tennessee's K-3 Class Size Study, Final Report.* Nashville, State Department of Education, 1990.

Wheelock, A.: *Crossing the Tracks.* New York, The New Press, 1992.

White, M.: *The Japanese Educational Challenge.* New York, The Free Press, 1987, pp. 68–115.

Wilkerson, I.: New school term in Chicago puts parents in seat of power. *The New York Times,* January 26, 1989, Sec. 3A, p. 1.

Wilson, W. J.: Parents and schools. *The Harvard Education Letter,* 4:1–3, 1988.

Wilson, W. J.: *The Truly Disadvantaged: The Underclass and Public Policy.* Chicago, University of Chicago Press, 1989.

Witte, J. F.: *Public Subsidies for Private Schools.* Madison, WI, University of Wisconsin, 1991.

Working together. *Newsletter of the Child Development Project,* Spring, 1987, p. 4.

Yale Alumni Magazine. Ethics in the Boesky era, Winter, 1987, p. 37.

Yankelovich, D.: *New Rules: Searching for Self-Fulfillment in a World Turned Upside Down.* New York: Random House, 1981.

Young, J. A.: Defining education to fit the advances of the future: Spring High Tech '85, *Washington Post,* May 5, 1985, p. C4.

Zaltman, G., & Duncan, R.: *Strategies for Planned Change.* New York, Wiley, 1977.

Zelditch, M. Jr.: Role differentiation in the nuclear family: A comparative study. In Talcott, P., and Bales, R. F.: *Family, Socialization and Interaction Process.* Glencoe, IL: Free Press, 1955.

Zuckerman, M.: Vanishing values. *U.S. News and World Report,* p. 88, August 8, 1994.

AUTHOR INDEX

SUBJECT INDEX